You Have to Pay for the Public Life

You Have to Pay for the Public Life

Selected Essays of Charles W. Moore

edited by Kevin Keim

The MIT Press
Cambridge, Massachusetts
London, England

This book was set in Adobe Garamond and Stone Sans by Graphic Composition, Inc., Athens, Georgia, and was printed and bound in the United States of America.

Library of Congress Cataloging-in-Publication Data

Moore, Charles Willard, 1925–
        You have to pay for the public life : selected essays of Charles W. Moore / edited by Kevin Keim.
            p. cm.
        Includes bibliographical references and index.
        ISBN 0-262-13373-3 (hc. : alk. paper)
            1. Architecture. I. Keim, Kevin P. II. Title.

NA27 .M66 2001
720'.9—dc21

                                                                            00-135247

Contents

"Place," Charles W. Moore wrote, "is the projection of the image of civilization onto the environment." Whatever promise or peril lies in that statement, as long as there has been civilization, *place* has been one of the most continuous cultural phenomena that we share, fundamental to what it means to be human, to enact society, and to imprint the condition of being *somewhere* on the surface of the globe.

Moore spent his life thinking about and making places, and was among the handful of twentieth-century architects whose prolific writing is as significant as his built work. He was even more distinct for the significant innovation he inspired through his lifelong commitment to teaching. Unlike many of his predecessors and colleagues, Moore did not write to devise an elaborate manifesto to prop up his architecture. Instead, for him, as one of his sources, Susanne Langer, once suggested, "a philosophy is characterized more by the formulation of its problems than by its solution of them." Moore wrote a great deal about the challenges of place-making at the end of a century when civilization changed so much and so rapidly. He felt that history could provide guidance, and he identified most with architects who faced similar challenges in their times. Indeed, one of the keys to understanding Moore's writing and architecture is that he did not search for a general aesthetic, style, or functional "solution" to solve an array of problems, but rather spent his life willfully absorbing influences, full of possibilities and infinitely variable.

Underlying all of his buildings and books, no matter how the quality may have varied (and few would deny that alongside works of great enduring power are ones far more ephemeral and less powerful), was a constant fascination with those questions that will always be a part of architecture and design: What does it mean to make a place, and how do we inhabit those places? How do we continue to build, but protect the landscape and the presence of landscape in our lives? What is original? What is the relationship between memory, the past, and the present? What is taste? What are the chances for the familiar and the surprising? What are the distinctions between familiarity and monotony? How do we balance community and individuality? How do we better educate students to confidently make places?

What is modernity? In what ways can inhabitants be included in the design process? Finally, what is public life in our time?

All of these questions, as he was the first to agree, are ones that nobody has exclusive right answers to (even if some thought they did), and they were not even questions that had to do with discovering "truth." He likely believed that such a truth didn't exist, that the fundamental nature of the world is unknowable. This position was not a kind of hopeless indeterminacy or uncertainty, but rather an acceptance that life is spacious enough for all kinds of ideas, that the world is filled with valid ways people have answered the question of making places, with gardens, buildings, streets, cities, houses, fountains. With every urge to make a place, to construct a house, create a garden, or embellish a city, there are a myriad possibilities. Questioning, looking, and writing were essential to his continual search for ideas, so that understanding what he wrote is essential to understanding his architecture.

This volume compiles forty years' worth of that questioning and looking, including published and unpublished material (book reviews, analyses, critiques, lectures, and interviews), beginning with his first piece, written in 1952 when Moore was twenty-seven years old and teaching at the University of Utah, and ending with the last piece he wrote (which actually revisits his years at Utah), two weeks before his death in Austin, Texas, in 1993. Essays are generally arranged chronologically to emphasize the evolution of Moore's ideas, with minor editorial changes to correct spelling errors or omissions, and with as many of the original illustrations as possible. To present all of the periods of Moore's writing life, selections are included from his graduate student years as well as selections of fairly straightforward reporting (written when he was a correspondent for architectural magazines), such as "Environment and Industry." These early works are critical because they either contain the seeds of later ideas or bring to mind the rhetoric of the high-modern, bureaucratic architecture that would motivate Moore's criticism and counterproposition. Since Moore continually revisited ideas, some essays have been excluded to avoid overlap. Some repetitions remain, however, such as the multiple references to Monticello, the Santa Barbara County Courthouse, and the Carpenter Center, underscoring Moore's enduring admiration of theses structures. The architects who meant a great deal to him, such as Thomas Jefferson, Sir John Soane, Karl Friedrich Schinkel, H. H. Richardson, Rudolph Schindler, and Louis Kahn, turn up often, since he identified with them as passionately involved, often in the face of difficult circumstances, in the thrill of making buildings that might evoke some of the aspirations of their respective civilizations. In the face of the serious questions, humor was always an important part of his writing (and of his personality, for those who knew him). Scarcely anyone saw places quite as he did, and these essays are endlessly enjoyable because we can, at least vicariously and with a little bit of transport, see the world through his eyes.

Pinpointing the precise nature of Charles Moore's legacy is impossible, since his influence was so broad, his willingness to collaborate so automatic, and his capacity for reinvention so constant. Critics and historians tend to classify (or dismiss) his work as "whimsical," though that falls short of its seriousness and depth. Moore was sharply antimodernist but admired and was influenced by the work of Aalto, Le Corbusier, Schindler, and Kahn. His novel method of practicing will likely remain unique—he established independent but simultaneously operating professional offices closely associated with the university studios where he taught, spread across the United States. Most of the practices he helped establish continue with their own work today. He eagerly absorbed influences from an array of sources, and the absence of a particular, easily recognizable "style" made him more elusive. He was an extraordinarily talented designer, whose skills were intensified by his penetrating memory and perception. Apart from Sea Ranch and other early houses, he was not a structural or technological innovator, although throughout his career he used materials in innovative ways. Episodes of exuberant ornamentation alternated with spells of decorative restraint. Spatially his buildings are complex—often fantastically so—and defy graphic or photographic depiction. He readily accepted that some of his buildings would be ephemeral, and that many would change and could adapt for new inhabitants. He wrote about a variety of topics. And Moore's refusal to attach himself to any particular school or region adds to the dilemma, making him the most elusive of moving targets.

Moore's precocious intellect, along with his childhood ventures to Mexico, Florida, and California, undergraduate education at the University of Michigan, apprenticeship in San Francisco, teaching experience at the newly founded University of Utah School of Architecture, service in the Korean War, and continued travels throughout the Americas, Europe, and the Near and Far East, made him a formidable graduate student at Princeton, where he was a master's and doctoral student and then postdoctoral fellow between 1954 and 1958. Moore arrived on the scene when the school was becoming a vibrant center of thought quite unlike comparable universities, especially Harvard under Walter Gropius. What distinguished Princeton was that history was not regarded as meaningless or merely incidental to the work in the design studio, but as *fundamental*. More specifically, history was not viewed as something that could supply models to be merely copied, but rather as a source of inspirations or references to be studied, abstracted, extended, reacted to, or reshaped; as Moore wrote at the time, it was a conviction that "we can learn from the past—indeed, that it is already a part of us, and that we cannot avoid learning from it." The result of this exploratory attitude was work utterly unlike what was occurring elsewhere. The period at Princeton, in fact, involved a set of young architects who would lead one of the most significant cultural revolutions in the postwar United States. Led by the director of design, Jean Labatut, and professors D. D. Egbert, George Rowley, E. Baldwin Smith, Enrico Peressutti, and later Louis Kahn, the group of students who emerged from Princeton at that time—Moore, Robert Venturi, Donlyn Lyndon, William Turnbull, Jr., Hugh Hardy, and others—were among the first to substantively question the rhetoric of modernism and formulate not specific solutions or rules of their own but a set of detailed observations about experience, hierarchy, ornament, scale, symbol, precedent, and past and present. All were themes of Moore's graduate research and design projects, his master's thesis on Monterey, California, and his doctoral dissertation, "Water and Architecture."

One research project at Princeton became the essay "Plaster in Architecture." Emerging from the surface of the dense prose are important insights that, together with other work done at Princeton, would coalesce in "Toward Making Places," written three years later. What better medium could there be to challenge the rigidity of modernism than plaster, at once common and ordinary but manipulable into curvaceous, sensuous, and intricately detailed architecture? And what would violate the strict taboos of the modern rulebook more than the use of plaster to cover, conceal, solidify into poché, "falsify," or, worst of all, to ornament? Plaster's malleability or "plasticity" allowed it to be used in many different ways: to be elaborately sculpted, smoothed into planes, or molded into modular blocks allowing in turn for all kinds of ornamental, spatial, and structural possibilities. Moore had first seen the monuments of the German baroque ten years before, and they captivated his attention, particularly Vierzehnheiligen, Wurzburg, and Wies. His descriptions of the richly ornamented spaces would ultimately lead to his suggestive phrase "space leaking up and out," or the feeling of being drawn into a space emotionally and then propelled upward: as he wrote in "Plaster and Architecture," plastic forms are able "to suggest movement, or to abstract the movement which our eyes and minds experience when they search out a space and imagine themselves around it and through it. Our reaction to spaces can be explained by this empathetic process, through which we imagine ourselves, when we enter a space, projected up and out into the space, searching out its farthest dimensions." Moore also made an observation here that can describe many of his own subsequent buildings: "Movement is one reason, then, for the creation of plastic form; the provision of aggressive enclosure, with a simultaneous unclearness of the space enclosed, is a second reason; and the desire for movement of light is a third reason."

In 1959 Moore went to Berkeley, where he became chairman of the Department of Architecture under Dean William Wilson Wurster. The essay in which Moore most succinctly outlined what would remain the essence of his work as an architect, writer, and teacher—the idea that architecture is first and foremost an act of defining place or "cultural domain"—was co-written in 1962 with Donlyn Lyndon, Patrick Quinn, and Sim Van der Ryn initially for *Landscape,* the journal founded by J. B. Jackson ten years before. Arguing against the core modernist doctrine of the *general* and *reductive,* the authors proposed instead the *specific* and *additive,* that buildings should relate to their unique sites and contribute to—not ignore—social and compositional hierarchies, in the interest of letting the culture of a place find layered structure, grow, and even flourish. Where the modernists sought to generalize, they preferred to be particular. Where the modernists avoided typology and precedent, they embraced the lessons of the vernacular and suggestive scenes of urbanistic allusion. And where the modernists sought to compress or flatten, they proposed layering with "aediculas" and "saddle-bags," to make symbolic cores for houses which could then expand outward, or to layer from a spine, as is done most strikingly in MLTW buildings such as the central California Jobson and Bonham cabins, Moore's own house at Orinda, and the Sea Ranch structures. Collaboration was another way of being "additive," of multiplying possibilities; to paraphrase Kenneth Clark (who was paraphrasing William Lethaby), a great building is "not one man thick, but many men thick."

"Past" and "present," "tradition" and "innovation," "influence" and originality" have been persistent dilemmas for the twentieth-century architect, and they are all themes that Moore continually revisited. Octavio Paz in his Nobel laureate speech called America the "womb of the future," recognizing, perhaps, the American restlessness for what is yet to come, and asked, "What is postmodernism if not an even more modern modernity?" The nature of modernity has much to do with the dilemma of twentieth-century culture and society and the struggle for relevance. If the modernists defined it exclusively as their interpretation of the present, free of the "limitations" of the past, then Moore felt that it was inclusive, that past and present are linked by memory and full of "possibilities." Time and experience, in other words, are layered. Referring often to T. S. Eliot's phrase "order *in* reality," Moore proposed that architecture needs itself to be related to reality, instead of mere geometric order or esoteric doctrines, if it is to be relevant to society.

Feeling that many of the basic qualities of architecture had been blithely erased by the modernist attempt to reinvent a whole new language, Moore and his collaborators wanted to go back to the beginning and reintroduce the most fundamental ordering principles such as "inside," outside," "center," "edge," "axes," "roof," and "opening," to name a few. When the essence of those principles was understood, then the actual forms of the buildings could be abstracted, so that the abstractions might in turn intensify the architectural qualities. What condensed the principles most provocatively into a simple but potent assertion of *place*, as they discovered in Sir John Summerson's *Heavenly Mansions*, was the aedicula. In his book Summerson pointed out the duality of the aedicula (or primitive hut, temple, baldachino): it could be a centrally planned four-poster or flattened into a door frame; could be very little to accommodate "imaginary little men" or very large to "express the superhuman character of a god." In all its forms, notwithstanding, the scale and symbolism relate to human beings. Moore and his colleagues were also intrigued with Louis Kahn's Trenton Bath House, the cluster of square pyramidal pavilions central to Kahn's own career-long fascination with the aedicula, which reached its zenith at the Kimbell Art Museum whose simple, elongated aediculas are repeated but never in precisely the same way. That ambiguity, the decisive but unrestricted organization of space, the symbolic establishment of a place with the human being as the focus, was the idea behind Moore's extraordinary house at Orinda; for Moore it was a way of "achieving almost infinite variety from a set of almost identical parts."

The condition of conflict, the ambiguous relationship of the past and present, may suggest why architect Charles Correa of India proposes that the Mexican experience was the deepest trove for Moore's thinking, images, and buildings. Moore began going to Mexico as a child, and then at Princeton he helped organize field trips to the Yucatán (led by Enrico Peressutti), where he made sketches and watercolors of the ancient sites at Uxmal, Chichén Itzá, Palenque, and Copán. By the end of his life Moore had visited every region of the country and possessed an encyclopedic knowledge of its ancient and modern monuments, landscapes, villages, and traditions. He also amassed a collection of Mexican folk art. He particularly liked Cuernavaca, Pátzcuaro, San Miguel de Allende, Oaxaca, Querétaro, and most of all Guanajuato, the colonial city that is jammed into a series of narrow canyons, its houses, plazas, and churches geodically encrusting the steep slopes and the dramatic sections, staircases, and *callejones* setting up spectacular views. If place is indeed a "projection of the image of civilization," then it is especially potent in Mexico, where the cultural tensions only seem to energize those projections: the pious Catholicism that tries to restrain the boiling, pagan pre-Columbian, the writhing depth of the Churrigueresque facades bursting from the smooth adobe and stone planes, the social and spatial layering enacted by the Laws of the Indies *plaza* and *patio,* the resistance to the "order" of the north, and the clashing hues of vibrant lead-based paint.

What Italo Calvino refers to as "the ancient rivalry between the civilization of America and Spain in the art of bewitching the senses with dazzling seductions" Moore extended across borders as "the doctrine of immaculate collision," where seemingly incompatible images, often plucked from distinct cultures, can collide and create novel, often witty aesthetic compositions. The Mexican experience was indeed a rich source for Moore, but so too was the German baroque; the work of Soane, Schinkel, and Jefferson (in one of his essays, reprinted here, he writes about their "simultaneous elitism and populism, the coexistent high art and low"); and virtually everything in Japan, a country that he described, after his initial visit during the Korean War, as captivating but "intimidating" because the buildings were so consistently magical and the chance that he would get close in his own work to the intensity of Japanese places seemed remote. The seeming weightlessness of Japanese spaces was the antipodes of the *gravitas* of the masonry-based Hispanic architectural culture, and none of its features escaped his attention: the tectonic timber joinery traditions, the carefully orchestrated layering, the preoccupation with the miniature and simultaneous development of a whole poetry of the infinite, expressible in water or bonsai or gravel or light, and the appreciation of the *thin,* of shoji, tatami, and ink wash. To combine these images and types in new ways, a visual and typological pluralism, was for Moore an inevitable and appealing condition of modernity—not the modernity of the International Style's invariable replication of culturally neutral buildings, but the modernity of ideas and images (and people) moving freely between cultures, and colliding, mixing, merging, and competing. As he wrote in "Impressions of Japan," "Neon and tatami can coexist, to the destruction of neither. This, damn it, is the conceptual triumph that may save the world, if there's any air left in it to breathe."

This pluralism, or the eclecticism of "being contemporary" while absorbing the "presence of the past," seems especially related to the art and culture of California, a meeting place of Eastern culture carried from Japan and China and the more familiar Western traditions introduced by the Spanish or carted across the continent by the pioneers. This fusion became an important theme for the Bay Region architects, in whose tradition Moore served his apprenticeship in San Francisco, and would remain a subject of his thought and writing, beginning with this passage:

Along the highways on the West Coast are billboards advertising a kind of beer, which announce, "It's lucky when you live in California." For over half a century this has been quite literally true, especially for architects. There have been magnificent sites, plentiful good wood, a benign climate, quite a lot of money, and a way of life which is perhaps more comfortably informal than any way of life that has ever existed before anywhere. On top of this has been a native tradition of putting together pieces of wood to make buildings which are easy, natural, and highly decorative. The building tradition is so easy, and so attractive, that for this half century, while it has scarcely changed at all, it has been thought excitingly "contemporary" by the rest of the world. It was "contemporary" in 1908, and the same thing is good "contemporary" design in 1958. But the architect in California working in the local idiom has two new problems to cope with. There is on the one hand the 1200-year-old Japanese tradition of putting together pieces of wood similar to his own with refinements and excellences which he can scarcely ignore, however different the two cultures are. On the other hand the architect has to face California's explosively expanding population, and the attendant urbanization, the need for buildings in cities, bigger than ever before, made of a new set of materials, and calling for a kind of organization more formal and less picturesque than he can manage in his present idiom. The West Coast architect has behind him a tradition which includes some of the pleasantest houses in the world. But he cannot any more create his buildings on a feeling for that tradition alone. He is faced with choices among other manners and other accomplishments, if he is to do his best with his materials and for his changing environment. Like it or not, he is an eclectic. He is faced with problems which have never existed for him before, and it is incumbent on him to understand them and the influences acting on him, to be able to crystallize their meaning for himself and only then to be able to push them to the back of his mind, to practice "creative forgetfulness" so that he is free to create architecture which will be the answer to these problems.

The "seeming rightness" of places that are familiar and recognizable would be essential to Moore's work, and his writing can be understood in a large sense as his continual probing of familiar and exotic images. The "choreography of the familiar and the surprising," as he would later put it, proved to be an evocative metaphor for Moore's ideas about architecture and urbanism, where there could be the datum of the familiar and then "carefully added surprise" to give form and expression to whatever patterns and hierarchies the culture deems suitable.

Documenting these patterns and their possibilities was the subject of a great deal of Moore's writing. *The Places of Houses,* with Lyndon and Gerald Allen, was an exploration (inspired by nineteenth-century pattern books) of the typology of houses and of notable examples such as Mount Vernon, Stratford House, or the Russell House—recognizable forms that, once tested and understood, are adaptable with infinite variation to accommodate new ways of making houses. *The Poetics of Gardens,* with William Mitchell, was a truly unique book that documented the typologies of gardens (illustrated masterfully with Turnbull's drawings) and the variations that could extend from the types. And in *Body, Memory, and Architecture* Moore and Kent Bloomer wrote about ways in which space and form relate to the human perception of order, disorder, pattern, chaos, the rational and irrational, starting from the premise that, "at the very beginning of our lives, we measure and order out from our own bodies." What made the insights in these books so clear and vivid was that Moore had actually been to all of the places he wrote about, and had, as Henry James had written in *The Art of Travel,* "formed the habit of comparing, of looking for points of difference and resemblance." This constant going out and seeing places, absorbing their lessons, comparing, resisting, rejecting, celebrating, returning for more experiences—and remembering—made a storehouse of continually accumulating images for his writing and buildings, and it centered his teaching.

J. B. Jackson was known for his travel, too, and his own investigations of the "natural" landscape, "cultural" landscape, and the vernacular made a lasting impression on Moore's early essays, as did Labatut's "creative forgetfulness," which Moore referred to in the passage quoted above. Like Jackson, Moore acknowledged the transitory aspects of American life, and he even celebrated the speed of travel made possible by the airplane and freeway, but only so long as the asphalt didn't spread too uncontrollably. Jackson, however, often wrote that architecture was no longer the primary way we sense place, since Americans lift their roots so readily. "I'm inclined to believe," he wrote, "that the average American still associates a sense of place not so much with architecture or a monument or a designed space as with some event, some daily or weekly or seasonal occurrence which we look forward to or remember and which we share with others, and as a result the event becomes more significant than the place itself." Moore might have partly agreed with that statement (in "Plug It In, Rameses" he admitted that his own life was most regularly cadenced by his visits to certain airports), but he also urged architects to endow physical places with meaning and connections to inhabitants' experiences, even if those inhabitants didn't linger for too long in one place.

Despite the inherent restlessness of American society, Moore always felt that buildings still had great potential to help people establish places over time and that physical settings could provide chances for memorable encounter. Contrary to the dreams of social engineering envisioned by the modernists, Moore did not regard architects as white knights who could suddenly rescue society with buildings or create social or political order, and certainly not that they could establish utopia. Places need time. They need continuing attention to meet the challenge of becoming permanent parts of the landscape. For as many times as Moore criticized the failure of modernist urban renewal plazas to attract people, his own plazas at the Beverly Hills Civic Center are equally empty, and the streets that were to support a sense of community at the Church Street South housing complex in New Haven (discussed in the interview with Heinrich Klotz) never worked; like most housing projects of the period, it was destined to become a slum, and it may soon be demolished. The Piazza d'Italia was meant to be a festive setting for public celebrations for the New Orleans Italian community, and a place, city leaders hoped, that would spark a renewal of its depressed neighborhood. The anticipated renewal never materialized, however, and with civic negligence the Piazza lapsed into what Moore agreed was "a perfectly Roman state of decline." Decay is certainly not unusual for New Orleans, but was this an indication that people were yet unwilling to pay for public life? Or was the mercurial balance of architectural intention and public spontaneity wrong? Whatever the case, once a place loses the confidence of people and is enclosed within chain link, its chance to welcome involvement drastically diminishes. What is obvious is that places need attention and care if they are to support lively activity. Now at least there is hope in this case: a private hotel, planned for construction on an adjacent site, may contribute to the public interest and rejuvenate the Piazza d'Italia as a pedestrian promenade and gathering place, an element in the public domain.

Four of Moore's most substantial, considered essays were written for Yale's architecture journal *Perspecta,* the latter three coinciding with his tenure as chairman and dean of the School of Architecture between 1965 and 1972, and the simultaneous founding of Moore Grover Harper, which later became Centerbrook. The first was "Hadrian's Villa"; then "You Have to Pay for the Public Life" (the namesake for this collection and arguably Moore's most influential essay), followed by "Plug It In, Rameses" and finally "Southernness." These four essays explore sense of place: how we perceive it, how time may alter those perceptions, how worthies such as Hadrian and Jefferson shaped it in Tivoli and Charlottesville.

What did Moore mean by the enigmatic statement, "You have to pay for the public life"? Was it a criticism of the privatization of public life that made it available only for those who paid admission? Or was he saying that if places are to have public life they need to be supported with money and interest and care and effort? And why are these questions—and these essays—relevant still?

Moore in the 1950s saw public life rapidly changing, often disintegrating as a result of a modernism that discarded the patterns, recognizable parts, and familiar language—again, the basis for communicating meaning—that had previously supported public life. Architects, grown increasingly exclusive and obsessed with originality, were producing buildings, whole cities even, that people found alien, cleansed of any shared memory, and uninhabitable. Now, forty years later, public life is even more challenged as the world grows smaller and prone to mass homogenization and as environmental destruction, personal anomie, and urban sprawl do not diminish but accelerate. The effects of consumerism and capitalism are evident everywhere. Population grows frighteningly out of control and places are faced with bizarre imbalances, typified by Mexico City's residential population exceeding all of Australia's. That overpopulation destroys natural habitats, and it is commonplace to hear of development directly causing biological extinction. The sprawl America has popularized amplifies the most dire of all problems, global warming, and the threat that we may simply pollute and consume ourselves out of existence. Racial, religious, and territorial violence persists, and people continue to segregate themselves (often behind gates) by ethnic and economic differences.

The electronic awakenings Moore quipped about in "Plug It In, Rameses" in 1967 are now fully unleashed, so that what we regard as "public" now exceeds more than ever what is physically close to us, or even connected to us through personal relationships, and often does not engage the architectural space of our cities but rather the architecture of transmitted image, demonstrated most astonishingly by the spontaneous global act of public life following Princess Diana's death. People are encouraged to turn inward to computer screens ("who needs places anyway?"), the television has effectively replaced the hearth (and the conversation that used to occur around it) in nearly every American house, and a whole new academic discipline is rushing to explain whether and how the Internet and mass media are *replacing* place.

At the same time, many architects have finally responded to the public's desire for towns and cities that seem like towns and cities. A great deal of exciting work is being done, and design has become more popular and accessible. The attitudes that inspired such proud statements as "when [our corporation] moved we provided one parking space for every two employees. We shall celebrate our first anniversary in the new building by constructing a large new parking area" (reported by Moore in "Environment and Industry") would now be regarded as grotesque. (Or at least the candor would.) To have subjects like suburban sprawl at least on the national political agenda is an accomplishment. People are more aware of the kinds of cities and towns they want, the support for "downtowns" and streets and parks is stronger, and a resurgence of active public life in places throughout the United States shows that people want public life and that it is still possible to have vibrant urbanity.

But where does that leave us? What is the state of our American cities and towns at the end of the century? There is general consensus now about the negative impact of suburbia and the damage that has been done to the center city. Many cities now face the challenge of designing themselves out of a bag, retroactively, hoping to revive central cores and restrain sprawl. Where once we had wretched slums (where there was a little *too much* life), the prematurely aging products of urban renewal (where there is *too little* life) are desperately in need of reconstructive surgery. There is a renewed sense of what seems "out of place," and when there is political will and money, intrusions in the landscapes and cities are being rethought. For instance, when people felt that the observation tower at Gettysburg violated the sanctity of the Civil War battlefield, it was demolished, restoring the uninterrupted horizon. Mistakes such as the typical crosstown freeway are being reconsidered too, with positive results, such as the decision not to rebuild San Francisco's earthquake-damaged Embarcadero Freeway (which formed a wall to the bay), or the Big Dig in Boston where, in a move anticipated by the residents of Guanajuato a century earlier, a major vehicular artery (I-93) is being sunk in a tunnel, with some of the regained land where the freeway once cast its shadows to become public parks. Constructing the freeway as an evisceration of Boston in the 1950s was a costly blunder, and they are indeed now paying for the public life.

Moore celebrated buildings or places that, however modest, give something back in the interest of the public realm or extend beyond themselves to project something into the public domain. He saw modernism wiping out whole layers of these kinds of buildings and places, but ultimately doing very little, if anything, to give something in return or advance the civilization of places. In one interview here, Moore speaks about the depressing experience of visiting his hometown of Benton Harbor, Michigan, and finding that much of it has been literally erased, torn down. Without physical places, people themselves can hardly give back to further the social good; indeed, a part of the problem is that once you deprive people of a public domain, they are more likely to question whether public life is worth having in the first place. The problem is compounded by the fact that compared to other societies, Americans have become an overwhelmingly private people. The mass media and the unprecedented comforts of domestic life have elevated our expectation of privacy to the level of fetish. Could television be the cause of this, in that people have little need for public interaction, and forget that they are even visible to others while in the public realm? (As Michael Benedikt once pointed out, "Televisions don't look back.") And have Americans, in their rejection or confusion about at least a minimum standard of public involvement or decorum, subsequently lost with it a sense of mannered sociability, so that there is little to start from in even beginning to build public life? Decorum once meant a tacit cultural agreement that people took seriously the shared space of the city, and with it accepted some level of responsibility for the activity in it. In Rome, for instance, people still largely accept a standard of decorum in dress and demeanor for appearing in the civic public realm, helped along by the language and rituals such as the *passeggiata,* which, through the simple act of walking and sliding past one another, ensures a continuity of public life.

Louis Kahn once said that cities should be places where children can discover what they want to be as adults. That notion, of the city as a metaphor for life itself where diversity is evident, would seem to require a healthy, thriving public realm, open to everyone. Indeed, in *The Death and Life of Great American Cities* Jane Jacobs wrote about the importance of a child's experiences of the city for learning how to participate socially in public life as a grown-up: "In real life, only from the ordinary adults of the city sidewalks do children learn—if they learn at all—the first fundamental of successful city life: People must take a modicum of public responsibility for each other even if they have no ties to each other. This is a lesson nobody learns by being told. It is learned from the experience of *having other people without ties of kinship or close friendship or formal responsibility to you* take a modicum of public responsibility for you."

While some would assume that Moore's enthusiasm for Disney's Main Street in "You Have to Pay for the Public Life" was mere staging for new urbanism, his work and his writing certainly do not advocate the recreation of "traditional" villages or towns as something that would automatically ameliorate placelessness. At the same time as he was writing many of these essays, he was designing Kresge College as a *metaphor* of a village, full of abstractions. Moore wrote about Disneyland as an example of how public life was being engaged, minus architects, and how people responded with wild (and continuing) patronage. Would Moore have advocated the replication of Disneyland beyond the turnstiles of Anaheim, as Ada Louise Huxtable fears? Certainly not, for his admiration of Disneyland was for its cleverly quaint recreation, albeit for an admission charge, of a setting where people could participate without being embarrassed in a kind of public life that had otherwise been removed from most people's lives. Highlighting Disneyland emphasized how dismal and lifeless cities had become. Moore was critical of the culture of detachment and privacy spreading through southern California ("whose only edge," he wrote, "is the ocean"), and indeed through most of the country, but he sought positive solutions that would fit the needs of society instead of rejecting them.

To think that people could revert to traditional, preindustrial villages was a fantasy, even as it was impossible to ignore some people's hopes of having more traditional towns. What was critical was for architects to pay more attention to endowing the places our society needs with aspects that help people to take part in public life. Moore would have been the first to agree that places like Seaside or Celebration are not "real" in the sense of being fully operating villages, autonomous economically and culturally in the nineteenth-century sense. Plainly, they are not. They depend on tourists and rentals, and on highways to carry the inhabitants away to jobs and hospitals and grocery stores. But judging from the cost of real estate in Seaside, some people obviously enjoy living in places that reflect their notions of what a town is; and even if they do not buy their groceries at the corner store or gather in the town square for a political debate, why begrudge them the opportunity?

In "Toward Making Places," the authors suggested that "the right democratically to determine the shape of our environment is the real freedom at stake." That issue remains, as people feel more and more disenfranchised from the complex processes that go into the shaping of the environment. Moreover, many now wonder to what extent the capitalist, globalized free market should determine (or outright destroy) the urban and natural environments, and further render places indistinguishable one from another.

In one way or another the conflict between traditional urban patterns and ad hoc, zoned, free-market urbanism has been at the center of the architecture debate for the last twenty years. When an interviewer asked Moore about the general state of American cities and the impact of urban renewal in particular, he replied:

> Well, there are kinds and kinds of city design. There are clearly conflicts between the masterplan makers of the last decades and people like us who are characterized by David Lewis as "urban tinkerers." It seems to me that the proper role of a person engaged in urban design is to start from the conventions—houses and streets and squares and city halls and things that people recognize—and diddle with them, improve them in ways that don't tear up the fabric, but try to mend and extend, starting with the familiar and carefully adding surprise. The kind of plans that there have been so many of from the bulldozer and urban renewal people of the last decade seem to me to be engaged in a version of criminal rape that I'm not in favor of. It has caused me and them to say quite ugly things to each other.

The MIT Press preceded this volume with collections of Colin Rowe's and Robert Venturi's essays. These three contemporaries independently formed the most prolonged and impassioned critique of modernism, each arriving at similar conclusions from different positions. Venturi, through his highly observant writings on the baroque and mannerism, and later with Denise Scott Brown in their analysis of Las Vegas, challenged the depthlessness of the modern, its failure to be complex enough to sustain any kind of long-term interest or provide a stimulating setting for society. Rowe not only found the Marxian subtext of the modernists socially and politically ridiculous, believing instead that cultural hierarchies are essential to cities, but also found that the modern movement's lack of a sophisticated language left it ultimately incapable of confidently establishing legible cities. Moore saw in modernism a failure to provide the fundamental spatial, ornamental, and social qualities that vernacular (or monumental, for that matter) architecture had succeeded in providing for so long, and, as a consequence, left inhabitants unable to form lasting, memorable connections to their places. "I see architecture," Moore said, "as having a primary function of making its inhabitants feel as though they are inhabiting something as they are someplace and therefore somebody."

All three recognized the emergence of pluralism, describing it variously as collage, layering, variation, ambiguity, collision, possibilities, or the benefits of "more" as opposed to "less." Indeed the array of work being done today by many architects owes a great deal to Moore's advocacy of pluralism and his work to break a calcified profession open. That was the genius of his contribution.

Pluralism, because of our interconnection and movement, is now an indisputable cultural condition on the planet. But will the work to foster diversity and protect what's unique about places be overrun by the consumerist frenzy and the homogeneity and disconnection it spawns? Will things be able to coexist without melting into just another kind of gray, formless blur? And if indeed place is the projection of the image of civilization, are we getting the kinds of places we exactly deserve?

Acknowledgments

This book would not have been possible without two important sources of support: Furthermore, the publication program of the J. M. Kaplan Fund; and the Graham Foundation for Advanced Studies in the Fine Arts. A number of archives also have been of assistance: The Charles W. Moore Archive at the Alexander Archive at the University of Texas at Austin is the repository for Moore's slide collection (from which the majority of the book's illustrations were drawn) in addition to the material that documents his life as an architect, writer, and teacher. Additional illustrations were generously provided by Tony Merchell, Alexandra Sauvergrain (page 88), the estate of Morley Baer (pages 188, 194, and 254 bottom), Norman McGrath (pages 205 and 309), and Venturi, Scott Brown and Associates. Many people have offered advice and acted as readers: Hal Box, Alex Caragonne, Jeffrey Chusid, Stanley W. Hensley, Hilary Lewis, Leslie Luebbers, Donlyn Lyndon, Richard Peters, and David Weingarten.

Finally, this book owes a special debt of gratitude to the Charles W. Moore Center for the Study of Place, which was established in his extraordinary Austin home and studio to extend his enthusiasm for architecture, places, scholarship, teaching, and collaboration to new generations.

You Have to Pay for the Public Life

Moore wrote his first published piece for The Forum, *a student publication at the University of Utah in Salt Lake City, while he was teaching there under Dean Roger Bailey and with professors Gordon Heck, James Acland, and Stephen Montgomery, between 1952 and 1954.*

New Hope for Local Art

A look at the fate of the visual arts during the last 150 years can be a depressing experience, if we start (as surely we must) with the belief that these visual arts are living things, which should contribute to the full existence of the civilization of which they are a part. We can watch the statues disappearing from the public squares and the murals being replaced by easel paintings, the more easily that both statues and easel paintings might be removed to vast caches (the Vatican Museum, the Louvre, the Metropolitan Museum, the National Gallery) of objets d'art, objects removed from their original contexts into a cluttered hierarchy in which the chief surviving relationship is with the dollar and the pound sterling. It becomes rather difficult, contemplating these artistic Fort Knoxes, to remember that a museum can be a living thing, with a local validity that can make the arts exciting again, contributing not to the esoteric delights of a few, but to the real and wholesome completion of a civilization in need of some civilizing.

If we were in Athens, we could find a pleasing and much alive validity in the little Byzantine Museum. In Florence the Uffizi, with all its earth-shaking contents, is interesting chiefly because of its important connection with the life of the city it represents. We needn't, though, go so far afield: In Salt Lake City the recent spontaneous and pyrotechnically successful appearance of the Contemporary Gallery can give us considerable hope that finally the sad and dusty procession of art off the streets and walls and into museum-morgues is about to reverse itself. For here a group of producing artists, inspired by a profound belief in the community's need for the arts, has swept by self-seeking pockets of opposition to found a democratic organization ready to find and show the work of artists working in Utah, to give encouragement to the producers, and to bring something equally important to the public at large, a public in need of art too. (At least the warm

Originally published in *The Forum* (University of Utah), April 1952.

public response to the Gallery's opening could make us hope that the need is finally a conscious one.)

In the Contemporary Gallery, according to its plans, there will be furniture, ceramics, architecture, photography, as well as painting and sculpture, all being shown to people increasingly anxious to see how these arts can affect their lives. In any such showing, of course, the act of selection is the telling one. The announced aim of the Contemporary Gallery is that, rather than harboring a set of prejudices in favor of a particular sort of contemporary visual expression (realism, abstraction, magic realism, surrealism, naturalism, or whatever), the juries will let standards of excellence in whatever of today's numerous visual languages a work is expressed be their criteria. The assumption is, certainly, that only by giving free play to the contemporary visual Babel can the long-lost standards of competence be resuscitated, as the first step in the establishment of our language of vision, universal among our creators and comprehensible to all the people, the universal language of vision (if you will, the style) that is the *sine qua non* of a complete civilization. The art forms of Italian Renaissance humanism, so long unsuitable, have finally receded far enough from us that the still unclear forms of our own visual language can begin to appear. The Contemporary Gallery, for one, is helping mightily in the process.

The "renewal" of cities, linked to the influence of Le Corbusier's Ville Radieuse, let the bottoms of cities fall out; this, combined with the shapeless expansion of suburbia, commonly linked now in many people's minds to Frank Lloyd Wright's vision of Broadacre City gone awry, compounded problems of isolation, social disintegration, and visual blight. Gateway Center in Pittsburgh (perhaps the closest embodiment of the Ville Radieuse built in America) is an urban island that turns its back on the streets, focusing inward instead on the featureless grassy planes stretching between the solitary towers. At night those spaces grow even more desolate as people go home to the suburbs, which offer few chances of their own for community or encounter. Overly stimulated renewal projects forcibly inserted into cities, mixed with the depressive effects of the suburbs, made for a deadly cocktail. And while the initial stimulant faded rapidly, the lethargy of the depressant proved persistent. One of the most perceptive chroniclers of suburbia, John Cheever, follows his character in "The Swimmer" as he travels across his forlorn suburb by drunkenly swimming from backyard pool to pool, only to arrive, at the end of the story, at his own house and discover that "the place was empty."

The next four pieces look at themes of city and suburb, written in 1958 while Moore was a reviewer and correspondent for Architectural Record. *His review of Frank Lloyd Wright's literary self-portrait is followed by reviews of George Nelson's* Problems of Design *and David H. Pinkney's* Napoleon III and the Rebuilding of Paris, *and finally by Moore's report on the Princeton conference "Environment for Business and Industry."*

Gospel According to Wright

Review of *A Testament,* by Frank Lloyd Wright

Frank Lloyd Wright's *A Testament,* the publishers point out, "consists of two major books. 'Book One: Autobiographical' begins with the story of a childhood influence . . . on through the challenging years in which he forged his own life and created a new architecture. . . . In 'Book Two: The New Architecture,' Frank Lloyd Wright presents an illuminating synthesis of the nine great principles upon which he has unremittingly based his life work." Running concurrently with these two books is the real work, and the

Originally published in *Architectural Record* 123, no. 2 (February 1958), pp. 58, 62.

reason almost every serious architect will want to own this volume: drawings, plans, and photographs, some of them never before published, of buildings and projects dating from as early as 1888 and as late as 1957.

Apart from some murkiness in the photographs, there is little fault to find with the magnificent corpus. The difficulty, for most of us, is that the World's Greatest Living Architect is by no means only a contemporary phenomenon. A number of buildings and projects bearing very recent dates attest to his continuing creativity; but on the other hand he has for a long time been a historical figure, and his book becomes, automatically, a historical document. He means it, apparently, to be even more: Tennyson is invoked, before the title page, to say that "Most can raise the flowers now, For all have got the seed."

In the text that follows, though, repeated injustice is done to the facts, and disservice to "organic" architecture by Wright's constant effort to make this architecture seem to be the product of his one-man crusade against the arrayed forces of pilastered Darkness. In fact, even if we allow the presence of columns and pilasters to disqualify as "organic" the consistent, natural, and very un-European town built in New England during the first two centuries of the continent's settlement, the history of American architecture since the 1840s produces a steady stream of attempts, often very successful, to build so as to express the nature of the materials, of the structure, of the site, and of the life within. The "Stick Style" and "Shingle Style" buildings in the eastern United States after the Civil War, Furness buildings in Philadelphia, skyscrapers in Chicago, the domestic buildings of Greene and Greene, Maybeck, Howard, and others in California after the turn of the century, and such subsequent developments as the "Bay Region Style," like the work of Wright himself, display the American genius for creating natural "organic" architecture.

Wright has every reason to be proud of his successes over the forces of reaction; it is only unfortunate that these successes, made so personal, are wrested from the mainstream of the development of an indigenous architecture. For if this American development is eventually to triumph, as one might fervently hope it will, over the "brittle box emphasized as brittle," it will not be entirely on account of the work of Frank Lloyd Wright. A Frank Lloyd Wright with a little humility could, however, help.

In the pages of *A Testament,* the flowering of the World's Greatest Living Architect is superbly evident, but the fact of a fertile seed, as advertised, would seem to remain open to question. The book's last sentence is perhaps more clue than enigma: "Growth, our best hope, consists in understanding at last what other civilizations have only known about and left to us—ourselves comforted meantime by the realization that all one does either for or against Truth serves it equally well."

The Shapes of Our Time

Review of *Problems of Design,* by George Nelson

Readers who have enjoyed the witty, engagingly written, and sometimes important articles of George Nelson in *Interiors, Holiday, Architectural Forum,* and a number of other magazines will be delighted to discover that twenty-six of them have been gathered into a new volume. Thus arranged, they are as pleasant to read as ever, and in places as provocative. The book is divided, loosely, into six sections: "Problems of Design," which includes observations on education, obsolescence, vision, and the intramural difficulties of the industrial designer; "Art"; "Architecture," including skillful appreciations of Le Corbusier's Villa Savoye and Wright's two Taliesins; "Houses," with refreshing approaches to housekeeping, prefabrication, and vacations; "Planning," observations about Main Streets, so much to the point a decade ago, when they were written, that they are architects' common currency by now; and "Interiors," where the light touch is applied. Some of the articles discuss matters of central importance to anyone with eyes and a mind in the twentieth century; in others, the eyes and the mind romp off into pleasant conceits. The articles are well illustrated with pictures of practically everything from high tension wires to "September Morn," with one surprising omission: Mr. Nelson has modestly avoided more than a very occasional illustration of his own elegant work. This is a great pity.

Something else, of even more importance, is missing. In Nelson's words, "The insights of today's greatest painters and sculptors cannot be other than profoundly disturbing." It would seem that the insights of one of today's best writer-philosopher-designers should be disturbing, too. And it is disappointing to realize, part way through *Problems of Design,* that somehow they are not. "It has been my own experience," Nelson writes, "that to begin to approach an awareness of the shapes of our time requires an extraordinary intellectual and emotional effort. Enlargement of his vision is one of the most difficult assignments an individual can assume." If he assumes the assignment, he can expect to arrive at a series of vantage points, some of them with frightening views. There is the vantage point, for instance, from which is evident the nightmare of endless suburban sprawl enveloping our countryside, or the adjacent vantage point from which William H. Whyte, for instance, in *The Organization Man,* notes the dissolution of

Originally published in *Architectural Record* 123, no. 6 (June 1958), pp. 60, 64, 348.

individual initiative in the inhabitants of these new suburban stretches. "The destructive aspects of this change," Nelson notes, "might indicate reason for profound pessimism, were it not for the fact that destruction and creation—here we have another example of the contradiction in action—are only two sides of the same coin. One therefore has the free choice of identifying himself with either the decaying or the new and growing elements in the process and then basing his personal philosophy and actions on this choice." This sounds rather like the free choice which used to be available on ballots supplied by Adolf Hitler, with a big square marked "Ja" and a very small square marked "Nein." This is not supposed to disturb our modern man, however. "He accepts his role as a member of a synchronized, cooperative group and one of these days he will arrive at a new comprehension of the many possible constructive relationships between the individual and the group. He is, in other words, a prototype of the non-competitive man about whom the religious teachers have been talking since 2500 B.C. He is one of the meek who will inherit the earth." Come to think of it, this *is* disturbing.

Everything in an age does seem to share in the spirit of the age. Even the columns of text self-consciously arranged on these square pages avoid the exposure of the outer edges, where they would easily meet the reader's eye, and seek the security of the bindings. Instead of seeking such security ourselves, we might stand ready to act on whatever our individual consciences demand, once we see what our enlarged vision enables us to see. We have still the right to do more than glide quietly with the spirit of the times. Mr. Nelson will not seem to encourage us to exercise this right, but he is pleasant stimulation while we prepare ourselves.

Emergency Surgery Was Necessary

Review of *Napoleon III and the Rebuilding of Paris,* by David H. Pinkney

This is an account of two energetic men, Napoleon III of France and the Baron Haussmann, and of how during two decades they applied their energies to a city. They found Paris an overgrown medieval town with a million people, slum-infested, ill supplied with water, congested with sewage, and choked with traffic. They silenced the conservative and the timid, turned finance into prestidigitation, and pushed through a program of public works which made Paris a model for the whole world for the better part of a century. Professor Pinkney is, to say the least, enthusiastic about their accomplishments. He weaves a fascinating account of the projects, the men who conceived them, the men who left the farms of central France to build them, the financial magic tricks that made them possible, and the men of the opposition who exposed the finances, routed Haussmann, and stopped the show. As the reanimation of that era, the story is a complete success. As an account of a city, street by street, it is a success rather heavily qualified by the absence of adequate maps.

It is probably captious to complain that this study, which does so well what it sets out to do, does not end up by illuminating our own problems. Washington has a sewage crisis which compares with the one Haussmann faced in Paris; New York's traffic tangle is as urgently in need of drastic measures as Haussmann's Parisian one was; and redeveloped Philadelphia's post-blitzkrieg look, with its frequent loss of comfortable human scale, poses problems which beset Haussmann, too. But Haussmann's solutions, bold as they were, do not emerge as much help to us because they do not emerge as the product of any real vision of a whole city. They appear instead as a kind of emergency surgery, a series of operations that were, even at their most brilliant, no substitute for attention to lasting good health.

Originally published in *Architectural Record* 125, no. 2 (February 1959), pp. 64, 374.

More Questions than Answers: A Report on the Princeton Conference

Princeton University sponsored, on March 4 and 5, a meeting of the Princeton University Conference concerned with "Environment for Business and Industry." Organized by Robert W. McLaughlin, director of the Princeton School of Architecture, with the late John Knox Shear, editor of the *Record*, and David Scribner of Joseph P. Day and Co. in order to bring together the points of view of architects and of business and industry, the meeting took its cue from Abraham Lincoln: "If we could first know where we are, and whither we are tending, we could then better judge what to do, and how to do it."

Accordingly a group of leaders in business and in industry presented their points of view about where we and our physical environment are, and about whither it and we are tending. Frazar B. Wilde, president of the Connecticut General Life Insurance Company, affirmed the desirability of "The Move to the Suburbs," while Adolph W. Schmidt of T. Mellon and Sons used the example of Pittsburgh to make the case for "The Redevelopment of the Central City." S. Westcott Toole, of the Prudential Insurance Company, also made "The Case for the Downtown Area." Laurence C. Plowman of Textron, Inc. discussed the "Shifting Locations of Industry in the United States," and David Scribner of Joseph P. Day, Inc. described the "Economic Analysis" of these locations.

A statement from the floor during the last session of the conference described what may have been a general reaction: "It seems to me that . . . the assumption has been that we're supposed to take sides . . . and I'm not going to take sides." Much more than in developing any area of partisanship for or against a move of business from a city to its suburbs, the effect of the conference was to suggest a civilization moving around so fast that even notions like "prosperity" and "recession" were left behind along the road. Mr. Toole mentioned the provision of a swimming pool in Prudential's new Houston office building to attract employees to the building's present location, while Mr. Plowman and Solomon Barkin, who represented the Textile Workers' Union, were describing some answers, and looking for more answers, to the acute problems of human needs in New England, where the removal of textile mills has created an army of thousands of "displaced persons."

Originally published in *Architectural Record* 124, no. 1 (July 1958), pp. 159–162.

"Since the wheel was invented," Mr. Plowman said, "thereby creating not only a major industry (the manufacture of conveyances) but making possible the movement of all industry on the wheels thus provided, the world's industry has been on the march." Where we are, in Mr. Lincoln's terms, seems subject to varying interpretations, and analyses of whither we are tending are various enough even to discourage sidetaking. The one thing clear is that changes are taking place with dazzling speed. "I think," the voice from the floor continued, after announcing his refusal to take sides in the city vs. suburb division, "the pattern of the future is like Los Angeles, which John Burchard has described as seven suburbs in search of a city, and we're not going to have the central city as we now conceive it and we're certainly not going to have the suburban-type thing. We're going to have an entirely new complex of living and industry and it seems to me the people who are most versed in these matters ought to be studying what we're going to have to deal with twenty years from now in terms of rapid transit, in terms of new governmental machinery and our financial base on this much broader complex. . . . I think we ought to look for the new pattern."

The question had been raised at other points in the conference: who is equipped to look for the new pattern, to synthesize the vast array of statistics, errant facts, and high-speed trends? It had been asked to members of a panel of Princeton representatives, made up of R. L. Johnstone, Professors Jean Labatut of the School of Architecture, Richard A. Lester of the Economics Department, John Sly of the Politics Department, and Harold Stein of the Woodrow Wilson School. Their answers, and some statements that had gone before, would have made frightening listening to anyone who had supposed that the great scale of contemporary projects was part of an overall plan. "After twelve years of intensive effort and a few dramatic results, it is quite clear to many of us who have been close to this situation that we have only scratched the surface," Mr. Schmidt had reported about the Pittsburgh development. "There is still no overall plan for the Golden Triangle (after all that famous development!) to determine its highest and best land use and suggest its best future development. Although we know that 90 percent of the population boom will settle in the suburbs and the periphery . . . we have done no broad regional planning to prevent encroachment upon strategic land areas. We have not been able to solve our mass transit problem."

Authorities

Various phases of the Pittsburgh redevelopment were accomplished by five
semi-public authorities: the Urban Redevelopment Authority of Pittsburgh,
the Public Parking Authority, the Public Auditorium Authority, the Allegheny County Sanitary Authority, and the Tunnel Authority. These pri-
vately supported civic agencies played the dominant role in the Pittsburgh
redevelopment: "In my own mind," Mr. Schmidt explained, "I have always
regarded the Pittsburgh Regional Planning Association as the left bower,
and Pennsylvania Economy League as the right bower of the Allegheny
Conference on Community Development, the action and coordinating
agency. The Planning Association makes the plans, the Economy League
asks where is the money coming from, and the Conference puts the plans
into action, by acting as initiator, trouble shooter, coordinator, catalyst. . . .
The work of the Conference is performed by eight officers and twelve members constituting the executive committee," on which are represented one of
the chief officers of the U. S. Steel Corporation, the Gulf Oil Corporation,
Westinghouse Electric Corporation, Pittsburgh Plate Glass Company, H. J.
Heinz Company, the Aluminum Company of America, smaller companies,
and banks.

The weaknesses in overall planning which are evidently inherent in
this complex of separate authorities were cause for concern in a variety of
connections. Mr. Barkin, concerned with the people displaced by the disap-
pearance of the textile mills from New England, pointed out that we do not
have institutions devoted to the problem of planning, and that we need desperately an analysis of communities that have lost their locational advantages. John Diehl reported, after a film supplied by Benacerraf and Guinand
of Caracas, who were unable to be present, that U. S. Steel's successes in the
development of the Orinoco Valley of Venezuela were not paralleled in the
Delaware Valley, where much more complex situations existed, because no
implements were available for synthesis. There is, for instance, he pointed
out, no unit equipped to study the New York region, to synthesize other
studies, and to focus them on one problem. The problem is not to *do* research, but to *take* research, and coordinate it so that it becomes useful. This
might well be the task of a university.

Professor Stein had discussed the large number of governments in the
United States, and the importance of politics as a solution to the problems

which exist. This brought up the inability of a jigsaw puzzle of governmental units to engage in overall planning, and the consequent need to set up separate authorities, which overlap governmental units but which leave in turn great uncoordinated areas between themselves. The problem of traffic, mass transportation, and parking, for instance, was raised by Kenneth Kassler. "I don't think," Professor Sly answered, "that there's any solution to this problem . . . unless we get a balanced transportation system." If we are dealing only with automobiles, he went on, we can never catch up; and while we are losing this race, rapid transit facilities are vanishing because they don't pay their way.

The very structure of most authority systems, which set up an autonomous unit to create highways, while other transportation languishes, has contributed to the gravity of the problem. "A few years ago," Joseph E. McClean, Commissioner of the New Jersey State Department of Conservation and Economic Development, had said at dinner, "we could afford the luxury both of the uncoordinated growth and of the uncoordinated attack on the problem. Today, we must coordinate all of our resources so that the major mission of each agency or department is made compatible with the major missions of the other departments. For example, a modern highway is not just a means of transportation, it may also be a means of eliminating a slum [or of causing one, as Lewis Mumford noted in the April *Record*]— hence, the highway engineers must see the challenge of eliminating blight and of substituting something constructive."

Mr. Scribner asked if the example of Toronto Metropolitan, which is a government able to institute a planned and coordinated program for the entire Toronto metropolitan area, was not one to look to in our dilemma. Professor Sly thought not: "We don't do that in this country . . . we fall back on authorities." Questioned whether the county government could be useful to combat metropolitan problems, again Professor Sly thought not, however useful the county remains in rural areas. Can other cities bestir themselves, a voice from the floor asked Mr. Schmidt, as Pittsburgh has begun to do? The cities "have to get really bad before people will do something about it," Mr. Schmidt had to say.

Economic Analysis

But if the body politic can afford for a while the wastes which result from lack of planning, business generally cannot. As David Scribner reported, "Ben Franklin once said that two moves for a business were worse than a fire. Today the industrial situation is in just that position. If we look through the shotgun marriages of industry, called 'mergers,' and the 'spun-off' plants which are 'surplus to the needs of the new corporation,' we see the after-effects of bad judgment. Bad judgment can always be determined by hind-sight; so, for that matter, can good judgment. To help make good judgment by foresight is the problem. This consists of a careful analysis of the industry under review, its future course, its place in our economy, and finally the role of the particular corporation in that industry. The next step is the analysis of the local requirements of this company and finally the selection of the many suitable places which should be considered. Too few industries attempt to make or have made for them an economic analysis of the city or region to which they intend to move. As testimony that this field is seldom touched upon are the many plants that are on the market for sale. Many of them are relatively new and in practically every case they will be sold at a loss because no economic analysis of the location and its suitability for a particular industry was made prior to construction. There are usually state as well as Federal agencies which collect data on manufacturing." This should be collected by the analyst. However, he "should not stop there, but should take a look at the nature of the industries represented and ask the question that any investor asks, i.e., 'Are these growth industries or are they dying industries?'

"Or, and this is important, the competition for employees may be tough in the years ahead, unless the service industries are able to grow in order to make it a place to attract people as a place to live. If there is adequate space for people to live and the region has all of the community services in sufficient quantity, the chances are that it will grow and that any manufacturer will be profitable growing with it, *if his products are the sort that should be made there.*"

When his products are no longer the sort that should be made there, disasters break out, of the sort described by Laurence C. Plowman, whose job has been to try to ease the shock to New England occasioned by the removal of the plants of Textron, Inc. "We must face the fact," he said, "that there is by no means a universal acceptance of acknowledged responsibility in this area.

"However, there are also some striking instances of industries, forced into a move by economics, voluntarily assuming responsibility for helping the community recover its balance through the acquisition of new industry to take up the payroll slack. My experience includes firsthand contact with case examples in communities in New England where the textile industry has been moving out and away—and to some degree these reflect conditions described by the reverse or 'other side' of the coin. However, despite this, the results obtained through industry-community cooperation have been beneficial. . . .

"In Textron it is policy, approved and adopted by the directors of the company, as a worthwhile expenditure for better community and public relations."

The job is one of salesmanship. In Nashua, New Hampshire, for instance, in 1948, disaster was averted when Textron closed its mills there because the "Nashua Industrial Committee" was formed of local businessmen. It bought the Textron properties (with Textron holding the mortgage), in order to lease them to other industries. "The next move was to tell the story of what Nashua was and what Nashua had to offer to industries outside of New Hampshire. Using every possible media within our modest means— newspapers, radio, and direct mail—we pointed out our ideal location, available space, and living and working conditions in Nashua. We visited prospects or invited them to visit us. We made no promise of subsidies, tax abatements, or special considerations. We had space to rent at reasonable rates and an excellent supply of labor to offer. As a result, we attracted industries which leased or bought space from the Foundation and provided more than 2,500 immediate jobs, in addition to other jobs provided by industries which could not utilize our space but found locations in other parts of the city at our suggestion. More than 5,000 people are today employed in some 23 different companies in this property as a result of this effort."

The prodigy of salesmanship must not, however, be confused with an economic study. Mr. Scribner pointed out: "The economic study to be effective must be completely objective. It must call the shots as they are seen. It should never be perverted to 'selling' the community or region." Mr. Barkin, of the Textile Workers' Union, doubted that the selling effort was successful: "The realtor approach for the industrial redevelopment of the distressed area is apparently inadequate" to rejuvenate or rehabilitate the areas left stranded, since the textile worker in New England is, in Mr. Plowman's words, "actually a displaced person."

The existing problems persist, though economic analysis may help avoid some new ones.

City and Suburb

Just as no ready answers seem available to the problem of planning the whole expanding metropolis, or to all the problems of rehabilitation and rejuvenation left behind by industry moving away, so no debate between city and suburb could produce a very determined opposition of ideas. Frazar B. Wilde of Connecticut General used the continuing operation of his company's building during last February's record snowstorm to point out its superior efficiency. "As much as any one thing that has happened since we moved into our new building back when the dogwoods were blooming last spring," he continued, "that storm brought into focus the picture of a business environment located just beyond the edge of town, in a pastoral setting where an ample site let us build as we thought best suited our needs and those of our employees. . . . Today, just ten months after we moved, we can expect no regrets. The values that we had hoped to derive from going to the country have materialized."

Connecticut General's move to the country was based on dismissal of a "balanced transportation system" and acceptance of the automobile as the one means of transportation, an acceptance which has grown even more complete during the ten months of occupancy. "We accepted the idea that most people wanted to drive to work. . . . Since we moved, the percentage of employees using the buses has gone down steadily; the percentage coming by cars has grown. When we moved we provided one parking space for every two employees. We shall celebrate our first anniversary in the new building by constructing a large new parking area. The ratio of one for two is not enough. It should be much closer to one for one."

S. Wescott Toole, discussing the Prudential's reaction to the move to the suburbs, listed an impressive series of reasons for remaining in the city. "All these downtown advantages . . . can really be confirmed," he said, "by the Prudential's own experience. Our company owns office buildings for home office use containing over 4,300,000 sq ft of rentable area. . . . In

1948 the company embarked upon a decentralization program. . . . I am happy to say that it has accomplished the objectives that we had hoped for. In providing office buildings for our decentralized operations, we have always located our buildings within the city limits. In some instances they are well removed from the downtown area. In other instances they are in the central city itself." Generally, though, they are on the edge of the central city, as in Chicago, for the light, air, and chance for the building to stand independently as a symbol, if not farther out, as in Houston and Jacksonville, where swimming pools and plenty of parking for the ubiquitous motor car can be provided. "We require," he said later, "a prestige location: environment, setting, and parking." Connecticut General, on the other hand, was not, Mr. Wilde pointed out in answer to a question, trying to escape the city limits. "Areas large and small need more metropolitan authorities," he averred, so as to arrive at a wider geographical tax base. Everyone in the metropolitan area should pay for its services. "Other pioneers" in Hartford thirty years ago "moved even farther out" than a mile from the Old State House. They "survived the warnings of their friends that people wouldn't think of going so far to work; that the main banking offices and the department stores had to be close by. The city has long since engulfed some of the pioneers. They are downtown now, because downtown moved out to them." The difference in Connecticut General's and Prudential's attitudes seems to be one of degree, not of any really sharp theoretical difference. Both want a prestige location, environment, setting, and parking, at a conveniently reachable point. The difference comes in whether the automobile's function is regarded as important or as vital.

What Is a City?

The question that didn't get much asked, significantly, in the numerous testimonials to the importance of the central city, from the floor as well as from the speakers, is "What is a city?" It was implicit—perhaps even partly answered—in a film shown at an evening meeting, a film of Chicago made by James Davis, of Princeton, in which there appeared the particular kind of life that makes a city, the raw excitement of elevateds, people, fire escapes, and busy streets. Mr. Schmidt had started his account of Pittsburgh's redevelopment with a challenge hurled at Pittsburgh in 1947 in *Fortune* magazine: "In an article reviewing the beginning of our post-war civic efforts, it concluded,

'Pittsburgh is the test of industrialism everywhere to renew itself, to rebuild upon the gritty ruins of the past a society more equitable, more spacious, more in the human scale!'" *Fortune* discussed Pittsburgh again in April 1958, after the Princeton conference, and to task the spacious equitable scheme for Gateway Center, because the human scale was not yet present. The center, unlike Mellon Square nearby, is an "ersatz suburb," covered with grass but not with people. People and their activities are shoved underground. Pittsburgh helps demonstrate that space and the movement of cars can be exciting but that spaciousness is not enough. In the very heart of Trenton, New Jersey, Professor Labatut reminded the conference, is a cloverleaf for the local freeway which is rather larger than the Place de la Concorde. The difference in urban amenity between the two spaces is alarmingly evident.

"We hope at this meeting to explore some of the important experiences of American business and industry as decisions have been made, to discuss some of the implications of those decisions, and perhaps to arrive at an understanding of the broad business and industrial statesmanship which forms the basis of architecture in its broadest sense," Mr. McLaughlin had said in the opening of the Conference. These important experiences of business and industry turn out to be kaleidoscopically various, heartily prodigious, and strongly averse to being pigeonholed. For an architect, it is no real surprise that some aspects of broad business and industrial statesmanship should elude understanding, and even credulity; opposing trends sometimes seem curiously to merge. This is not to deny, however, that from these counsels of industry often come the decisions which shape our design decisions and so our architecture, which in its turn shapes us.

Moore spent the years between 1954 and 1957 earning his master's and Ph.D. at Princeton University, and stayed an additional year as a postdoctoral teaching fellow. The subject of his master's thesis was an urban design proposal for Monterey, California, exploring the compositional unification of the historic adobe structures with the rest of Monterey and its bay. The thesis was presented at Princeton in 1956 and later became the subject of an article for the Journal of the American Institute of Architects in 1959.

"The Architecture of Water" was written for Canadian Architect in 1959. It was based on Moore's doctoral dissertation one year prior, and much later became the book Water and Architecture (New York: Abrams, 1994). The dissertation included a history of water symbolism, grouped under the headings "fountains and waterfalls," "rivers and canals," "pools and lakes," and "oceans and islands," as well as design projects for St. Bartholomew's Church, the Seagram Building, and Glen Canyon. The subject itself became a metaphor for the larger issues Moore was considering, as he wrote in the dissertation's introduction:

> Dissatisfaction is the provocation for every thesis—dissatisfaction, and the hope that the discovery, organization and possibly creation of ideas might do something to improve the situation. The provocation for this thesis was dissatisfaction with the aridity of much of our own architecture, coupled with the observation that water has just those qualities which arid buildings lack: it invites approach, and it remains captivating for periods of prolonged contact. But water is not often used in architectural composition in our time, and even when it is used it is usually unconvincing. The pathetic little shower heads which are beginning to grace our shopping centers are no more out of character with the composition around them than is the disappointing arrangement in front of Frank Lloyd Wright's Imperial Hotel.
>
> A Ph.D. thesis in Architecture seems the proper place to try to discover a possible place for water in our design. This thesis, therefore, will investigate the medium, its form, and its content, using the work of the past and the attitudes and ideas which produced it, which are the materials available for an investigation of this sort. Water has been an object of the deepest concern to man as long as he has existed. The control he has exercised over it, the forms he has caused it to take, and the meaning of those forms could lead to a cultural history of man. Such an undertaking

would be, to say the least, beyond the scope of this thesis; it would also be, in this case, beside the point, which is to try to see how water can be of use to us in our own architecture. The uses of water in the past will be examined, not to compile a catalog of effects which we could copy, but to try to arrive at a better understanding of the material, and how it has been expressive of the different points of view of the designers who used it. Our own point of view is again different, and our own uses of water in design will not correspond to those of the past. This thesis, then, is not directed toward the revival of any special water form, like fountains, which have been suitable in the past and may or may not be suitable for us; it is directed, rather, toward the discovery of whatever about water would be useful in the formulation of our own approach to design.

Architecture is, in its broadest sense, man's conscious ordering of his visual environment, indoors and out, whether his materials are land forms, or building materials, or plant forms, or light—or water. Current definitions which limit architecture to the creation of enclosed space, however useful they may be for other theses, are of little use in the problems at hand. Water very rarely contributes to the enclosure of space, but it contributes heavily to man's environment, and is therefore of concern to the architect, whose job it is to design that environment.

This investigation is motivated by a dissatisfaction with things as they are. The triumph of the unadorned forms, the simple statement, the "glass box" demands immediate attention to the problems of developing architectural character. The architect today must seek a richness and depth which will make architectural composition more than just clear, simple ideas, and will give them meaning not only for the seconds required to glance at them, but also for the minutes required to approach them and go through them, and for the years required to live in them, and for the weather to act upon them. Our economic situation renders the intricacies of ornament unpromising in the development of our architecture; but water offers constant change and movement coupled in a paradox with a suggestion of the infinity of time and space. It offers qualities of splash and play and delight, and other qualities of calm, profundity, and invitation to meditation.

Moore also had several concurrent research projects that he hoped to develop as books, including studies on Byzantine mosaics and the manipulation of landscapes at large scales. Contrasting his water research was an examination of *the solid but plastic forms of plaster architecture, research that would result in lectures such as "Domes, Neumann and Rococo."*

This set opens with a short commentary by Moore on the influence of Princeton's design director Jean Labatut (written for an exhibition catalog of 1976) and concludes with a review of two books about Louis Kahn, one of Moore's teachers there.

Commentary for *Princeton's Beaux Arts and Its New Academicism*

I got finished with the army in February [1955] in the middle of the school year, and was put into Class A. They don't have a Class A anymore. Hugh Hardy was in Class B at that point. Also in Class A were some ex-qualifiers like John Woodbridge and Ed Sprankle, who is now with Ernie Kump, and a variety of others. The first problem we had was two churches. Apparently, in the past they had been given with expectations of enormous subtlety. That is, there would be an Episcopal Church and a Baptist Church, or a Baptist and a Methodist Church—something that for the naked eye would seem indistinguishable, but one was expected to find subtleties of difference between them, as reasons for difference of architectural expression. Amazing!

There had been a short problem which I had done well on, which had to do with the entrance across the fields from Route 1 toward Princeton with the tower of the Graduate College in the left distance and Holder [on the right]. I had done a very simple thing with pictures through the windshield and windshield wipers and all, which seemed to me reasonable—it pleased Labby greatly—with very little done except moving some rows of trees around and making what turned out to be a typical piece of Labatism, very like his Johnson & Johnson stuff up the road which I didn't know anything about at that time. So he had liked that very much.

The next thing were the churches, I think in our case Unitarian and I can't remember the other one. I remember my Unitarian one because I thought it was just wonderful, I dug a pond and made what amounted to a Japanese pavilion that you went on little back-and-forth bridges to get to, and it had a little rail around it over the water and a big Japanese-meeting-room-shaped interior. In fact, I'm working on one for someone in Ohio right now which is a dead ringer for it. But Heath Licklider, Bill Shellman,

Originally published in *Princeton's Beaux Arts and Its New Academicism*, exh. cat. (New York: Institute for Architecture and Urban Studies, 1976).

and Labby were on the jury and they failed it. It got fewer points than anyone else by far. I thought they had not recognized the real importance of my Zen concepts.

Then in the fall of Class A, Labby was teaching the thesis and I had Enrico Peressutti during one of the golden moments, when we had the site at Yucatan and Peressutti was full of the new and the old. At Christmas time the whole class, including by then the ones who had been in Class B the spring before, Ham Niles, Joe D'Amelio, flew down there and had this incredible time, with Peressutti full of things way ahead of his time. He was very much interested in putting modern buildings with old ones in a friendly way at a time when people were saying that it was neither interesting nor possible.

He was extremely important to me at that time. I guess what I expected and what Labatut didn't seem to me to be delivering at that moment was some overall sense of what to do. And Labby had all these visions and perceptions that, in retrospect, seem enormously valuable and wonderful. But, at the time, there seemed to be something missing in that none of the students knew what they wanted to do, so that the buildings came out with lots of insights and never any exciting shape, and that was the fifties when that was what you did—have buildings with exciting shapes.

In the five years that I had [at Princeton], certainly Labby was the key figure; the subtlety and the breadth of his vision made it all work. What also made it work was the presence of people like Peressutti and Kahn who were also prepared to look at the past and who were much more specifically into their own formulation of it.

Neither made any requirements of the students that the projects had to look like what they had in mind. But they did offer a model of what you might get if you followed the lines they were operating under. I was Kahn's teaching assistant while Labby was in Rome (1955–1956). Lyndon was fighting Kahn every inch of the way, whereas Turnbull was very eager for Kahn to give "it" to him. The Kahn shapes and the Peressutti ones, too, were very powerful. The secret to Labby's long-term success, and occasional short-term discontent, was there were no such models. When I was there Labby hadn't done any buildings ever. . . . You know, with standard allowance for my failing memory, Vincent Scully used to say the most important thing about Princeton was that they didn't teach you anything wrong there.

Our relation to the past is not a simple one. We are not carrying on in our cities an unbroken architectural tradition; but the relics of the past are available to us as they never have been to a civilization before, and we find ourselves anxious to extract meaning from them, perhaps more anxious than any previous civilization has ever been. Our cities grow quickly obsolete and are rebuilt. Their buildings do not long retain their usefulness, though sometimes their power over our imagination increases with their age. We cannot seek the comfortable continuity of a medieval village; instead, as Henry James pointed out, "We are divided . . . between liking to feel the past strange and liking to feel it familiar; the difficulty is, for intensity, to catch it at the moment when the scales of the balance hang with the right evenness."

Monterey, California, like many other historic American cities, poses just such a difficulty. In the decades before 1848, Monterey was the capital of Spanish and then of Mexican California. It was at the very edge of the Spanish world, not far from where the Russians, coming the other way around, had established Fort Ross. So far from the sources of style, Monterey did not even look like a Spanish or Mexican town; its simple adobe houses, without patios but with balconies around, were scattered, undivided by streets or fences, on a curving greensward that swept down to a cool and lonely bay.

Not much over a hundred years ago, the Americans came to California, Monterey lost its importance, and there was no need even to tear down the old adobes. After a half-century, the town began to come alive again, first with sardines and then with tourists and retired people who came to enjoy the famous local scenery. Monterey remains proud of its Spanish past, but is completely separated from it. "That, to my imagination," as Henry James had said about something else, "is that past fragrant of all, or of almost all, the poetry of the living thing outlived and lost and gone, and yet in which the precious element of closeness, telling so of connections but tasting so of differences, remains appreciable." In Monterey, two dozen simple adobe houses, handsomely textured by time, stand in the middle and on the edges of the downtown area. The lonely greensward at the end of the world, on which they were once scattered, is increasingly urban, crowded with tele-

Originally published in *Journal of the American Institute of Architects* 31, no. 3 (March 1959), pp. 22–25.

phone poles and polychromed automobiles almost as long as the adobes. The difficulty, for intensity, is to balance the strangeness of these adobes, and their elusive loneliness, against their use in the living town.

I attempted an answer to the development of downtown Monterey in a master's thesis done under Jean Labatut in the School of Architecture at Princeton University. It is not an attempt, like Williamsburg, to rebuild a portion of the past. There is too much of the present in Monterey to make that desirable. Nor is there an attempt, as at Santa Barbara, to try to merge the present and the past in a set of forms inspired by the past. Instead, the attempt is to extricate the adobes from visual chaos, and to try to suggest, in the middle of the city, their loneliness and distance from us, so as to increase their special savor (fig. 1).

1
"The View toward the Past," panel from Moore's master's thesis at Princeton

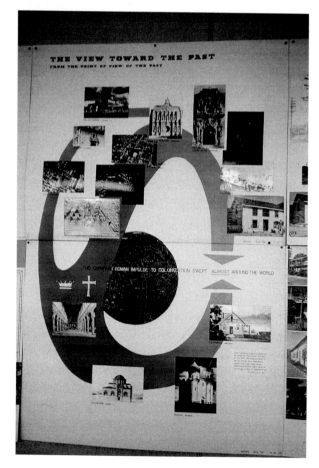

The adobes are concentrated in two areas: one, at the foot of the main shopping street, on the shore of the bay, contains the old Customs House, California's first theater, the two-story Pacific Building, and three houses; the other area, two blocks away, at the head of the main street, stretches almost half a mile, in a wide arc parallel to the shore of the bay. Between Colton Hall, at one end of the arc, where California's statehood was established, and the late eighteenth-century Royal Presidio Chapel at the other are some twenty adobes, dispersed among even more numerous gas stations and automobile agencies. At present, a tourist route past almost all of the historic buildings is marked by a stripe in the pavement; but this is no real boon. The motorist is faced with the physical discomforts of driving through a tangle of downtown traffic, and the visual fatigue from concrete, asphalt, telephone poles, parking meters, wires, and signs, through which, with luck, he can glimpse historic buildings. The adobes are too far apart for us to expect that an automobile-bound American tourist would walk between them, so a basis of the plan is a separate tourist road, a pair of grooves for tires, sunken some two feet below ground level, which connects the historic buildings, minimizes the intrusion of the tourists' own huge automobiles by sinking them partly out of sight, and enhances the feeling of openness and a romantic sort of loneliness around the buildings, by lowering the visitor's eye level, and by making possible the control of what the visitor sees between himself and the historic adobes. The attempt in this space is to use rocks, walls, trees, and a feeling of emptiness to evoke the mood of the loneliness and apartness which, with minimum destruction of modern buildings, would restore the sense of houses on a green. In the middle of the modern town there would appear then "the past fragrant of all, or of almost all, the poetry of the thing outlived and lost and gone . . .".

The plan uses the shaping of the earth first to create a ridge at the entrance to the town, behind which pine trees rise, through which automobiles enter the shopping area, and along the top of which, separated from other traffic, runs the tourist road. Walls, groves of trees, and mounds of earth planted with pines control vision around a series of dramatically empty spaces through which the sunken tourist road runs. The adobes are at the edge of the spaces, in contact with the life of the town, except for a very few, already museums, which stand in the middle of the emptiness. Otherwise, only a few solitary lampposts stand in the space, as they might in a De Chirico painting, to suggest a "nostalgia of the infinite."

The tourist road is one-way, well over a mile long, and accessible, except in emergencies, only at its entrance and at one intermediate point. Three small overpasses and some reorganization of the tangled downtown street pattern keep it free from any cross traffic. Concave grooves in the sunken pavement keep tires on the track, and limit speed to 20 miles an hour, so that even the driver is able to concentrate on what there is to see. Frequent parking areas, sunken and shielded visually from the empty space, make it easy to stop for photographs and to visit the adobes which are open to the public. The road skirts the downtown business section, to arrive at the cluster of adobes near the bay, where a great sand plain with rocks creates the empty space, larger than the grassy voids farther from the water. Here the drive ends. The plain suggests water as a Japanese sand garden does, so that the openness of the bay seems to extend to the area between the buildings. On the bay side of this void, an existing Fisherman's Wharf, lined with brightly painted and lit restaurants and shops, is retained, and space is set aside for similar establishments on the adjacent shore. Their lights and activity, seen across the sand, should further emphasize the emptiness of the intervening plain.

A serious traffic problem exists in downtown Monterey, because a tangle of streets and hills forces all traffic to the north past complicated intersections onto one street along the bay. This plan attempts a solution by reducing the number of intersections, channeling through traffic across rather than along the main street, establishing a loop parking road around the shopping section, and removing traffic from Alvarado Street, the main shopping street. Alvarado Street then becomes the link between the two historic areas. Small sand gardens, sometimes walled, create a rhythm of busy spaces and voids down the street, recalling the voids near the adobes and concentrating pedestrian activity. The downtown shopping area, currently in the doldrums while business expands on nearby highways, thus gains adequate circulation, parking, an impression of activity, and above all a kind of cohesion that should give it an edge in the competition for the Monterey Peninsula's business. The shopping is important, since any plan for saving the adobes must be based on a healthy economy for the downtown area; the risky alternative is to let the downtown choke itself off, as it seems ready to do, and then to count on clearing the slums.

A pedestrian walk with brick pavement links adobes and runs the length of Alvarado Street. It is slightly raised off the ground so as to emphasize pedestrian separation from automobiles in the historic areas and to control the movement of the pedestrian for the best sense of lonely and busy spaces. A colonnade covers the pedestrian walk in places. (It shows in the foreground of the sketch of the Royal Presidio Chapel, and in the background of the other sketches.) It is made of precast concrete units, with precast roof slabs laid over, to form fifteen-foot-square gable-roofed bays, meant by their small scale to enhance the importance of the adobes. The colonnade is used to enhance important or handsome buildings, to camouflage unfortunate structures, to describe pleasant pedestrian spaces, and to create a consistent form which will make a visit to Monterey a coherent and memorable experience, much as Pope Sixtus V installed straight streets and obelisks to give unity to the experience of visiting baroque Rome.

Continuity could come, too, though a scheme of dark colors for modern buildings, soft earth colors for the adobes, and white with copper roofs for the colonnades. Wires would go underground, and a family of related forms for street lights, traffic lights, and signs would support the visual calm. At night the lighting fixtures, set low, would provide incandescent light for pedestrian areas, and set high would provide mercury vapor light for areas occupied by automobiles. Mercury vapor lights in the standard fixtures, set to shine into the trees, would heighten their greenness, and gold fluorescent light shining very softly from the windows of the adobes would emphasize their antiquity.

The thesis includes a design for a museum, on the one hand to orient the tourist, and on the other to demonstrate that simple and honest contemporary architecture, carefully scaled, can more effectively enhance the simple little adobes than large-scale parodies of them could.

Perhaps the most surprising aspect of the thesis was its reception. It had been done, three thousand miles away, as an investigation of the relation of the past to the present, and how to make the most of it; it was done quite independently of any special local interests. Precisely, however, because it had been done free of pressures, it seemed to have considerable local appeal. Exhibitions of the thesis in the Monterey library and the AIA pavilion at the county fair, newspaper publicity, and a public lecture sponsored by the Monterey History and Art Association all stimulated interest, and study is presently under way for an Urban Renewal project meant to achieve, in the cluster of adobes near the bay, the goals toward which this thesis is aimed.

The Architecture of Water

In the ruins of Pompeii there stands a drinking fountain which served for donkeys and for people. It had a faucet and a basin, and over them was carved a cloud with a rain god sitting on it. For the donkeys the carving was not necessary; for the people, though, the cloud and the god must (at least sometimes) have given added pleasure and meaning to the water they drank.

In a cold climate, the value of water lies very largely in the cloud and the rain god. The water itself is likely to be frozen solid, or at least a chilly and forbidden thing. In deserts this is not so. There, the sight and sound of water—looking cool, sounding cool, and actually cooling the air with its spray—becomes a real physical pleasure. In a climate like Canada's there is no such need. But there is a real use for it, stemming not from a physical need but from a state of mind. This use, so far largely ignored in North America, results from a unique property of water: a trickle, a stream, coming from somewhere and going somewhere else, is capable of suggesting a mountain far away and the mysterious depths of the sea. In a sense, all the water in the world seems to share in the same identity: as the cloud and the rain god enhanced the importance of the water in the Pompeiian basin, so the water in the ocean adds a dimension to the trickle in our stream.

For us this state of mind about moving water is based on a knowledge of the cycle in which it moves. From the sea, we know, it is evaporated into clouds, to fall on the mountains, to seep into the springs and streams, to flow into rivers, and so back down to the sea. This quality can make running water particularly useful in our sprawling cities, where physical escape gets more and more difficult every day. Then water in a stream fills a real need, providing (for the imagination) the wide and distant places that the suburbs have physically choked off. The streams in the ravines of Toronto, for instance—as Herman Melville long ago pointed out about streams everywhere—link the mind not only with wide spaces of the lake but with the harbor front, the ships from exotic places, and the mysteries of the sea.

On top of this, bodies of water often provide open space where a city needs the feel of open space but has no use for vast plazas; we have little need for rallying points for mobs or armies, but cities become much more beautiful when they contain wide spaces. Stockholm on its islands, or Paris with its spinal river, are enhanced by their watery settings, as San Francisco is.

Originally published in *Canadian Architect* 4, no. 11 (November 1959), pp. 40–45.

Given the need for water flowing into our cities, even the cold ones, what conditions should be filled to make the water most effective? One device worth attention is *paradox,* to attract the observer by putting at odds what he thinks he sees with what he knows is true. A more general need is *immediacy*—establishing the closest possible contact between the observer and the water. Past this, a sense of *distance* is of course essential if the experience we are discussing is to work. And since water is a flowing, moving medium, at the root of its effectiveness is the way it is composed in *time.*

Water, since it obeys a set of rigid rules with which we are all familiar, provides an excellent opportunity for the designer to play with paradox. Water flows to the lowest available level and stays there. If a play with optical illusion can make the surface we know to be level seem to tilt, the paradox immediately catapults us into the picture. Much more simply, an underwater barrier (as at the mill at Fergus, Ontario) can cause an apparently stable body of water to break suddenly away and fall (fig. 2). A celebrated Chinese garden of the Sung dynasty was based on such a paradox: three still ponds on a tiny island on the windswept water of Lake Si reflected the moon; smooth water lay above the rough water, and the moon lay way below them both.

If paradox is a rather particular way of attracting an observer, immediacy is the quality that must always be present if the water is to be worth having. "Immediacy" was defined by Gordon Cullen some years ago in the *Architectural Review* as "a mental leaning-out-over." The sense it includes of

2
Mill, Fergus, Ontario

contact, and closeness with the water, must be established before any waterworks become effective. Roman fountains offer an ideal example. They invite contact; people seem irresistibly drawn toward them, to dangle their
fingers in the water, then to plunge in their arms. Some of this attraction is
without a doubt a function of their settings. Two of the most potent attrac-
tors, the Barcaccia in the Piazza di Spagna and the Trevi Fountain, are located below ground level, so that people step down to them and are thus
given a strong sense of being immersed in them, even in the middle of city
traffic (fig. 3). The contrast somehow comes with the sense of being drawn
down into the water; but the design of the edge of the fountain basins plays
an important part. The water in these Roman fountains fills the basins to
their very brims, or even splashes over. The edge, on which people can sit,
often dips down under the surface of the water, so that observers and water
are very close. In direct contrast, most North American fountains, ringed
with uninviting vertical walls, the water below the edge, manage to recall
water in the bottom of a bathtub, or rain water in an unfilled swimming
pool, so that the sense of immediacy eludes us.

3
Barcaccia Fountain,
Rome

Immediacy can be there on a much larger scale as well. Portofino, on the Italian coast, has a harbor like most harbors were before the industrial revolution (fig. 4). The line between the water and the land is filled with chances for contact: sometimes the pavement dips below the sea, so that small boats pulled ashore find themselves in the central square; sometimes the water is deep enough, at the edge of the quay, for bathers to dive into it (it is crystal clear) and swim among the boats. Farther along, cranes hang out over the water and there is all the activity of cargoes from larger ships being lifted ashore. The variety of activity itself, the animation of the line between land and water, all contribute to the sense of contact, of "mental leaning-out-over," for the passerby at the edge of the sea.

At Elora, in Ontario, the activity along the river front is much more limited than at Portofino, but some of the same sense of closeness exists. Buildings rise directly out of the river, whose smooth surface (paradoxically, again) suddenly disappears over a falls. Windows and balconies open over the water, while a tiny path with the thinnest of railings skirts the falls and provides, frighteningly, the sense of "leaning out over."

4
Portofino, Italy

Contact can be maintained even across space. The parapet at the edge of the Dufferin Terrace in Quebec serves to make the observer soar, in his mind, high above the St. Lawrence, and unites the terrace with the water as effectively as actual physical contact would, and rather more dramatically.

In Toronto, on the other hand, all sense of contact between the water and the people on the land is lost, destroyed by uninterrupted stretches of industrial buildings and throughway rights-of-way. All the possibilities inherent in the line between land and water are lost.

The sense of contact, the immediacy of water, important by itself, is immeasurably enhanced when it goes with the sense which water is almost uniquely able to give, that sense that makes us, in a cold climate, most interested in using it: it evokes the image of great distances and far places. This image, which we can call the sense of distance, acts not only on our senses but on our imagination, like theater, to take us past the limitations of visible space. The water cycle, from sea back to sea, was not really understood until the eighteenth century, but for thousands of years men have been fascinating themselves with fantasies about where the flowing water comes from, and where it goes to, and how it finally gets back to the place it started from. When it was discovered, the water cycle soon provided the theme for one of the richest and most exciting exploitations of water's forms and qualities in the world: the Trevi Fountain in Rome (fig. 5). Here, in a whirl of allegorical sculpture and richly varied rock forms, water squirts, slides, splashes, and tumbles down to a wide, calm basin. In the allegory, these are the streams and rivers, and this is the sea. The composition juxtaposes water flowing, water falling, water shooting up, water suggested by the pattern of erosion carved into the rocks, and then water still; the designers enjoyed to the limit the shapes that water can take and the things it can do.

When the site allows, the sense of distance can be achieved much more easily by water flowing out of sight. Garden designers in China and Japan long ago made into a rule the idea that water should proceed from an unseen source, flow by us, then, suggesting unlimited distance, flow round a corner and out of sight. Bernini, in the Fountain of the Four Rivers in Piazza Navona in Rome, lets the water disappear through the mouth of a dolphin (fig. 6). Remarkably, instead of seeming like an ordinary drain and killing in our imaginations the continuity of the water's flow, the dolphin manages to emphasize contact with the vast depths of the sea to which the water must be on its way.

5
Trevi Fountain,
Rome, Nicola Salvi

6
Fountain of the Four
Rivers, Rome, Gian
Lorenzo Bernini

Architects are used to composing buildings in space, and in the time it takes the observer to circulate around and in them. Water, because its impact on the senses and on the imagination depends so much on movement, makes the designer concerned even more than usual with composition in time. The surf pounding on a beach, especially if there are rocks for it to break on, can keep us fascinated for as long as we watch the infinitely varied rhythms of the waves, but a mechanically timed sequence of events, of jets or squirts, loses much of its fascination as soon as we discover the sequence (in most cases, a matter of a very few minutes). A man-made sequence not so easily predictable can hold us as the sea does: a fountain in a garden in Philadelphia by George Howe did it very simply, with only a basin and a single jet of water, whose outlet was just under the surface. The surface tension held back the water coming out of the underwater pipe, only a slight bulge showing on the surface, until the pressure built up enough for the jet to break free. Then it would shoot up into the air until enough water had accumulated aloft to fall back down on the inlet and recreate the surface tension. Even so simply, the fountain managed to suggest a natural timing, measured, like the ocean's, in terms of infinity instead of the measured tick-tock sort, which is good for many things but of little use for the kind of play of distance and time that water is capable of making.

Since water moves and people move, the possibilities for composing the two motions are immense. The Villa d'Este at Tivoli, near Rome, is such a composition. It is on a hillside, and a sizable river has been diverted into it to make possible a series of waterworks. When it was built, late in the Renaissance, it was entered from below and the visitors passed up through the garden to the villa above. The path of the visitor upward did not coincide with the path of the water downward but frequently crossed it, at points marked by fountains and cascades (fig. 7). At the entrance, a trickle of water could be seen and heard; on the way up, the volume of visible water and of sound increased to a climax just below the villa; in the courtyard of the villa, then, a trickle in a tiny fountain recalled the torrents below. Later, more bombastic additions have destroyed the clarity of the earlier scheme, and the entrance is no longer from the bottom of the garden; but the continuity that comes because of the water's coherent relation to its source, and the complex relation of the spectator's path to the water, makes a visit to the garden still a fascinating experience in time.

7
Villa d'Este,
Tivoli

All these uses of water, though they may employ the physical pleasure of its bubble and splash, are mostly concerned with images we form in our minds. They do not depend on a hot dry desert and the need it generates for the cool delights of fountains. In a climate like Canada's, though, the images we form become even further separated from the physical qualities of the water itself, since there are long months when water, frozen solid, cannot move. Much can still be done: on the one hand, as is demonstrated whenever a fountain is left in temperatures much below freezing, the fluid forms of built-up ice can be beautiful themselves, just as the pans of ice in partially frozen streams take on a series of streamlined forms of great beauty; on the other hand, water (at least its contemplative qualities) can be suggested even when the water itself is not present, as, in Japanese gardens, a sunken rocky plane suggests a stream, carefully placed rocks in a field of sand evoke the images of islands in the sea, and two vertical rocks can powerfully suggest a waterfall (fig. 8). The physical delights of water, bubbling and splashing, or falling, or still, are a function of the season; but the states of mind that the skillful introduction of water can induce, the evocation of distance, of freedom from cramped space, and the mystery of far places—these can last the year round.

8
Ryogen-in, Kyoto

This essay is written in the conviction that we can learn from the past—indeed, that it is already a part of us, and that we cannot avoid learning from it. It follows that a look at the uses of plaster in the past should throw some light onto our own attempts to benefit from new uses of it in the future. None of us, certainly, is interested in historical material assembled into a source convenient to copy from. Nor is it necessary to establish plaster's legitimacy by belaboring its antiquity (the Egyptians used it). If, however, a look at its uses in the past can point to some needs that these uses were created to fill, and if the needs in some measure coincide with our own, as we might expect them to, we may well be able to benefit from the experience of others.

The experience of others with plastic materials extends over a long period. Plastic materials and "plastic form" must have entered the human consciousness when someone discovered that a handful of moist clay would change its form under the pressure of his fingers, and then would retain the form that bore his imprint. Since the first discovery that a layer of plastic material spread over a rough surface would create a smooth one, or that a layer of plastic material spread over a complicated set of shapes would simplify them, plastic material has been applied, indoors and out. And since someone first discovered, on the other hand, that these same plastic materials could be fashioned into shapes which could make building surfaces more interesting, they have been pressed or cast into decorative shapes, and applied to enrich the simplicity of architectural forms.

Plaster is one of the most important of these plastic materials. As a building material, its special quality is its ability to take and retain the form impressed upon it, or upon which it is impressed. As it happens, during the last half-century architects and critics have been paying particular attention to the "nature of materials" and its expression in architecture. There has been a strong insistence on the need for a stone building to demonstrate its stoniness, or a brick building its brickiness. Into such an atmosphere plaster does not fit very well; its essential quality is not its "plasteriness" but its ability to take—and make—architectural forms. Our own development of the uses of plaster, it seems likely, will then be a product of an interest in and a search for form, at least partly for its own sake. This search for form—on the one hand, through the simplification and clarification of shapes that are

Previously published in John R. Diehl, *Manual of Lathing and Plastering* (n.p.: MAC Publishers Association, 1960), pp. 4–30.

38

complex and confusing, and on the other, through the enrichment of shapes that are too simple to interest us—should be our concern here. Examples are available to us from a wide variety of times and places. Through the ancient Near East and in Egypt, plaster was used to make surfaces smooth for decoration. The Romans used it both in smooth walls and to make sculptured relief. It appears in Romanesque churches and in Renaissance palaces. Finally, in the late baroque and rococo periods in western Europe and America it became the basis for a whole system of design, even as much earlier the Moors in Spain had based an entirely different system of design on its use. Chronologically, we should note, the development of our own plastering traditions seemed, to late nineteenth-century historians of the craft, no development at all, but rather a retrogression from the exuberant heights of expression reached late in the Middle Ages by the plasterer himself. Gradually since then, they lamented, designs had become more and more specific when they came from the architect until, in the nineteenth century, they were reduced to ready-cast plaster decorative elements which the plasterer on the job needed only to install, and the craftsman's initiative had almost vanished. Now, with handicraft processes stifled more than ever by the increasing industrialization of the entire building industry, we are in need of a whole new evaluation; the tear shed so eloquently by the nineteenth century for the departure of the "happy" medieval craftsman need not be shed again. Our own techniques can scarcely be turned backward in time. But the ways people in the past (and the past extends up to the present moment) have used plaster in their search for architectural form, and the successes which met their efforts, are nonetheless illuminating. We are fortunate that there are so many examples to look among.

The Creation of Plastic Form, and the Articulation of Form

As we have noted, there seem to be two principal ways to compose buildings. There seem, too, to be two ways to make use of materials: whether buildings are composed by simplifying complex forms or by enriching simple ones, they are either put together of separate pieces or are made of something continuous. Ordinarily, the separate pieces fastened together best result in a series of straight-line forms, distinguished from one another; that is to say, the forms are "articulated." On the other hand, it seems desirable to emphasize the continuity of continuous materials, so that smooth curves lead from one surface to another, and angles do not break the flow of the eye over the form. The resultant curved continuous shapes may thus express the quality of plasticity which was the original nature of the material, and reinforce the impression that the material has been squeezed into place. A piece of plastic material squeezed into a round ball is a very different thing from a Chinese wood-block puzzle whose separate pieces interlock into a round ball. Although they have the same shape, only the form is "plastic." And even plastic materials, like poured concrete, which are put into place between forms of non-plastic materials are apt to seem non-plastic, as they retain the shape imposed on them.

In the American past, which offers mostly examples of buildings made of pieces of wood, masonry, or metal, it would not be difficult to conclude that articulated form, resulting from the expression of pieces put together, was the norm, and the plastic form an aberration. The 1957 *Progressive Architecture* Award Jury, for instance, thought it wise to withhold prizes from two buildings by John M. Johansen which it admired, because their plastic forms, so different from standard building shapes, seemed to the Jury to be fraught with the danger of being repeated by unskilled hands. This conclusion, though, would be hasty; the history of American building is full of examples of continuous form. The Southwest American tradition of building, for example, with adobe bricks covered with renewed layers of mud plaster, has for centuries produced buildings with curved surfaces, rounded at the corners, which look as though they had been modeled or squeezed into shape. The Ranchos de Taos church in New Mexico, built in 1776, is such an example. In the eastern United States, especially in the decades following 1870, even wood shingles were applied as a continuous flowing skin, which created the impression of plastic forms. Contemporary with these plastic forms of shingle, the heavy masonry forms of H. H. Richardson, Furness and Hewitt, and other architects, though they were pieced together of separate stones, created forms which seemed carved from a single block, and therefore seemed continuous. Techniques following on the development of metal lath and new methods of blowing concrete and plaster onto it might well give new importance to plastic forms in the architecture of our own time.

The use of plaster does not depend entirely on the creation of plastic form. Today, in fact, plaster appears in millions of houses and offices on planar surfaces divided by angular corners; it appears, in fact much more frequently this way than as a material which creates plastic forms. But if we are to distinguish the ways plaster has been used in the past and ways it could be used to advantage in our own work, the differences between the two uses become important. New techniques increase our ability to create plastic forms, and a glance at the architectural periodicals indicates a growing interest in these forms during the last several years. Just possibly this is happening because the designer, separated by a lengthening set of mechanical processes from a finished product, feels the need to achieve the same kind of immediacy as exists between the hands of the potter and the work that takes shape under his fingers. The creation of a set of forms which seem as though they had been squeezed and patted into place helps fill this need. Then, for the designer, there are still other reasons to create plastic forms: these forms create a continuity of structure, of experience, and of movement of light; they intensify a sense of enclosure, while they render unclear the relation of the observer to the space he is in; and they can heighten a sense of movement.

Continuity of structure is important even in stressed-skin systems made of plywood and other unit materials. It is generally essential to a structure made of plastic materials. In such a structure, as we know, stresses do not act neatly at right angles to one another, around right-angled corners. Instead, a force applied at any point in the system creates lines of force which flow through the structure. Natural forms such as morning glories, turtles, and walnuts, as the structural engineer Fred Severud has pointed out, are curved, and while "we cannot . . . completely abandon right angles and straight lines in favor of nature's curves . . . what we can and should do is to understand that her use of curves is merely the expression of a principle of structural continuity; and this latter quality is what distinguishes her designs." A multistory rectilinear cage, on the one hand, which is an adequate demonstration of the structural nature of steel, is not a particularly reasonable form in concrete, because it is unrelated to the structural nature of plastic material; and for people in the middle of the twentieth century, interested in an honest indication of the nature of the structure, a serious dilemma has appeared which must be resolved. In the works of such engineers as Pier Luigi Nervi, on the other hand, or of others interested in the structural properties of concrete, men like Felix Candela or Eduardo Torroja, the shapes are related to the curved lines of flow of the stresses, and are generally continuous; the plastic form works to indicate the nature of the structure (fig. 9).

9
Gatti Wool Factory,
Rome, Pier Luigi
Nervi

Another characteristic beginning to emerge in the middle of the twentieth century is a special concern with the observer's reaction to a building over a period of time, so that the whole process of arriving at a building, of seeing it from far away and up close, from a variety of angles, represents part of one continuing experience, in which the forms instigate the observer's movement, so that one view slides into another. At Le Corbusier's chapel at Ronchamp, for instance, each facade folds into the next, and even the facade full of windows set into deep reveals is arranged so that the observer inside, drawn by the desire to see through each window, is impelled from place to place. The curved tower, on the left as one approaches, turns around the corner to become, with only the slightest break in the continuity, the gargoyle-accented west wall, which in turn slides smoothly around a curve to become a tower for the smaller chapel. This simple continuous experience of one surface is enlivened by variations in the texture of the plaster, and by the constant modulation of the light that falls on it (fig. 10).

10
Notre-Dame-du-Haut,
Ronchamp, Le Corbusier

A third concern, which is now only beginning to interest us, is for the continuity of movement of light; if movement of light is to have continuity, a continuous plastic form for it to fall on is strongly indicated.

Earlier in this century, it was as if light and the sun were newly discovered; glass walls opened up to face the sun, and the more light came in, the better. Now the decorative screen has intervened, so that the light from the outdoors is tempered and patterns of light and shade are formed on the walls and floors inside, as they had been in the eighteenth-century church at Wies, in southern Germany (fig. 11). When patterns of light fall, the nature of the surface they fall on becomes important; it can be smooth and simple, as at Wies, to emphasize the pattern falling; it can be smooth but not planar, as is evident in other parts of the picture at Wies, so as to add variations to the patterns: or it can introduce, as at the Alhambra in Granada, a pattern in counterpoint to the pattern of light. In any of these cases, an important characteristic of the light that makes the patterns, if it is sunlight, is that it changes its direction from minute to minute, from hour to hour, and from

11
Pilgrimage church,
Wies, near Stein-
gaden, Dominikus
Zimmermann

season to season. Here the continuity of plastic form again offers the opportunity to take advantage of movement of light, as it slides gradually from surface to surface. The interlocking plastic forms of the light-intercepting screens of Erwin Hauer are among the very few contemporary attempts to take advantage of this opportunity. For decades, though, the apse of the church at Ranchos de Taos, New Mexico, has been a favorite subject for painters because of the way the sun slides across its surface during the day, forming changing shadows and picking out, as its rays almost become parallel with the wall, the concavities and the subtle curves of the adobe plaster, and its irregular texture (fig. 12). The nave at Wies is an even subtler demonstration; here a pattern of light shining past other forms falls onto the multiple surfaces of the wall, creating a fascinating double modulation of the pattern. The same kind of effect occurs at a larger scale as the light, patterned by the shape of the south windows of the nave, hits the floor and the wall beyond and picks up the leading edges of plaster decorations, so that even within a few minutes, as the sun moves through the sky, the movement of light on the plaster forms makes the space come alive.

12
San Francisco de Asis,
Ranchos de Taos

A second reason to create plastic form is in order to intensify enclosure, to create areas in which the intellectual relation of the observer to the

space around him is destroyed but his emotional relation to the space is enhanced. "There is," as Heinrich Wölfflin pointed out, "a beauty which has its roots just in the not fully comprehensible, in the mystery which never quite unveils its face, in the unassimilable which seems to change at every moment." Trinity Church in Newport, Rhode Island, built in 1725, and Touro Synagogue, also in Newport, built in 1763, create in their beautifully proportioned interiors such a dissolution of intellectual relationship with the space. In each of them a system of columns and entablature, painted white, rises for perhaps three-fourths of the height of the space. The carefully defined members of this trabeated system bear, down to the last molding, a directly measurable relation to one another, and to the human observer. But above these columns and entablatures there is, in each building, a simple smooth blue-green plaster vault, which suggests a vast indefinite incommensurable space very like the sky, a kind of reasonable infinity.

Plastic forms, as well as rendering unclear the sense of forms receding, can intensify the sense of enclosure. The cavelike, womblike form seems more effective than any other for providing the reassuring sense of solidity at one's back, a sense whose absence is suddenly coming to be noticed. John MacL. Johansen's project for a house with a plastic shape, mentioned before, or especially Frederick Kiesler's "Endless House" illustrate the ability of plastic forms to produce buildings which, though small, are not oppressive because their size is unclear. Because of their cavelike continuous forms, they provide a sense of enclosure which is phenomenal.

A third reason to create plastic forms, a reason which other times have understood, perhaps better than our own does, is in order to suggest movement, or to abstract the movement which our eyes and minds experience when they search out a space and imagine themselves around it and through it. Our reaction to spaces can be explained by this empathetic process, through which we imagine ourselves, when we enter a space, projected up and out into the space, searching out its farthest dimensions. This empathetic process causes us, too, to project ourselves into the structure, which perhaps helps account for our thinking of Gothic piers as rising, rather than as pressing down into the ground as they actually do. The imagined motion, like expressed lines of streets, is likely to have a pattern of flow made up of curves rather than of angles and straight lines. Such suggested motion can flow around the outside of a curved form as well as into or through an enclosure, as the example from Ronchamp demonstrates.

The next step in the suggestion of movement comes with the desire to get the forms themselves into apparent motion. It is a desire, surprisingly, which our own architecture does not yet often show, although the sweeping forms of our new superhighways have a hold on the public imagination which the static "architectural" forms at their sides do not possess. (On the highways, to be sure, the mind's imagined sweep through space can be physically duplicated at the wheel of a car.) Some new buildings come, ostensibly by way of structure, to forms which seem to move: Eero Saarinen's hockey rink at Yale University, for instance, suggests rather more motion even than the very plastic Einstein Tower of Erich Mendelsohn, built in 1921. But in order best to discover the conscious development of forms which seem to move, we must look to the buildings of central Europe of the seventeenth and especially the eighteenth centuries, when the plaster masterpieces of the later baroque and rococo periods were conceived. In the Würzburg Residenz, for example, are pilasters and a cartouche, delicately formed of plaster but caught up nonetheless in an illusion of wild writhing (fig. 13). The background of the cartouche swells broadly, then divides itself with fine furrows and curls up again. Consoles curl over the cornice, and feathery leaf forms flutter down over the doorway; other forms slide and dance down the pilasters, and whirl around the candelabra, while out from behind the swelling cartouche prickle spiked objects. More than that, in the architecture of this period whole interiors swirl into motion: the nave of the pilgrimage church of Vierzehnheiligen, in southern Germany, comes into moving life, and the facade of San Carlo alle Quattro Fontane in Rome, symmetrically organized as it is, weaves in and out (fig. 14). In the nineteenth and early twentieth century in the work of Gaudí, such as Casa Milá in Barcelona, as symmetrical organization and simple geometric forms are discarded and the plastic shapes become more free, the movement becomes more complex—and more violent—than ever (fig. 15).

Movement is one reason, then, for the creation of plastic form; the provision of aggressive enclosure, with a simultaneous unclearness of the space enclosed, is a second reason; and the desire for movement of light is a third reason. The creation of plastic form is by no means synonymous with the use of plaster; stone, concrete, clay, and many other materials beside plaster can create such form, and the use of plaster on forms which are not plastic is common, as we have noted. It is important to us, however, to distinguish between the kind of desires which produce plastic forms and those

13
Residenz, Würzburg

14
S. Carlo alle Quattro Fontane,
Rome, Francesco Borromini

15
Casa Milá, Barcelona,
Antoni Gaudí

which produce articulated forms just because plaster is such an extremely flexible material, because it can do, and has done, such a wide variety of things that its use does not suggest specific forms. Indeed, instead of letting his material determine the form, as a steel beam or rough stone determines form, the designer using plaster must decide himself, on these other bases, which kind of forms he wants. If there is in these pages a particular emphasis of plastic form, it is because recently the future of plaster in its creation looks particularly promising.

As soon as forms begin to take shape in the mind of the designer, the development process begins, either simplifying complex ideas and forms to bring order and clarity to them, or amplifying simple forms to bring richness to them. Through both these processes, the natural material can give form to the designer's idea.

The Clarification of Form

In a complex world, a world of complex architectural programs and a riot of complex forms, the process of simplification should be of vast importance to the designer. The plan complexity of a hospital program, for instance, demands an orderly modular repetitive unit if the solution is to be comprehensible to the eye and the mind. Just so, the visual complexity of almost any urban scene requires simplification and organization, if the eye and the mind of the observer are to be satisfied. Articulated forms can be simplified ordinarily so as to emphasize whatever rhythm is inherent in the ways the pieces are put together; plastic forms can be simplified, too, so as to emphasize basic rhythms and relationships in space.

For the clarification of articulate form there is required the establishment of an order in which parts maintain their own identity but are organized into units, which in turn are combined (without loss of the identity of the unit) into the whole. It is important, for clarity, that the parts be commensurate, and that their relation to the unit of which they are a part be understandable. The Chinese long ago formulated for these purposes the "law of five." In a set of observations corresponding closely with those of more recent Gestalt psychologists, they noted that it is impossible instantly to understand a relationship among more than five objects. It would follow, then, that for clarity each unit should be made up of not more than five such parts. For clarity, too, the identities of the separate units must be maintained, and insisted on. The recessed joint, increasingly in evidence, is a means for separating panels from one another by a small recess, instead of hiding the separation with a molding. In this way the panel is established as surface in its own right, so that attention falls onto its proportions and on the plane of its surface. In an example in Los Angeles by Richard Neutra, the proportions and the plane surfaces of the plaster shapes are emphasized by their isolation from one another, either in depth or, when they occur in the same plane, by the glass walls. In a Japanese example, on the other hand, a complex wall surface achieves clarity by its use of plaster wall panels as negative elements. No clear planes of plaster are established by any definition at the edges; instead the insistence is entirely on the dark wood forms, balancing one another in acrobatic symmetry. Numerous examples in western Europe since the Renaissance have used the same negative quality of plaster panels, by putting them between pilasters of the same material, in order to throw emphasis onto the proportions of the pilastered bays, onto their relation to the window openings within them, and onto the proportions of the whole facade, of which the bays are a part.

To clarify plastic forms, the designer must shift his attention from planes and their edges to volumes, so that the attention of the observer will be drawn to the relationships of solid forms in space. Greek island villages such as Mykonos are, for their size, extremely complex aggregations of tiny dwelling units and even tinier churches, with tortuous paths of circulation winding among them (fig. 16). If these complexes were built of a variety of materials, or even of a few materials which called attention to themselves, the visual result would be sheer chaos. As it is, however, a coat of plaster painted white is applied to almost all the surfaces and the result is an exciting kind of visual order. In Alberobello, in southern Italy, the coating is simply a lime wash, applied frequently. The result at both places is that the emphasis is all on the forms themselves, and not on their relationships in space. Added to this is the tactile pleasure suggested by the plaster; it acts as though it had been patted into place, and welcomes further patting. The very whiteness, accented by an occasional blue door or window frame, increases the contrast between sun and shadow, so as to put more emphasis than ever on forms standing in space. The detailing is crucial to this impression of solid forms: in contradistinction to the kind of recessed joint which emphasizes the fragmentation of planes, at Mykonos the planes merge into one another, so that a sharp angle is avoided, the juncture is almost lost, and the sense, as at the Ranchos de Taos church, is not of planes but of solids. Even when changes of material occur, as they occasionally do in villages such as Mykonos, the order brought about by the continuous surface material persists. Often, for instance, the whitewash on parts of a wall of rubble stone merges with the white plaster areas of wall, so that in the bright sun the only variation is the appearance of shadows where the rubble walls cut back out of the sun. The sense of order which comes from the continuous material brings visual calm to the riot of complex form.

A sophisticated version of this play of forms in space against the unifying element of a single plaster texture, used almost everywhere, appears in the rear view of Le Corbusier's chapel at Ronchamp, where sun, shadow, and oblique light play on the plastic forms of the curving wall and on the bulge in it. Here the strong sense of the total form is modified but not destroyed by the recessed joints where the curved wall meets the towers. The recesses

16
Mykonos, Greece

create a sense of separation among the varying shapes of the wall, so that there does not seem to be one surface with an irregular bit taken out of it, as the absolutely unbroken combination of towers and wall would otherwise have produced. On the other hand, these recesses are not so strong that they overcome the powerful continuous curved flow of the wall and tower; they do not fragment the sense of the whole as one plastic solid. They modulate it without destroying it, which is a very sophisticated accomplishment indeed. The same subtlety of modulation without contrast is to be seen in the introduction of unsurfaced concrete forms under the downspout. The color and texture of the exposed concrete underline the fact that the walls are not concrete but a rough-textured plaster. The plaster, therefore, is not the negative foil for the positive wood, as it was in our Japanese example. Instead it receives some attention for itself as well as for the form it creates—but not very much. It is the form which is important.

The work of some twentieth-century sculptors, particularly Constantin Nivola, illustrates the same unification of disparate forms with a consistent negative material, a sand-textured plaster. As it is used at the Olivetti showroom in New York (whose architects were Belgiojoso, Peressutti, and Rogers), joints between pilaster panels establish a rhythm in the wall without destroying the powerful plastic continuity of the sculptural forms.

A much different use of a plastic volume, designed to show itself as the simplest possible mass in bright desert sunshine, occurs in a new store for Joseph Magnin in Las Vegas, Nevada, by Victor Gruen. Here the problem was to try to vie with an urgent and chaotic set of roadside signs; the solution was the simplest possible block, with an overall plaster texture and with surfaces merging into one another, so as to emphasize their solidity (against the dancing signs nearby) and create an almost primitive strength of presence which, like the building of Mykonos, would carry a sense of calm, as an antidote to the chaos around. A complex program housed in a smooth plastered shell has been rendered almost as simple as it can become.

The Enrichment of Form

Architecture complicated by budgets, schedules, limited land, and other restrictions of space, time, and money is, in our own day, rather more in need of simplification and clarification than of the counter processes, amplification and enrichment. But our age has developed a set of "pure" and simple forms, and now we feel strongly the need to enrich these forms, to make the simple complex. At this juncture we run headlong into three problems, whose common quality seems to be that they all have to do with time. There is, first, the problem of the value of the craftsman's time, second, the problem introduced by the need we feel to express the relationship of the product to the time during which it was created, and third, the problem of the changes wrought by time and the elements after the building is built.

To a historian of the plasterer's trade, such as William Millar, the whole "development" of English plaster from late medieval times to the twentieth century is in some important ways no development at all but rather a decline, as the freedom of the early plasterer to create his patterns as he worked was gradually removed. The early designs of the English plasterer were his own creation; he was artist as well as executor. Then some of the design initiative was taken from him, and he was put to work interpreting the design of someone else, the architect. Finally, the crucial parts of the design became prefabricated units, which the plasterer merely inserted, and he was left with only the simpler routine areas to work. It is easy enough to regard the process as inexorable decline, and to regard the mid-twentieth-century state of affairs, which would hardly allow for any hard-done ornamental plasterwork at all, as the absolute end of the art. What has happened, of course, is a decline only from one point of view. The emphasis has shifted: the plasterer, like everyone else in the industry and the building trades, must produce a great deal more than his medieval counterpart did if he is to earn the correspondingly greater return which is his in our society. Some sort of multiple production does seem indicated. Richard Neutra points out in *Survival through Design* that our society, unlike former ones, does not regard uniqueness as essential to quality. An item of value in the Renaissance was the only one of its kind: our machines turn out quantities of identical products, all of them "perfect" within extremely close tolerances, so that the perfection which resulted from extreme manual skill creating the unique object has lost some of its value. Indeed, as Neutra notes, although the pre-machine craftsman applied his labors toward making a round pot perfectly round, we are frighteningly likely to make the round pot lopsided, in order to make clear that it has been "hand-crafted." A plasterer cannot ordinarily work all day perfecting the surface of a tiny area, by hand, if his day's labors are to earn him the house, car, washing machine, steak, and other manifestations of the "good life" which can be his.

In this situation, one of the notions which has disappeared is that plaster is useful to imitate some more expensive material, like marble. It is simply not worthwhile for a well-paid man to work the imitative material by hand. Unfortunately, no such restriction applies to products of the machine, and we have an increasing array of surface materials in imitation of everything from wood to gold mosaic. But during the last century the notion has gained force that the "nature of materials" is worth considering, so in our best work what looks like wood is wood, and what looks like stone is really stone. This was not always the case, and numberless historical examples exist of plaster carefully formed and painted to look like wood or marble, as well as of stone carefully cut and joined to look very much like plaster.

Besides the kind of time for which the craftsman is so well paid, there is a second kind of time, the time required for the creative act, which seems to me more important to us, perhaps on account of the remarkably accelerated tempi of our lives, than it has ever been before in the West. Since in China for centuries the visual arts have been intimately related to the passage of time, it is there that we can turn for some parallels with our own urgencies. In China, for instance, the media used for painting—brush, ink, and silk or absorbent paper—establish that the visual form of a painting will be determined by the speed of its creation, since an ink-loaded brush drawn swiftly across the paper produces a very different shape from the one that results if the brush is allowed to hesitate. It is not impossible that this whole set of materials was found sympathetic because the painters were likely to be not humble craftsmen but calligrapher-littérateur-courtier-officials, whose time, however calmly passed, was valuable. Chinese stories abound in which the famous painter, ordered by the Emperor to paint a thousand miles of Yangtze scenery, spends years in thoughtful reflection (with perhaps a province or two to run on the side) until at length, the night before the Emperor's patience is about to run out, he suddenly paints a shorthand representation which so evokes all that stretch of Yangtze that the Emperor is speechless with amazement.

This kind of urgency of activity is evident in some of the work of Picasso or Matisse or Klee and seems to be of special interest to our high-speed generation. Even the Western past, moreover, offers examples of artistic activity conditioned by time, when time influenced the medium itself. In such a technique as fresco, for example, tempera colors are applied to plaster while it is still wet: plaster background and applied colors then dry together. This ordinarily produces a far different expression from, say, oil paint on canvas, which can be worked and reworked over an indefinite period of time. The Roman "impressionistic" technique, for instance, in the Yellow Frieze in the House of Livia, with such realistic sparkle at a distance, is evidently, from close up, the product of a shorthand technique eminently suited to the relatively quick-setting medium. The simplicity of a Giotto fresco, too, may well be regarded as stemming from the techniques required by the plaster and the tempera, as they quickly set together.

Another technique of surface decoration depending on the drying of plaster is graffito, in which a top layer of plaster is spread over an underlayer of contrasting color, and then while the upper layer is still wet, portions of it are scraped away to reveal the color of the layer below. The plaster facades of late medieval English houses often used this technique. A recent example, a labyrinth at the Milan Triennale, designed by Belgiojoso, Peressutti, and Rogers, contains a graffito mural by Saul Steinberg which illustrates well the headlong quality that the drying plaster seems to generate.

In addition to the time contributed by the workmen, and the time of creation expressed in the work of art itself, there is a third kind of time which must be considered in connection with the enrichment of form. That is the time which will pass after the building is built, while obsolescence sets in (which happens very rapidly in our time) and while, at the same speed as they always have, water, the sun, and dirt act on the building.

Plaster does not have, in our minds, the symbolic permanence of stone, although some extant plaster surfaces are thousands of years old, and even exterior plaster exposed to the English climate has lasted since the Middle Ages. We are more likely to remember what a plaster wall meant to be temporary, as on a world's fair building, looks like the year after (or what a struggle San Franciscans have had with the temporary plaster Palace of Fine Arts, built for the season in 1915 and too beloved to be torn down yet). In other circumstances, however, plaster rather more protected from the elements, or of a more permanent sort, can improve its looks with age since simple unbroken surfaces can give rich play to the discoloration and textures of time. On simple buildings, such as the plastered adobes of the Southwest, the very texture of time, the patterns made by waterborne dirt, become a part of the enrichment. If the texture of the plaster is rough, as at Ronchamp, the accumulation of dirt assumes particular importance. And if the relation of the wall to the weather can undergo variations, on account of overhang, or change of exposure, patterns to enrich the surface are introduced at an entirely different scale.

With the three kinds of time in mind which can allow us to consider the enrichment of simple forms, we have occasion to note that, as buildings are "articulated" or "plastic," so the enrichment of them can be either, and plaster can be used in either way. Applied to surfaces with traditional plasterer's tools, or with a machine, it can serve as plastic enrichment: and cast in blocks, it can be assembled as a set of interchangeable pieces. Mayan temples in Yucatan used stone in this way, in a series of blocks which functioned as abstract decoration, or as the eyes, nose, mouth, and ears of a ritual mask when they were properly assembled. This system is of obvious interest to us on account of its simple interchangeable parts (parts whose counterparts could easily be made by us by machine) and the enrichment these simple parts are capable of producing. Perhaps the most impressive development of this idea occurred among the Moors in Spain. At the Alhambra, in Granada, the Court of the Two Sisters has a fantastically elaborated faceted ceiling composed of 5,000 precast plaster blocks. The 5,000 blocks which create this richly elaborated effect are of only seven different shapes, based on just three plan forms with similar curves in elevation, so that the pieces fit together in an incredible variety of ways. The process, achieving almost infinite variety from a set of almost identical parts, is of direct interest to us, as we begin to look, within the limits of the three kinds of time that concern us, toward the enrichment of our simple forms.

One of the recurring twentieth-century notions which could slow down this kind of enrichment is a narrow interpretation of the dictum that the "nature of materials" should be "expressed." This can mean that the natural materials must be put together as little changed by the hand of man as possible: rubble stone wall and untreated wood, preferably sawn rough, are most acceptable. There is a curious notion based on this dictum that even manufactured materials, like steel I-beams, must manifest themselves as decorative as well as structural elements, undeviating from the state in which the standard product comes from the steel mill. But plaster does not come in any standard shape, so the import of this approach is to doubt that it has any nature and to mistrust it therefore. Central to plaster's nature, of course, is its ability to take almost any form, and it is this interest in *form,* succeeding the prejudices hinging on a narrow interpretation of the "nature of materials," which bodes well for a new understanding of neutral materials like plaster, materials that are capable of taking almost any form without themselves attracting much attention.

Our interest in enriched forms leads us, along the way, to an interest in the unadorned surface, calculated to give importance, by contrast, to enriched areas. Here the ability to create surfaces unbroken by joints is essential, since the forms of the enrichment must establish their own relationships of size and scale, and plaster, not subject to any modular unit size, is able to be formed into whatever surrounding the enrichment requires. At the Joseph Magnin store in Las Vegas, the absence of visible joints again contributes to the almost primitive monolithic strength of the statement.

With time in mind, and the weather, the faceting of surfaces implied in, for instance, the Alhambra becomes of particular importance, since the play of light and shadow is augmented by the contrasts among dirty surfaces, where dirt can land but water cannot fall, neutral surfaces, where dirt can cling but cannot settle and water cannot fall, and clean surfaces, washed by the rain. These variations carefully exploited can bring added interest to the surface, and minimize the adverse effects of weathering and decay.

Articulated enrichment is of particular interest to us because of the possibilities inherent in it for the mass production of parts, and its consequent congruence with our industrial capacities. But the possibilities and the importance to us of plastic enrichment should not be minimized. For the same reasons that we are interested in creating plastic forms, it becomes important that the same plastic material should enrich the forms, so that the nature of the forms themselves is amplified and enhanced. The sense of continuity of the forms then remains unbroken, as in the interior of Wies, and the movement of light becomes a continuous one. The sense of enclosure is not destroyed by fragmentation, and the movement suggested by the large building forms, as at Vierzehnheiligen, is continued into the very details, as in the cartouche from Würzburg which we have examined.

This continuous plastic enrichment, however, introduces all the problems in time that enrichment brings up in our society. Continuity of enrichment of this sort demands one-of-a-kind creation, since by its very nature it cannot be pieced together of prefabricated parts. The value of the craftsman's time becomes important, therefore, and the need arises to express his creative art as something happening in time. The craftsman, of course, is not limited to hand tools; he is as much a craftsman if he operates a machine for spraying plaster onto surfaces as if he held a trowel: and the variations of texture, of shadow, and of form achieved with the larger tool are as full of meaning as those achieved with the smaller one.

As a matter of fact, the sense of urgency introduced by the machine recreates the same kind of excitement in time as the absorbent Chinese paper under the brush, or the soft plaster changing its consistency under the graffito tools. The enrichment which follows on the techniques of plaster forming can be, as at Ronchamp, as exciting, as urgent, and as full of movement as the forms done by hand in another era at Wies or Würzburg. But the underlying needs are the same, and the control of light on the plaster at Wies, or the control of water on the plaster of Ronchamp, or the built-in control of dirt on the plastered walls of an English cottage are all responses to them.

These notes on the creation of forms, plastic and articulated, on their simplification and clarification when they are complex, and on their enrichment when they are simple, are not meant to make rigid definitions of modes and working. Neither are they meant to promote any special new uses of plaster. However, since plaster is particularly capable of taking on an almost infinite variety of forms (so that the design process must start with forms more especially than with the limitations of material), and since plaster is an old material, and the world is full of its uses in response to demands for forms, it has seemed appropriate to examine some of these demands, and to note some of plaster's uses which resulted. Our own demands, which may be very much the same, and our own techniques, which will be very different, will suggest new uses for plaster, and new forms. They will be different from anything ever seen: but they will not be unrelated to what has gone on before.

For those of us who knew him, Louis Kahn was the center of our lives. My own years of being around him were in the late fifties, when he taught some thesis groups at Princeton and I was his teaching assistant. Those late fifties, I believe, were the great Kahn years, when he was searching for the architectural truth with a dedication and a fervor that I've never seen matched, before or since. I saw him often in New Haven, a decade later and more, but by then he seems to have found some of the truths he had earlier been searching for; he would clutch his little notebook as though it contained holy writ, and would look upward to where he seemed to have made some connections not yet established in the fifties.

Kahn had said in those earlier days that the reason he thought he was a good teacher (and he was proud of being a good teacher) was that design did not come easily for him: he had to struggle for it, so could appreciate the students' struggles. Maybe, I have thought, after Salk it got easier. Maybe, too, that difficulty that lies at the heart of Kahn's greatness is what makes it so difficult to get at him through books. In successful biographies, the character takes on new dimensions, as the biographer reveals new aspects to his character. In *Louis I. Kahn: L'uomo, il maestro,* edited by Alessandra Latour (Rome: Kappa, 1986), a book of interviews made with great seriousness and care, we get the sense instead that we have come upon a hall of mirrors, where we are watching numbers of people, mostly in Philadelphia and New Haven, holding mirrors up to themselves as they knew Lou Kahn, while Lou himself slips modestly out the back, and we know him less well than when we started. There are a few fascinating exceptions: William Huff tells more of the story of Kahn's problems with Yale than I managed to learn in ten years there. And Bucky Fuller's telegram to Esther Kahn when Lou dies is included:

> Now Lou is even more vividly present in the thoughts and hearts of all who have known him and even greater numbers who have known his work without having the privilege of experiencing him personally. So long as any of his buildings stand, and most will stand for a long, long time, Lou will be speaking directly to the living humans whom he

Previously unpublished; written 1986.

loved and all who loved him and when the buildings are gone forever after will his indirectly assimilated wisdom continue to bless humans.

Each of us who knew Kahn, or didn't know him but thinks of him anyway as the great architect of our time, has, I've come to believe, his or her very own Lou Kahn, and I, for one, am not really enlightened by reading about all those others.

In *What Will Be Has Always Been,* on the other hand, collected by Richard Saul Wurman, we have a big and beautiful book dedicated to the words of Louis Kahn himself (New York: Access and Rizzoli, 1986). For those of us for whom the words recall the man there is a thrill on just about every page of this giant work. Its faults are the faults of a major book: you can't find anything, for instance, but then how could you expect to since Kahn's talks were as elliptical as his thought, and the same unfluency that contributes to making his work and his teaching so important makes the search for the right words tentative and provisional as well. The best bet is probably to employ the same method people used to with the Bible: let the book fall open, and think for a while about what you see. I just did that, and got a paragraph on page 177, about the Kimbell Museum in Fort Worth:

I look at my work with a sense of what is forthcoming. The yet not said, the yet not made is what puts sparks of life into you.

Like Louis Kahn, Moore was inspired by the ruins of Hadrian's Villa. The following narrative tour of the villa was the first essay Moore wrote for Perspecta. *He first saw the villa in 1950 on his initial tour of Europe (the result of winning the Booth Travel Fellowship), again on subsequent trips, and during his two residencies at the American Academy in Rome. The complexities of the plan, the colliding and overlapping geometries, the very shapes of the ruins and fragments, along with the decay and disintegration, the excavation and reconstructions, the loss of memory, and the way the villa absorbs interpretations depending on what each visitor wants to see, all appealed to Moore and his preference for layering, manipulations of scale, and anthropomorphic space.*

Moore sometimes invented fictional explanations for design moves, such as with his Austin house in 1984, which was partially a renovation of an existing bungalow. Through a process of "selective erasure" he peeled away the former occupant's linoleum to "discover" (though he really painted it himself) a square and circle floor pattern—evidence, he mused, that the Romans had actually made it to Texas. So the links between Hadrian and Dulles might not be so far-fetched.

Hadrian's Villa

Entrance to Hadrian's Villa at Tivoli is usually made against a stream of tourists pouring out looking very hot (if it's the season) and very tired (always) muttering, if they still have the strength, about how stupefyingly big it all was. It turns out, a few hundred yards later, that they were right; for sheer exhausting extent, rendered infinite by the blazing sun, the place has no peer. And yet architects flock to it, fascinated. This account is meant to examine what we see there, or perhaps what we think we see, in areas whose ruin is nearly complete, in order to try to find out why the villa has the meaning it has for us as twentieth-century architects. This is not meant to be a historical account; but one personality so dominates the place, and so affects our reaction to it, that any account must start with him. The Villa is still very much Hadrian's.

A classmate of mine whose experiences I found awesome once noted that he was revolted by perversions to which he was not addicted. Similarly, we are likely to be fascinated when someone else's vagaries coincide with our

Previously published in *Perspecta,* no. 6 (1960), pp. 16–26.

own, however repellent they seem. Ancient Romans are forever trotted out as worthy of our attention because they were, for ancients, so incredibly American. What's worse, the comparison seems to hold up in detail to a point which encourages us to extend it even farther. Hadrian met with the Parthian king in a successful attempt to avert a war in an atmosphere which has a remarkably twentieth-century air; and even a comparison between Hadrian at his villa and Thomas Jefferson and his may not prove to be too far-fetched, though Hadrian, to be sure, is something of an enigma. He has the reputation of having been a splendid sort for a Roman emperor, able and efficient, in possession of most of the qualities valued by nineteenth-century members of the British Liberal Party; but we also hear that he was especially interested in having himself worshiped as a deity (not very good form) and that his efforts to this end were remarkably successful in the eastern portions of his empire. His zeal, too, to deify his favorite Antinous after that young man had evaded the problems of aging by drowning in the Nile would strike us as even worse form in a Victorian. But the size of his undertakings, the avidity of his search for culture, and the gold-plated quality of his success at finding it are nothing short of Texan. And the sheer endlessness of his construction at Tivoli outdistances Versailles (which was, after all, based on a fairly simple idea) and competes with the scale of the twentieth century. The G.M. Technical Center will be equally exhausting to walk among the ruins of, though probably not nearly so much fun.

Hadrian's entry in the megalomania division, though, since it bears so heavily the stamp of one man, seems to come much closer to the edge of madness. It is the product, as Eleanor Clark pointed out, of a craze to build, very like those nineteenth-century follies in the United States whose owners, obeying only the dictates of some irresistible inner urge, added crazily, continually to them, and were generally stopped only by death. But this is not crazy in quite the same way, because this is often beautiful. It is perhaps much more parallel with Jefferson's efforts at Monticello, the work of a man moved to establish himself firmly on a piece of land, and to reaffirm the establishment constantly by building there, while his duties and interests kept him far abroad. For Hadrian's conduct of his office, rather like John Foster Dulles's, was based on travel. He strengthened the Roman Empire by traveling through it, and formed his own character along the way. He had been born in Spain, but Athens was said to be his favorite place, and the art of Greece, some of it already over five centuries old, his ideal, though he collected art from Egypt and the east, and many other places too, and seems to have found the vaguely oriental charms of a Bithynian more to his taste than whatever Greek talent was available.

Indeed, the most striking point of rapport between Hadrian and ourselves is this eclecticism. Eclectic has been a dirty word for most of the twentieth century and it is very recently, if yet, that most modern architects have been willing to drop the pretense that their work springs to life full blown from the problem and their uninfluenced imaginations, or that it is the product of a new tradition, a twentieth-century version of a medieval craft. A medieval craftsman could work within his tradition, developing it, unmindful of the work of other times and other places. A Renaissance man could form his images from Roman antiquity as well as from the local tradition; and nineteenth-century designers succumbed to the lure of a variety of rediscovered manners of building, which they sought to reproduce. But Hadrian was in another boat, very like our own. We are treated, every time we sit in a subway car and look at the ads above the windows, to maybe thirty different kinds of appeal—from abstractions in the manner of Mondrian on behalf of a bank through figures shaped like Life Savers or cigarettes to a delicate line, vaguely Botticellian, which outlines a lady left clean and delicate by the right kind of shampoo—and what is more, we respond to all of them. Books and magazines, movies, television, and easy travel flood our mind's eyes with an incredible array of things. We could not shut them out, even if we wanted to, nor can we pick among them. Instead we have to transform them in our own visions, absorb them into our whole selves, and then create, not from a fragment of our experience but from the whole thing. It is Hadrian's triumph that he did just this (fig. 17). He created at Tivoli, his biographer Spartian says, representations of celebrated buildings and localities which had impressed him on his extensive travels; but he did not reproduce them into a Disneyland of exotic forms. He transformed them. Not only are they all Roman; they are a whole new kind of Roman style, less Greek, if anything, than what had gone on in Rome before. The orders and the marble revetments, to be sure, which were once applied to portions of the masonry forms are gone now, but they could never have been the whole show: there is too much excitement in the masonry forms themselves, in walls and vaults and especially in domes, and in spaces that must once have been domed. Behind it all—and once again we are looking at ourselves—is the search for order in geometry. Circles and squares and a riot of combinations

17
Hadrian's Villa, Tivoli,
photograph of model:
view toward Canopus

of the two are the ordering devices which bring unity and continuity to the vast establishment. They are additive, though, as we would expect from a complex that was, for the few years of its building, constantly and obsessively added onto. It is not the sort of place which insists, for its beauty, that nothing could be added or taken away. That sort would have been done in by several centuries of use as a quarry. But it is not, on the other hand, as far as we can tell, the sort of place subtly keyed to the varied dictates of function. Countless hours have been whiled away by archaeologists assigning uses to the spaces, and guessing what specific exotic locale they were meant to recreate, but the archaeologists cannot agree, because the spaces are not thus specific. To take the terms from Louis Kahn, the villa is a realm of spaces, designed as spaces, domed and colonnaded, and made to evoke their use. The use, to take it from E. Baldwin Smith, would have been for the solemn palace ceremonies based on those of the Hellenistic east which deified Hadrian, in the setting of the royal symbolism of the colonnade, the divine and celestial symbolism of the dome, and (I suspect) the fertility symbolism of flowing water. Professor Smith, who must often have been at

Tivoli under the sun of noon, opined that "without the solemn formalities of a court ritual, which presented him as a manifest god, his architectural creations at Tivoli would have been as empty, meaningless, and tiresome to him as they are to the casual visitor who wanders aimlessly from one unused structure to another."

To animate the spaces beyond what we can see today, or perhaps beyond what we can even imagine, would have been the rush and the splash of flowing water, which was everywhere. It is possible to trace its presence, but almost impossible even to surmise what special delights each fountain offered (fig. 18). Did some of them bubble, or jet up to support balls and dancing objects in the air, or splash in pretty rivulets, and did some quietly moisten mosaics, or lie still and mysterious, in deep pools? Scholars have noted that a recurrent feature of the villa would have been long vistas down straight axes, along which there would have been alternate pools of light and shade, so that moving from one area to another would begin to be an ordered experience in time. The sight and sound of the water, and its flow, must have contributed even to this processional quality, toward bringing

18
Hadrian's Villa, plan

A	Palace and Library Court
D, E	Libraries
G	Maritime Theater
H, J	Poikile
M	Cryptoporticus
O, P	Baths
Q	Vestibule
S	Piazza d'Oro
T	Academy
W	Belvedere
X	Canopus and Temple of Serapis

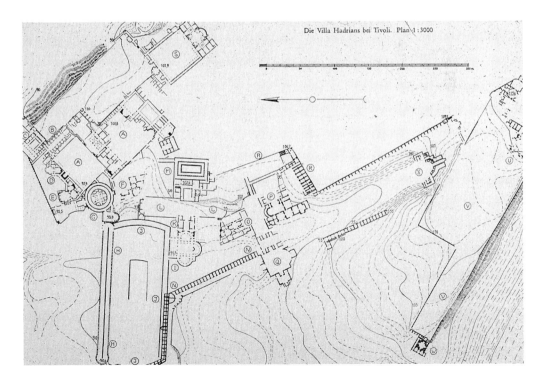

Die Villa Hadrians bei Tivoli. Plan 1:3000

some coherence into the passage from space to space. This coherence now, in the passage among the ruins, is of all qualities the most elusive.

The site for Hadrian's villa in the foothills at the edge of the Roman campagna raised an immediate question: why would a man with an empire to choose from have picked this one? Jefferson chose for Monticello a hill-top which commanded the widest and most beautiful prospect he knew. The views from the town of Tivoli, not far up behind Hadrian's villa, are magnificent, the weather is better, and surely the site was available to the emperor. Hadrian's view of the campagna does not extend quite so far as Rome, and is, whatever the enthusiasts write, totally unremarkable, while the "Vale of Tempe" which lies between the villa and the mountains behind it has been accurately described as a gulch. The gulch owes even its present size, it turns out, to excavation made there for material during the construction of the villa. The Touring Club Italiano's guide suggests, without conviction, that the unimpressive site was selected because the property belonged to Sabina, the wife who played such a negligible (or negative) part in Hadrian's life. That seems little enough reason, but then there was little enough reason for all the fuss over the Bithynian shepherd boy Antinous, who was bland and pudgy, sulky, and very probably quite brainless. It was the emperor's energies that turned him into a deity. Perhaps it does not force the issue too hard to suggest that the site below Tivoli was as tractable as Antinous, capable of being molded to the emperor's design, something fairly positive to start from but capable of being, in the end, swallowed up into the grand scheme. For here nature is dominated by geometry, more even than at Versailles. At Versailles a system of axes imposes a formal order on the grounds, but at Hadrian's villa there are no grounds, only the architecture which contains it all and includes spaces roofed and unroofed, open to the outside and enclosed.

The mound which this architecture occupies, and must once have come close to superseding, runs roughly north and south for almost a mile, though it seems longer, and is about a third that wide. To the east, beyond the so-called "Vale of Tempe," lie the Sabine mountains; to the west stretches the flat Roman campagna, visible almost, but not quite, to Rome, which is fifteen miles away. The villa wrapped around the north, west, and south sides of the mound, cut well below its surface in places, especially at Canopus and the Inferi (fig. 19), and extended well out past it at other places, notably the Poikile. There, especially, the hill has been superseded by

a multistoried wall filled with cubicles for guards or slaves, which retains a vast earth terrace at a dizzy height above the slope, a lovers' leap, as someone has called it, shored up on slave quarters. It all seems frightfully undemocratic, a horror, mitigated for us, perhaps, because Jefferson did exactly the same thing on a much smaller scale at Monticello, where a semi-underground level of service rooms builds up the top of his hill, and makes a base for the geometry of the pavilions he places above. At Tivoli, it occurs, as it does perhaps even more powerfully on the arcades which form the face of the Palatine hill above the Roman Forum, that the scale of the natural formations and of man-made structures coincides, so that the hills become in a sense man-made, and the structures take on the quality of a natural formation. Farther on top of Hadrian's hill, more such merging of scales takes place. A valley was dug for Canopus, and a ravine hewn in the rock, supposedly for the River Styx, was connected with a set of subterranean passages. Natural formations become almost indistinguishable from man-made ones, but the control is in a man's hands (though proper Roman usage, and certainly his own wish, might require us to call God's hands the controls of the deified Hadrian).

The foregoing might be regarded as remarks made en route to the site (although the ride is scarcely that long), so that the next step is to examine the site itself, fragment (as is inevitable) by fragment. A plan of the whole is not so helpful as we could hope, since it can suggest neither the original scheme, which would have been much less random than what happens to have survived, nor the quality of the ruins, which are much more picturesquely vertical than their incredible horizontal extent would lead us to suppose. Much of the excitement of the spaces, in fact, comes from slight changes of level between them. The plan is but remotely suggestive, too, of the play of light and shade, of covered area and open, of hall, portico, and peristyle, which would once have been an important part of the experience of being in the palace, nor can it any more follow the watercourses which might have brought another kind of order to movement through the complex. The plan does suggest how big it all is (though there are many more buildings off the plan), how strong the geometry of the individual pieces is, and how axial organizations form. Notice especially the one from the Poikile through Canopus, reinforced by later excavations there, and the one into and through the Piazza d'Oro, on the eastern side of the villa.

Some areas are named on the plan, but this is in most cases for convenience only, and to commemorate the endless effort of archaeologists to find places in the ruins to accord with the description of Hadrian's biographer Spartian, who related how the emperor "created in his villa at Tivoli a marvel of architecture and landscape gardening; to its different parts he assigned the names of celebrated buildings and localities, such as the Lyceum, the Academy, the Prytaneum, Canopus, the Stoa Poikile, and Tempe, while in order that nothing should be wanting he even constructed a representation of Tartarus." A few places, especially Canopus and the Stoa Poikile, are clear enough. The rest of the names at least facilitate discussion, and recall how well these spaces defy labeling.

The modern entrance to the area is from the north, toward the Poikile. The ancient approach, supposed to have been between the Poikile and Canopus, is the most satisfying place to imagine entering the villa itself, since the approach would have to pass under the huge retaining walls stuffed with rooms (the Hundred Chambers) which support the Poikile high above the slopes of the hill, and entrance is into a vestibule big enough to celebrate the Advent of the deified emperor, with a portico and semicircular apse forcing the juxtaposition of a square and a circle, to set a theme around whose recurrence the geometry of the whole villa is organized.

Right from the vestibule, along the long axis of the complex, lies Canopus. The axis followed to the left would lead to the Poikile. And just across the axis, to the left and right, lie two baths, variously labeled "men's" and "women's," or "summer" and "winter," or "large" and "small." One of Piranesi's *Vedute di Roma*, of the larger baths, comes as close as any one drawing can to showing the excitement that attended the translation of Hadrian's two-dimensional piling up of vaults and domes. Piranesi's splendid foliage creeping over the bared masonry doubtless pleases us more than the sumptuous materials that would once have covered the surfaces, although this is the area where some stucco decoration does survive, and it is very fine. During the century and a half which preceded Hadrian the Romans had fallen into the habit of hanging their structures with fancy-dress systems of columnar decorations, generally banal enough, and very nineteenth-century; poor Hadrian seems to have had even the same crosses to bear that we do, furnished by the taste of his predecessors. Pretty clearly, though, in such a place as these large baths, no cosmetic application could veil the clarity and strength of the arched and vaulted forms. The frigidarium was covered, over its square center section, with a cross vault, and was elongated north and south with barrel-vaulted sections. North of this extends a semicircular apse the full width of the room. Niches in the walls of the apse held fountains. To the east, the frigidarium was extended by a rectangular swimming pool, with fountains, and to the west is a circular caldarium, whose diameter equals the diameter of the semicircular apse, or the side of the square high vaulted area of the frigidarium. Opening from both the frigidarium and caldarium is a square tepidarium, of the same dimensions, its roof essentially a barrel vault. Some of the frigidarium opens another square of the same dimensions, this one cross-vaulted. All this is very simple geometry—the circle, but with its face further extended in three directions—but it is a geometry that is immensely effective, capable of containing without dissolution huge quantities of bejeweled and polychromed jazz. To judge from the quantities of objets d'art found here and mercifully spirited away, it must have had its hands full, even so.

The small baths don't have much ruined grandeur, but their plan is intriguing to trace. The shapes are not quite so simple, and run to rectangles with convex ends. The tepidarium was such a shape; from it opens a circular caldarium, entered from an octagonal hall whose alternate faces curve into the space. From it a small room of the characteristic rectangular shape with concave ends leads to a much larger room of the same shape, extended at its side into wings which in plan are deepened semicircles.

The small bath, built along an axis established by the part of the retaining wall which holds the Hundred Chambers and which includes the larger baths, the vestibule, and Canopus, are distorted at their north end to pick up a new direction, on which the stadium, the cryptoporticus, the Poikile, and the buildings between them are laid out. All this, of course, is to make the villa fit around the brow of its hill, as Frank Lloyd Wright disclosed that a villa should; but on a scale as vast as this, the clanging together of geometries, at least on the plan, is a strange thing to see.

The space referred to as a cryptoporticus on older maps has a raised pool restored in its center, with a double portico around. The pool is the size and shape of a good-sized American swimming pool, and as appealing in the heat, but it is not sunken restfully into the ground. It is raised, so that the water seems to hang there in the middle of the court. Low around the outside, giving the weight it all needs, is the cryptoporticus, with openings looking out toward the pool, and on top of this are set up some columns from the high upper portico, which manage to create a really outsized Texan look. After this the Hall of the Doric Pillars nearby, with (probably) no water ever, and with a few rectangular Doric pillars, freestanding, seems chaste and refreshingly clean-cut, although it is self-consciously archaic (fig. 20). It is neither Greek nor modern (second-century) Roman, and has whatever mixture of virtues we might be able to attribute to a white clapboarded "colonial" church in one of the flashier reaches of Dallas or Beverly Hills.

All this is several hundred yards from the Poikile, for which the change in geometry at the little baths had prepared us, and to which we should return, past a long narrow space below the cryptoporticus whose shape suggests that it was once a stadium, and past a structure where we can trace in plan a system of half-circles around a square.

The Poikile is a huge colonnade, 330 feet by 750, suggested, we are told, by the Stoa Poikile, or painted porch, at Athens. In spite of the general agreement about its name, it is hard to understand on architectural grounds. The orientation, as we've seen, of this part of the villa has been shifted from that of Canopus and the baths, in response to the curve of the hill. Now this great field, perfectly level, leaves the hill, and soars to the west out over the

20
Hall of the Doric
Pillars

valley, retained high above the slope by the Hundred Chambers. The mag-
nitude of all this undertaking is hard to realize from on top, and of course
the need for a vast flat field right at this point is lost on us, though the power
that comes from the simple geometric form is not. The shape, the same kind
of rectangle with concave ends that we saw in the smaller baths, is echoed by
a large pool in the center. Around that, some say, would have been a hippo-
drome, or, as it has been hypothetically restored, a garden. Around that is
supposed to have been a kind of cloister, which would be less moving than
the fragment left standing along the north side of the field: a great wall, 250

yards long and almost 10 yards high, which runs almost due east and west, so that the south side is in sun, and along the north is shade. The simple strength of this statement—a long slab surrounded by space, which divides sun from shade—amasses a grandeur which, in its ruined state, is more than just Roman.

At the east end of this great wall, past the Hall of the Philosophers (a rectangle with a semicircular apse and seven niches for statues), is the circular area that makes a pivot point on the plan and is, more than any other single place, the focus and the heart of the villa. It is called the Maritime Theater, or the Natatorium, but neither of these names makes any sense. It is a round island, surrounded by a moat which is surrounded with a colonnade, which in turn is backed by a circular wall (fig. 21). In Hadrian's time, the island was reached only by two retractable bridges. As we've seen, in the villa water was used everywhere, creating with its flow an image of distance, creating, especially in some of the sections cut into the hill, an image of immersion, but here in this round place the water is made to create the image of an island, with all the sense of withdrawal and independence that an island implies. Here in this vast jungle of ruins is an inviolate place, a perfect circle surrounded by water, with a stronger sense of place than anywhere else in the world. Gertrude Stein said of Oakland, California, that "there's no there there." This island, has, above all things, there.

On the island are incredibly small rooms, and in the center of it all is a tiny atrium, square with concave sides, which must have held a fountain, a source of active moving water which would have lost itself in the still waters of the moat around. What went on in the rooms is anybody's guess, but it was surely something very special.

The concentric circles of island, moat, and colonnade make what seems like a pivot point in the plan, but two affairs called libraries invite a series of spatial problems by continuing the direction of some structures south of the island into an area where everything is oriented in a new direction, along the northeast slope of the hill, facing the "Vale of Tempe." This is the area of the Imperial Palace, so called, with large numbers of buildings and courts, which were once, it appears, particularly lushly appointed, and where the arrangement seems especially formal. The presence there of a couple of major buildings heading in another direction is particularly surprising, but they are at the edge of the hill, and have fallen into ruin in a highly picturesque way. The importance they gain because of their odd direction

and the skill with which they have been fitted into the rest are both remarkable. The whole villa defies understanding as a place where people might
live, and these Libraries, Latin and Greek, seem best to be suited for that,
since they have at least some privacy. The Ospedale, a set of rooms which occupy the adjacent side of the rectangular courtyard against which the Libraries are wedged, are shown as guest rooms, but it would take a peculiarly
eccentric Texan to stuff his guests into cubbyholes like this, even though water channels there suggest heaven knows what sort of hidden delights.

(This is perhaps time to point out that the hidden delights in all this mass of masonry have been poked among not only with archaeological skill, as we would expect by now, but with skill and verve and high excitement by Eleanor Clark, in *Rome and a Villa,* and Marguerite Yourcenar, in *Hadrian's Memoirs.* Their own monuments are not to be sliced into but must be taken on all at once, like Hadrian's. Their fantasies, however, as well as their insights, have become, as Piranesi's did earlier, a part of the place, in the way that more recent residences gain fame for the guests they have sheltered. So their speculations appear here.)

On past endless rooms of the Imperial Palace, past the Hall of the Doric Pillars, lies the Piazza d'Oro, so grandly named because the objects taken from here have been even more sumptuous than the ones from anywhere else. The Piazza itself is a rectangle, whose 68 columns were alternately of Oriental granite and cippolino. It is entered through the center of one short side via a vestibule which is octagonal, so that it looks in plan like a square with rounded corners, which would have had a domical vault, for the celestial implications of the ceremonies when the deified emperor arrived here. Flanking the vestibule, opening into the Piazza, facing northeast, a half-round area faces the Vale of Tempe, but opposite the vestibule lies what must have been a square reserved for what must have been the most elevating ceremonies. In plan it is a large octagon, with sides alternately concave and convex, not walled but suggested by arcades, as San Vitale in Ravenna was to have its form suggested four centuries later. On the concave sides, splayed rectangles helped fill a square. On the side opposite the entrance, which was convex, the form was echoed by an apsidal wall concentric with the convex arcade bordering the octagon. The two remaining sides, at right angles to the entrance and the apse, gave onto rectangles whose ends were concave. These rectangles had no walls, but only arcades into still other spaces. It is the baroque-like summation of the simpler geometries of the square and circle which the whole villa has developed. And it was alive with water, flowing from everywhere. The water used in the rest of the villa and the geometry of the rest of the villa must here have reached a ceremonial crescendo, though at the center of everything, hundreds of yards away, lies the island.

The Piazza d'Oro lies at the end of the Imperial Palace portion of the villa, so that past it to the south and east lies the brow of the hill itself. Our steps retraced toward the vestibule and the baths, where we started our tour,

might well take us past a nymphaeum, an exedra with a fountain, a set of cubicles called a barracks, and a grander set, behind the great baths, called a
praetorium. From the vestibule and baths to the south, along the great axis
we previously followed north, lies the Valley of Canopus, artificially cut into
the tufa rock of the hill. This is one part of the villa whose special affinities
are in little doubt. "Canopus," according to Strabo, "is a town 120 stadia
from Alexandria . . . containing a highly reserved temple of Serapis. . . .
Troops of pilgrims descend the canal from Alexandria to celebrate the festivals of this goddess. The neighborhood of the temple swarms day and night
with men and women, who spend the time in their boats dancing and
singing with the most unbridled merriment, or find accommodation in the
town of Canopus and there procure their orgies." Hadrian's Canopus, too,
has cubicles along the sides of the valley and a temple of Serapis at the end
of a panel of water. The area furnished quantities of Egyptian works of art,
now mostly in the Vatican, which made more positive its identification; but
perhaps the most surprising thing about the valley now is how Roman it all
is. The "canal," recently restored and filled with water, is not really a canal
at all (and Hadrian could certainly have afforded a canal if he had wanted it,
if need be with water running uphill). It is a pool, in one of the characteristic shapes of the villa, a rectangle with convex end. At its north end a colonnade with architrave alternately flat and arched has now been restored—a
form new even to Rome, and unheard of in Egypt. Opposite it the temple
took on an even more remarkable form, a melon-domed circle sliced off at
the front with a plane which would have produced an arched opening divided with columns. From behind the circular space came a tunnel, alternately roofed and unroofed (therefore light and dark), through which a
major source of water flowed and splashed in fountains, in the tunnel, in the
niches of the domed temple, and in front of it, toward the pool. Only the
rear half of the dome exists now as it did in Piranesi's time, made of convex
segments as some domes were to be in Byzantium much later. The look here
is forward, not back. The festivals in this Canopus were said to copy Egyptian ones, and they may have, but neither the building forms nor the plans
were copies of anything.

The rest of the villa, to the south, looks fascinating in the books, with
a ravine cut into the rock in order to recall, it is said, the River Styx, and mysterious underground passages connecting it with other underground phenomena, including one named after Tartarus. Then there are other ruins,

the Academy, the Odeon, the Lyceum. The Academy, or Small Palace, especially, has a fascinating plan, squares and circles and a portico, with a main space made of circles intersecting the sides of a square, with round-ended rooms to fill out the corners. But they are private property and not a part of the visit, and anyway there has already been, on even the coolest days, enough. The row of eighteenth-century cypresses that leads away from the hill is beautiful, its shade is deliciously cool, and we will want refreshment. We will probably not remember to look back. It will be later, when we need refreshment of another sort, that we will want to look again at the whole hill made over, devoted to the privacy of forms and a serious game of space, a game based on the subtlest permutations of the possibilities inherent in a circle and a square, and transforming with a circle and a square the objects and impressions of a whole world.

This set explores themes of technology and craft, science and myth, architecture as engineering for function and architecture as instrument for imbuing sense of place. It begins with Moore's coverage of an ACSA education forum at Sagamore, debating the advantages and disadvantages of teaching architecture as the science of technology or the art of design (or both), and concludes with Moore's review of Vincent Scully's The Earth, the Temple and the Gods.

Moore co-wrote "Toward Making Places" in 1962 with Donlyn Lyndon, Patrick Quinn, and Sim Van der Ryn, and in 1965 Moore and Lyndon proposed a book for the Ronald Press that would be an expansion of the essay (first called "Introduction to Architecture," then renamed "The Architecture of Place") and would be illustrated with drawings by William Turnbull, Jr. The book was never published in this form, but the proposal and outline reveal the direction of Moore's thought in the early sixties:

> Architecture is considered almost always as a land of extension of the other arts, as functional art cast in succession of styles following those of painting, as sculpture you can get inside of, even as "frozen music." These considerations ignore the fundamental purpose of architecture, what Susanne Langer described as the creation of ethnic domain, the extension of man's image of himself and his society onto the face of the earth, in order to take possession of some part of the face of the earth, to create a controlled inside surrounded by layers which select for admission only certain aspects of the outside. In the process, man has often made an abstraction of this act of taking possession, by symbolizing the world as he views it, within a framework under his control, as in the temples of Angkor Wat, which are a diagram of heaven, or the city of Peking, which was a diagram of the organization of his earthly kingdom.
>
> This book seeks to introduce the ways in which the ethnic domain is given form and made habitable, visually, thermally, acoustically, and in other ways as well, then carefully to examine, in diagrams and photographs, a limited number of examples (Itsukushima, Peking, Khajuraho, Angkor Wat, Carpenter Center, the Villa Savoye, Copley Square, Fatehpur Sikri, Chartres, Wies, Conques, and the Santa Barbara County Courthouse), to see them not as shapes betraying a certain style, but as skillfully manipulated examples of man's extension of his civilization onto the face of the earth.

I. *Making place*

    A. *Accommodating or celebrating human activity; participation*
        Main Street, bus stop, church
        Palaestra, forum, bath, r. r. station

    B. *Taking possession of space; territoriality (of individuals and societies)*
        Chinese wall, Silverton, Colo.
        the human bubble of space

    C. *The symbolic extension of this act: order*
        The symbolism of column, cave, mountain, gate, tent, paradise, garden and machine
        Angkor Wat, Peking, Barcelona Pavilion, Kepanji

    D. *Establishing a hierarchy of importance*
        1. *In the landscape: man and nature*
            Greek temple, Italian hill town, Spanish farm
        2. *In the city: public and private realm*
            Main Street and courthouse square
            Medieval cathedral town
            Georgian square and city
            Arab town, Italian piazza
        3. *In the building—entrance, hearth, aedicule*
            Served and servant spaces (Salk Center)

II. *Distinguishing inside from outside*

    A. *Boundary and the in-between realm*
        Alhambra, porches on Main Street

    B. *Axis*
        Karnak, Peking

    C. *Marker*
        Borobodur

    D. *Up and down; the manipulation of ceilings and floors*
        Medieval cathedral vaulting, Baroque vaulting, Mont Alban

    E. *The land and the water*
        (Portofino, Lyme Regis, Bamberg, Alhambra, Villa d'Este, Trevi Fountain, Itsukushima)

III. *Conditioning the inside: light and dark, heat and cold, wind and sound*

    A. *Thresholds (Baths of Caracalla)*

    B. *Light for drama, and for seeing, dark for comfort*
        Wies, 1000 pillared mandapa

    C.   *Keeping cool in the tropics*

    D.   *Keeping warm—central heating vs. the medieval castle*

    E.   *The price of quiet (Peking, N.Y.)*

IV. *Manipulating scale: the big and small*

    A.   *Proportion (Palladian villas)*

    B.   *Openings in walls*

    C.   *Space in Frank Lloyd Wright houses*

    D.   *The landscape and the freeway*

V. *Manipulating space and shape*

    Bramante, Mannerists, Guarini, Palladio, Mies, Kahn, action architects

VI. *Manipulating sequence in time*

    A.   *Sequence*

       (Japanese Temple Gardens, British townscape, Frank Lloyd Wright houses)

    B.   *Weathering*

    C.   *Time in space*

       (Bibiena, Piranesi prisons)

VII. *The building as narrator: the influence of the particular*

    The diagram—Louis Kahn

    Vauban fortifications

    Butterfield, Stirling, Carpenter Center, Harvard

    Style—Santa Barbara County Courthouse

*Moore continued to develop the set of observations further in essays such as "Architecture—Art and Science" (*AIA Journal, *1965); in his course on Oriental architecture at Berkeley (with Lyndon) and his first-year course at Yale University (with Kent Bloomer); and in a lecture series he gave at Harvard University as a visiting professor, titled "Flights from the Dialectic: Recollections of a Watermelon," subsequently presented as an issue of* SD *in 1986. (The watermelon was in reference to his house at Centerbrook, Connecticut.) Later, Moore and Lyndon explored similar themes in the book* Chambers for a Memory Palace *(Cambridge: MIT Press, 1994).*

Last summer's ACSA-AIA seminar on the teaching of architecture, the fifth such seminar so far, was the first to hinge on a single subject: technology and what to do about it in schools of architecture. The setting was Sagamore, built by the Vanderbilts as an elegant Adirondack camp, and more recently makeshifted into a conference center for Syracuse University; it was highly appropriate on several counts. Independent of any college campus and free of any dead hand of authority, it allowed for the continuation of the robust tradition (quickly established and all the better for that) of the R-17 seminars; debate was sharp, wide-ranging, and free. Sagamore's remote location, nowhere near distractions except a small and icy lake, suited well the intensely serious group of speakers and participants. The accommodation of the Vanderbilt lodge to mid-twentieth-century conference paraphernalia even fit the occasion; it demonstrated the same grudging lack of conviction with which most pretechnological architectural curricula appear to have embraced fragments of technology. Even the weather was mostly as ominous as James Marston Fitch pointed out the implications of technology have become.

Technology, indeed, was approached by most of the participants with a circumspection described variously as discomfort, incomplete understanding, or just plain fear. The wall, in the profession and perhaps especially in the schools, between the space-shaping (or more extremely, form-making) designer and the nuts-and-bolts technician was almost always apparent. Though frequently individuals broke through the wall, it seemed worth while, eventually, to risk a generalization (like most generalizations, more illuminating than precise): that there have been in the last decades just two groups of students for whom technological processes and the shaping of space have been integral parts of the same architectural whole; one of these groups studied with Walter Gropius in the late forties and early fifties, the other with Louis Kahn in the late fifties.

For most architects, though, the wall between design and technology has been a high one and unclimbed, and the result has been what Robert Newman of MIT and Harvard called "the sad condition of fashionable architecture in the United States today." James Marston Fitch of Columbia in

Previously published in *Journal of Architectural Education* 16, no. 2 (Summer 1961), pp. 3–7.

his keynote address discussed the gravity of the problem. The implications of technology, he pointed out, are more ominous and obscure than they were a hundred years ago, when the Crystal Palace so resplendently inaugurated the modern era. Even institutions of the very highest learning are throwing up buildings which constitute "a definitive catalog of error." The question is whether, in our unthinking application of mechanical gimmicks to unsuitable forms, we won't become the blind victims, rather than the masters, of all the technology we have espoused. Mies's glass-sheathed buildings, he pointed out, are designed for the climate of Plato's *Republic*. Human comfort is ill served by a fashionable glass wall facing west in Houston or Chicago, and any available skin for a building controls comfort only very crudely compared with the equivalent covering on animals. (There was a suggestion that many a lesser architect otherwise indifferent to climate did maintain an ear cocked to which way the wind was blowing.) In the generally bleak picture Louis Kahn was singled out for praise, as he was frequently to be in the ensuing weeks, for his capacity to suspend his judgment and let the form determined by technological and spatial needs force itself.

Richard Stein, from Cooper Union, contested the assertion that environmental control is the key to the total environment. Mr. Fitch's counterassertion was that environmental control, though no guarantee of good architecture, is an indispensable base for it; and the provision of the base of course is where the education comes in. The crimes being committed by architects, Mr. Fitch went on, are not crimes of malice, but come about partly because our students are taught as though they were all being prepared to be individual residential architects, preferably in the Bay region. Technology, he intimated, passes them by.

That afternoon, a study group, fighting its way out of semantic snarls, became the first (but by no means the last) to ask from the floor of the conference: What is Technology? And what is this business of the separation of design from technology, when everyone evidently thinks he is training the whole man? Nobody ever ventured an answer to the first question, but the separation came under close scrutiny. King Lui-Wu of Yale characterized it the following week as the fight between the head and heart of the architect, who must be an artist, but cannot afford to be an ignorant artist. Ulrich Franzen opined that the central problem is the marriage of the mechanical arts and the visual arts; though Robert Schenker of Tulane likened the marriage of art and technology to a horse pulling an automobile, and Donald

Jackson of Auburn resented altogether the notion that we must call things technical or artistic.

J. Walter Severinghaus of Skidmore, Owings and Merrill described early in the conference some of his firm's work in order to emphasize the importance of coordination between the architect's office and its consultants, in a time when mechanical and electrical work can total 35 to 50 percent of the cost of buildings. From the beginning of the conference, though, a gulf had opened up between the "conceptual designers" and the "nuts-and-bolts men." Bernard Miller of Smith, Hinchman and Grylls noted "much interest here in concept. As soon as it gets off into technology, you are uncomfortable," while from another point of view, that of Frank Frybergh of Skidmore, Owings and Merrill, "technological man alone is a monstrosity." "Why," asked Ulrich Franzen, "do we assume all art will take care of itself?"

At Smith, Hinchman and Grylls, Bernard Miller explained, the distinction is made between design and architecture. Architectural designers do preliminaries, while architects do working drawings. The educated product is not the total architect but a member of a team, and good engineers are not presently forthcoming as members of the team. Architects, therefore, must save the day, and architectural schools must reshape themselves to produce top-flight engineering talent, so that electrical, structural, and mechanical engineers will be in the profession, trained in, or at least oriented toward, architecture. Donald Barthelme, of Rice Institute, called this a proposal for a team of straddlers, and debate ranged from warm to acrimonious. Keith Kolb of the University of Washington summarized the points of view: either (1) that engineers are being provided (but are these the best available men?) or (2) that engineers are not being provided. And if (2), then should the training of engineers be at the hands of engineers or architects? Joseph Passonneau, Dean at Washington University, discussing later the mediocre capabilities of most structural and especially mechanical engineers, put the recruiting difficulty on a more basic level. "The issues that the building engineer faces," he said, "are trivial. They are codified to the point where they are not challenging to a first-rate mind," since the history of science follows a pattern of scientific ideas taken over by engineers, codified, then taken over by schoolchildren; and the best brains are attracted by the ideas. "Building technology does not merit a place in a first-class engineering curriculum."

This did not mean, for Dean Passonneau or for the participants who agreed with him, that training for architects should stay on the design side of a wall separating design from technology. It meant that the wall had to go. It meant, for one thing, that students interested in technical areas could learn from design. As Richard Stein from Cooper Union phrased it, students would learn more from Gropius's plaster cracks than from sand-lime ratios. And it meant that the knowledge could flow another way, too. In the words of James Yarnell of Cornell, "the need is for discipline. Design alone is not a discipline, Architecture is."

To this end, the problems of teaching about architectural materials were cause for extended concern. As John Hill of Louisiana State University put it: "If you don't talk about materials in relation to design, what the devil *do* you talk about? Raymond Caravaty of Rensselaer Polytechnic Institute spoke from the point of view of the teachers of materials courses, and the problem of what to teach. There seem to be some 40,000 items available today for construction use. At one minute each, using the cookbook approach, a 9-hour course would cover 6,600 items, leaving the rest untouched and a method for coping with them undeveloped. But "the biggest function of schools," according to Frank Frybergh, "is to impress on students the need and love of materials." "How could you possibly design something," asked Donald Jackson, "if you don't know what material it was?" (To which Kenneth Sargent, Dean at Syracuse, retorted, "Look about you!") Roger Montgomery, of Washington University, using the Fröbel blocks of Frank Lloyd Wright's childhood as an instance, made the point that it is *materials* which begin the teaching of design (to which Dean Sargent's retort was "Then we teach paper").

The point remained, however, that building technology or materials, taught out of a code or a cookbook, do not attract even the attention, much less the thoughtful consideration, of good students. Richard Stein described the need for a materials text or supplementary text like D'Arcy Thompson's *On Growth and Form.* An exchange between Roger Montgomery and Kenneth Sargent focused on the same point, and hinged on Montgomery's conviction that the student of university age is still susceptible to moral issues, and indeed only becomes really involved with problems when moral issues are at stake, as they seldom are in a cookbook. Later, he suspected, we lose some of this moral fervor, but in the university an area without moral involvement is not worth having. Sargent asked, "Who'll do the architecture?" and Montgomery replied, "Give me an IQ of 175 and enthusiasm, and I'll figure out the nuts and bolts in real jig time."

(The point had been spoken to earlier in the conference, after J. Walter Severinghaus had stressed the need for coordination between the architect and his consultants. James Marston Fitch had asked him, "What do you want from the architecture schools?" and Severinghaus had asked for enthusiasm, ability, and judgment. There is still a need to draw, and more thinking would be acceptable.)

An object of frequent concern during the two weeks was the nature of the education process: *who* should teach and *what. How* to teach, as James Acland, of Toronto, announced in the introduction to his lecture about vaults, is something we have no business telling each other, since how to teach grows out of the subject matter and the teacher.

George Boguslavsky, from Rensselaer Polytechnic Institute, spoke to the seminar as a professor of psychology, about education. Pointing out the rather special nature of architecture education, he distinguished between education for the reproduction of the type, and education like an architectural one where emphasis is on creativity, which is to say growth beyond the type. (But creativity originates in experience.) Two types of growth are worth distinguishing. One is growth *in* the field, encouraged by teachers at the frontier of knowledge, making the nature of our ignorance known to the student. The second is growth beyond the field, which demands of the teacher versatility and humility, which are qualities temperamental rather than academic. If humility is lacking, provincialism results. In spite of the differences in education for reproduction of the type and education for growth beyond the type, Dean Passonneau made the point that art and scholarship are closely related; that they are in fact an identical intellectual quest. In each it is the function of a teacher to take a position.

The question of who should teach, at least in rather special areas, came up following talks by Robert Newman on acoustics and Felix B. Graham of Syska and Hennesey on lighting. Newman thought that anyone who reads and observes (a sort of parallel to Roger Montgomery's man with an IQ of 175 and enthusiasm) would be in a position to do a good job. Felix Graham thought this idea dangerous, and stressed the amount of time and special effort required to encompass the knowledge in an area such as lighting in order to reduce it to a capsule suitable for architects. Engineer Fred N. Severud, after a talk about structure in which the big role of enthusiasm was underscored, drew one of the fortnight's heartiest rounds of applause when, asked what his training had been, he replied, "I play the violin."

One of the main functions of the architect, it was asserted, which ought therefore to be incorporated in the aims of his education, is that he be alert to what is given him. Joseph Watterson, editor of the AIA *Journal,* extended that to say that the architect must be literate, articulate, and well informed—a reading man. Donald Barthelme of Rice Institute put it in terms of stripping away nonessential functions to try to discover "what is the last thing you'd give up," which would be the ultimate function of the architect. The last thing, he had concluded, would be "the serving of those intangible human values deriving from environment. The clear implication is that young people should be prepared whose function is not limited by time or social change."

During the first week of the seminar, groups of participants had been formed to question the speakers—and each other—more closely, and to report back to the whole group their areas of agreement, or bases of disagreement. The second week the participants were issued a kind of design problem, and they regrouped to develop solutions. The problem postulated an architecture school in a typical small university and asked for a reorganization of its first and fifth years. The school described in the program, meant to be an abstraction of typical smaller schools of architecture, apparently was not abstracted far enough; it so appalled the participants that they chose instead to develop the full curriculum of a more palatable (which is to say entirely imaginary) institution. One group did examine the abstracted typical school and recommended closing it. Other groups, projecting full new curricula, seemed often to wind up with systems very similar to the existing ones, but with an extra attraction, or an area organized. One proposal, for example, concentrated its attention on a technical sequence. Another proposed a sixth year, spent on a world tour. Another proposed a curriculum culminating in a thesis not in architecture, but in the humanities. Still another relied (in a remarkable recall of the chapel of another area) on spending the first hour of the day in assembly with a visitor. Seldom, if at all, were the basic premises of the case study architectural curriculum questioned. But, the assembled critics agreed, almost all the projected programs tried to include too much, to train the architect as dilettante, not as a profound man.

The need for the profound man was developed in Lawrence Anderson's closing address, as he outlined the awesome challenges the environment poses. The future seemed ominous still.

An editor must somewhere editorialize, and to editorialize about the paradoxes of the most recent R-17 seminar is a ticklish business. On the one hand is the free-wheeling marvel of the seminar itself; on the other, the curious conservatism of many of the participants. It is surely an editor's duty to complain about stereotyped reactions, not very thoughtful narcissistic images, and young men whose view of the future of architecture is limited by conditions already defunct. Yet to do this would be to suggest that the R-17 seminars had become what they very easily could have, and by a miracle have not: indoctrination courses where the existing image of the profession could be stamped on the impressionable minds of young teachers. It is to the everlasting credit of Harold Bush-Brown, Christopher Wadsworth, and a number of others that they have managed, in just a few years, to establish a free forum for the exchange of points of view, hewing to no line, and giving the best kind of chance for teachers of architecture to take a clear look at each other. (Even if nobody had an idea at all, the chance to see that a number of other people, in their separate ways, are coping with related problems would be enough to make the seminar worth while.) It is truly remarkable that they and five sets of participants have made the seminars so quickly into a very much alive tradition. And it is really amazing that the concentrated effort of two solid weeks of discussion, day and night, could be sustained with such seriousness of purpose, and at the same time with such spirited enthusiasms as they are.

And yet some of the older hands present were saddened by the conservatism, not to say the timidity, of some of the younger teachers when they approached "ominous and obscure" implications of technology. A cocktail-hour classification of the participants seemed at the time pointedly accurate, and therefore great fun. In retrospect it is rather more sobering. It divided us into four categories:

1) The Space Man. He is not technological at all. His outer space is not interstellar, but interstitial. He may have gone to MIT, but his concern is with design, the molding of space, and he is delighted he may do that, and teach about it, while others, unaccountably, concern themselves with technical things, and teach them.

2) The Well-rounded Man, the universal man, the man of the Renaissance. The very possibility of his existence was denied by Bernard Miller, who espoused a team organization, and by many others. Curiously enough, many of the recruits for this category have been trained by Walter

Gropius at Harvard, where teamwork was probably invented, and where at least artificial boundaries must have been removed. The younger men in the category most seem to have come in contact with Louis Kahn, so that they have come to regard the study of materials and techniques, the processes of building and serving space, as indivisible parts of the same whole, and are prepared to suppose that technical as well as spatial attributes of building are subject to thoughtful analysis and moral fervor.

There were proposed in addition some dubious subcategories of the universal man (cf. Bernard Miller's "well-rounded man with the thin-shelled veneer" and someone's "dormant universal man").

3) The Half-round (or Romanesque) Man. This category was devised by Renaissance men to fit their well-rounded colleagues in whom they had discovered flaws, but to whom they wished to be charitable.

4) The Clod. This group named itself, and rather insisted. Variously titled "nuts-and-bolts man," or "watts-and-bolts" if their area was electrical, their attitude toward conceptual designers varied from awe to ill-concealed distaste, but the separating wall seemed always there.

The classifications are partly caricature, but their mood is unmistakable, their implication clear, as senior speakers issued warnings about the future of the profession. The possibility of failure, as a profession, and its price (socialism) were invoked by Philip Will, and the challenges and almost overwhelming difficulties of shaping the whole environment, with the catastrophic possibilities which failure could let the future hold, were developed by Lawrence Anderson in his address which closed the seminar. But the rumblings of change caused little stir among most of the serious young teachers of architecture, whose developed images of things as they are included the past but excluded much of the future, chopped the problems of the world down to intramural size, and made solutions into something that would eventuate when the catalog got properly rephrased.

Toward Making Places

with Donlyn Lyndon, Patrick Quinn, and Sim Van der Ryn

Architecture is in a bad way. It is taught as a craft and its best disciples are craftsmen. They learn to respect the nature of materials, to organize surfaces and solids. Sometimes they master the molding of space, and a few can learn to manipulate the magic flow of light (while others learn to manipulate the magic flow of money). Our magazines are filled with handsome photographs of buildings. But, with all this, our environment grows messier, more chaotic, more out of touch with the natural world and inimical to human life. The order of the existing natural world is destroyed, but no order closer to human understanding is introduced to take its place. The chaos shows up alarmingly clearly when numbers of our most distinguished architects are loosed on the same area, from the Berlin Interbau through the Brussels Fair to the Lincoln Center for the Performing Arts, at which a coating of travertine is expected to insure superficial uniformity for a disparate collection of very careful designs.

The more fashionable all this is, the better is the chance that it will be thought "expressive" of something or of somebody's self. In this chaos of self-expression, careful or sloppy, the basic function of architecture has somehow been forgotten: past the provision of merely shelter, past the expressive manipulation of materials or even of space, it is the creation of place, of what Susanne Langer calls an "ethnic domain." This creation of place amounts at first to taking possession of a portion of the earth's surface. Then, architecture being an act, that process of taking possession is abstracted, as life is abstracted by the playwright.

It seems evident, to people who study such things, that birds sing not for the joy of the morning or the beauty of the season but in order to take possession, to establish acoustically the limits of their domains. The Chinese more ponderously achieved the same sort of demarcation with the Great Wall. But, since men are subtler than birds, they long ago elevated this act of taking possession into an art, abstracting the act. Ryoan-ji garden in Kyoto, for instance, contains just fifteen stones in a walled area of sand about the size of a tennis court, meant to be seen from an adjacent veranda. Thus seen, they are merely rocks in the sand, or tiger cubs crossing a stream, as some say, or turtles, or islands in the sea, or points fixing the cosmos, as in

Originally published in *Landscape*, Autumn 1962, pp. 31–41.

the equally celebrated Japanese teahouse at the edge of the sea, from which the sea is only visible through one small window, placed low and over the bowl where one washes one's hands. So the message is clear: to have (by empathizing with it) the water in the bowl is to have it in the sea as well.

This is all thrilling, but disappointing too, like a play which brilliantly brings into focus a life that no longer exists. For us, it is not a natural world only which needs to be thus possessed and abstracted but a world formed too of man-made forms and ideas, where we have to ask, all over again, questions of what constitutes meaning and what is capable of being abstracted from that (what is real?) and what constitutes somewhere. Who is taking possession of what, and in whose name? So far, we are uneasy about this; we experience some discomfort when the land is taken over for "the people" on 60-by-100-foot pads, and we experience even more discomfort when the people's institutions can seem to assert a reasonable act of possession—like New Orleans's new Civic Center, which is on the edge of town, in deference to an obscure hierarchy of values which is apparently based on the act of parking automobiles.

22
Angkor Wat

As both cause and effect of our confusion, there exists a strange hiatus in our architectural language: experience, which used to be a teacher (even innovations of the lightning Gothic sort took generations), was firmly rooted in the chance to study existing building forms as they weathered, and as they were used, and to modify them as they needed it, and as the newly changing situation demanded. Our famous architects, and many not so famous, seek always the magic moment. They innovate with each job, and with almost no experience, since we have no real way of saying how a building or a town—a place—works, and what effect it has on the people who use it. We have carefully developed techniques for describing what buildings look like, both in words and in two-dimensional monochromatic abstractions by celebrated architectural photographers. The talismans of these gentlemen have such value that, in curious annual rituals, they are examined by panels of experts who bestow awards on the buildings from which the most elegant abstractions have been made. Meanwhile, nobody—critic, architect, teacher, or other theoretician or technician—has so far communicated any interest in the way these buildings work, the way they have taken possession of someplace for somebody and the way in which, in turn, people take possession of them. It would be hard to communicate such an interest; there is no technical language to do it. But the language, presumably, does not exist because the need for it has not yet been urgently enough felt.

Lacking experience of the old sort, and the basis for achieving any, we need a body of theory, a formulation of a way of working which will let us consider how, and for whom, our structures are to function, what they are and how they figure in the lives of the people who use them. The forms which the famous "form givers" give, and even the spaces which some of those forms enclose, become far less important than the places which we establish and of which we establish possession.

Charles W. Moore

The General and the Specific

The "form giving" of fashionable architects of the fifties and sixties is particularly susceptible to lionization on museum walls and in the pages of glossy magazines. Its opposite is generally taken to be the "anonymous" architecture of barns or the Bay Region Style. (One takes it that museum attendance would run lower for a demonstration of this sort of thing.) A more useful distinction might be made between the *general* solution and the *specific*. The general solution, whether curvily sculptural or puritanically cubed, is the diagram of an independent idea, conceived in isolation; the specific solution starts with a place, makes it habitable, and enhances the qualities of the specific place by making it responsive to the needs of the people who use it (in all those ways we find so difficult to communicate). A-frame churches and all-glass office blocks are in the first category. Some industrial buildings, and the orphanage of Aldo Van Eyck, are in the second. A third category, more rarely found, firmly rooted in the specifics, manages to generalize these specifics so that they take on a universal importance transcending the importance of the place itself, just as characters in a play, superbly aware of the nuances of the situation they find themselves in, yet create a frame larger than this situation, large enough to hold us all. Chartres Cathedral is a candidate for this third category.

We can leave this category to occur when it will; our troubles start from too much that is general and too little that is specific, too much that is expression and too little that is response, too much that is invention and too little that is discovery. The richly varied places of the natural world are structured in an ordered relationship that is yet full, for people, of drama and surprise (see "The Cross Valley Syndrome," by Paul Shepherd, Jr., in *Landscape* for Spring 1961). They are rapidly being obliterated under a meaningless pattern of building that is monotonous (the tract house and the glass office block) and chaotic (those fashionable forms) all at once. The new structures will fall down one day but the obliteration of the natural order is permanent. We are in urgent need of understanding places before we lose them, of learning how to see them and to take possession of them.

C. W.M.

Boundaries

There is still great power in the traditional ways of ordering and establishing places, though with something of the poignance that attaches to a departed view of the world. Some of these ways remain essential to the making of place, though the lapses in our language cloud their very existence. Landmarks have for centuries ordered our sense of position (but monuments are essentially landmarks, and the FDR Memorial competition discussed in the book reviews demonstrates how chaotic are our thoughts about all this).

The obelisks, for example, which Pope Sixtus V had set up in the medieval tangle of Rome, and the straight avenues he had cut leading to them, were quite specifically to let the pilgrim understand where he was and where he was going, as he proceeded from basilica to basilica (fig. 23). A processional way, passing from landmark to landmark along an axis (not the standard long narrow empty space leading from nowhere to nowhere, like the malls of our housing developments, but an axis on the way from someplace to someplace), can coalesce space, so that such a city as Peking, sited as casually,

23
Piazza del Popolo,
Rome

according to Sir Hugh Casson, who was there, as "a dog biscuit on a beach," can gather up importance as the processional way from gate to gate to increasingly sacrosanct precincts intensifies the importance of being *there*.

The demarcation of edges, as well, is crucial to this gathering up and enclosing of importance, and the absence of edges may well be responsible for the disappointing sense of nowhere in some of our newer cities. The urbanity of island-bound Manhattan is unquestioned, given the clarity of the boundary formed where the water meets the land, and the strong sense of place and of city in downtown San Francisco is, I suspect, at least in part a function of the half-forgotten real estate feud which established rival gridiron plans on opposite sides of Market Street, where once roared streetcars four abreast. To cross this mess has been, for almost a century, immensely difficult; just possibly, like a medieval wall or a river, or like similar convulsions of the gridiron in Dallas and Denver, it has held the life of the city in place, and if it went the life might leak away.

A sense of place might conceivably exist independent of such traditional ordering devices as processional axes, boundaries, and landmarks; but basic to it is the division of inside from outside.

C. W. M.

Inside and Outside

The first, and simplest, act of possession is to establish an *inside* that is separate from the *outside;* to set apart one section of the environment as secure against the hostile, uncontrolled *outside.* Such are the snug houses of our Anglo-Saxon dreams, the sacred compounds of Oriental reality, and the staked fortresses of the frontier.

Inside doesn't necessarily mean "indoors," it is not dominated by where the fresh air is; it is dominated by where the participant thinks he is. An interior court that forms part of a complex of spaces may be *inside.* The Court of the Lions at the Alhambra is a very good example of such space (fig. 24).

Inside is partly a function of the participant's attitude and may even be variable. The lobby of a theater is outside at 9:00 P.M. Inside may be very simple, as in a primitive hut or a Philip Johnson building, or it may have an elaborate hierarchy of development, as in the progressive stages of *inside* in an Egyptian temple, the walled cities of Peking, or the Barcelona Pavilion.

24
Court of the Lions,
Alhambra

Being *inside* is knowing where you are. Supermarkets have very little *inside. Inside* may belong more to the "outdoors" public spaces than to the rooms which surround them, as in the Place Vendôme or in the more spontaneous commonality of the western silver towns, where the genuine false fronts emphatically define the space of Main Street, making a place for law and order, gunfights and bustles in the midst of the desolate and desperate wilderness.

Once the architect has established *inside*, it's his responsibility and right to select and screen the view out. It is, indeed, one of the advantages of being *inside*—being *in* is being selective.

Donlyn Lyndon

The Frame

A work of architecture is a statement of beliefs, a projection of our attitude toward reality into a three-dimensional environment. The importance of this must be kept in mind. We each know only a small portion of what is. Environment is that piece of reality which gets through to us; which passes the highly selective screen that sifts the world into comprehensible experiences, a screen lodged partly in each person's brain and partly in the specific spinning of circumstances. What we do, the way in which we respond, is a projection of that screen—it brings it into the open for scrutiny and in turn selects and sifts the experiences of others.

In architecture, the real challenge of this lies not in the expression of ourselves but in the effect that our work has on determining its user's "fix" on reality.

The importance of architecture lies in a building's capacity to determine the way in which its occupants see the world. Our world is exceedingly complex and impossible to comprehend in its totality. Each science is an attempt to hold reality still long enough to think about it. A painting, or a piece of music, isolates a coherent set of visual or aural relationships to encourage and reward more than normal undisturbed attention. It creates a minute insulated world where the mind can dwell untrammeled in order, thriving on consistent care and systematic response, until that order becomes a means of grasping reality.

Architecture when consistently and provocatively ordered can do the same. It can establish a coherent *inside* environment and, in addition, it can screen and select the view of *outside*. We must get into a frame (or a "frame of mind") in order to make any sense out of the world.

The "view of outside" is much more than a photograph out the window. What we see through a selected opening is one indication of our relation to surroundings. Our entire attitude is at stake, however. The "view of outside" includes the taste of the air, the level of sound, recollections of other places and people, and knowledge of the town structure.

What we "let in" to our selected environment should help us to "place" ourselves specifically in a broad context. By directing attention to specific events and processes, the frame that we build can remind us of a total order, an order which includes both the worlds of nature and the worlds of man. We should be reminded of an order that is not our own, the simple facts of the natural world that nurtured our growth and on which we still depend. The daily cycle, the change of seasons, the movement of air, are all healthy evidences that we are caught up in processes more important than our appointments calendars. The changing direction and intensity of sunlight is a continual gauge of our "place" in time. A building must emphasize, not destroy, these variations.

Natural growth is also a record of the processes of nature and of the conditions of any particular locale. It is symbolic evidence of the dynamics of organic process. In addition, it makes us aware of the constituents of the natural environment. Trees and bushes reflect and modify the sun, move and flicker in the breeze, suggesting the world's animation.

That which we make becomes part of this all-encompassing process and enters into the flow of time. It should show evidence of this. It is here that man's synthetic development comes into conflict with the natural processes of decay and regeneration which initially created the world we know. Much of our technological effort is directed toward eliminating the effects of time. The aluminum barns that glitter disturbingly in golden fields stand out because they are not in phase with their surroundings; they remain essentially aloof from organic change.

The world is being made over to fit man's rhythm of development at an alarming pace. As we consume and destroy more and more of our natural world, we are learning to carry our environment with us. Instead of perfecting the earth we are discarding it. In this process each generation thinks as though it were an end in itself, giving the illusion that no other existed and, incidentally, that no other will come. Our technical needs and capabilities in many cases do demand highly specific temporary structures whose destruction is an integral part of their economic life. But temporary structures in most cases permanently alter the land. The "luxurious" plaster hovels, for which the hills of California are being leveled, will soon vanish, but the hills will not return; and the thoughtless network of service lines from which they spring will remain to inhibit the growth of future development. Whatever its virtues, Disneyland is a pathetic and shortlived substitute for the natural beauty that has been squeezed out of existence by its parishioners.

The existing structure of the land is a resultant of unseen natural processes operating over a long period of time. We must respect the structure and work to have our constructions be a continuation of that process, letting the present landscape play an evident role in the determination of suitable form for each place, respecting the impact that any structures have on the land. Similarly, the existing structure of a community is a result of many, often conflicting processes, and is analogous to organic growth. Again, what we do should be a part of an interacting process which includes and respects what has been done, what there is to do and there could be to do. Whatever we build significantly affects neighboring structures and the overall sense of place. We must attend as much to this reshaping of the existent environment as we do to the shaping of our own building. In this sense there is no *outside*.

What's *inside* should also make us conscious of the resources that man has created. The form of a building should respond to the systems that produce it, whether by implication or dramatization. The elaborate service systems, mechanical, transportation, and communication networks that give sustenance to our daily lives should not be buried in oblivion. We ought to be reminded of our dependence on man's technical know-how and to recognize the part it plays in our lives.

D.L.

Participation

Most importantly, we must "let in" the user, not as a hapless occupant filling a chair in the "living room," or "giving scale" to the elevation, but as an active participant. He is the person who really defines what's "in," the person who uses the architect's clues to establish a world for himself.

Architects must learn to understand the tension between actual possession and abstract possession. The architect abstracts the act of possession, clarifying it through the discipline of selected observations. He establishes an ordered frame for the random, chaotic movements of thought and body: a frame whose form is an intermediary between the participant's *inside* and the *outside* world of existing environment and technical capacity. It should be neither an arbitrary generality nor a glovelike translation of specific activity. The user must be allowed to participate, to reclaim through his acts that which has been abstracted for him. The ghats at Benares are the most striking example of this tension. As great cascades of steps they plunge out of the narrow streets and down to the sacred Ganges (fig. 25). As an edge to the river, their simple geometric forms indicate the annual rise and fall of the

25
Benares, India

river and its tremendous importance to the town, providing with one gesture an infinitely adaptable base for activity. Each step is a potential place: place to worship, place to wash, place to sell, place to sing, place to sleep, place to die and be burned. Every day the people come to bathe in the hallowed water, to repossess the river's edge. The steps remain, the act is daily repeated.

The places that we build should also keep us aware of the conjunction between natural order and synthetic form that is at the base of human activity, establishing an abstracted frame that gives meaning to, and is given meaning by, our personal acts. In Hindu temples the Being beyond all time is each day presented with a flower.

D.L.

The Search for Order

Science and art, it has been said, search for unity in hidden likenesses. The establishment of our domain requires us to give meaning to external realities and experiences. We seek patterns of order and search for essential unities within the seeming chaos of life. We require architecture, as distinct from building, to create a singular sense of order: a sense of *place.* The qualities of place are dynamic, temporal, and personal. Our response may vary but our feelings about place are real. *Place* and architecture communicate to all who use them the essential meaning of a particular environment.

The creative act of architecture abstracts intrinsic qualities of an existing natural environment and, together with components of our mechanical world, synthesizes a new place, a harmony of human and natural environments.

When we are at a *place,* we know it. If our image or perception of a specific environmental order is confused or unclear then there is no place. We don't know when we are *there;* we don't know *where* we are. Organic synthesis, human possession have not occurred. Our lives are increasingly spent in just such meaningless environments. Mechanically contrived "order" is substituted for environmental synthesis and becomes our reality. Immobility replaces action. As personal images blur and dissolve, a vacuous culture replaces human experience with instructions on how to live.

Sim Van der Ryn

A Need for Testing

The system of experiences, spatial and temporal order created by architecture, is dynamic and open-ended. Architecture becomes relevant and real only as it involves its users, imparts meaning to their experiences and elicits response. The reality of architecture is the process of interaction between *place* and inhabitant. This essential reality is most often ignored in current practice. Most architects just don't seem to be interested in how people use and respond to their "solutions." Yet the only way to determine the validity of hypothetical solutions is to test them operationally. The current test of successful architecture seems to be the number of pages of architectural garnish garnered in the trade press. Concern for the real process of architecture is evidenced by the inclusion of people in photos as elements of scale and background.

The history of modern science is a history of testing assumptions as accurate approximations of external reality. Science demands that the test of truth be operational. This is precisely what the latter-day alchemists of architecture will not do. Somehow they intend to produce gold. Simulated ends, preconceived and untested theories all substitute for a logical process of organizing conceptual images. The Pure Food and Drug Act forbids the marketing of a new product until its effects on the innocent public have been tested and observed. We need a Pure Architecture Act!

Recently the AIA proposed that the architect's responsibility today extends to all facets of community design. This pronouncement sounds rather hollow until the profession can establish means for evaluating architecture as an environmental process, which is something we expect of every scientific discipline. We need clearly to integrate our methods with the work of both behavioral and social sciences and the natural environmental sciences. Systems technology may provide the technical means to integrate knowledge from these fields with the particular problems of architecture.

The AIA position sounds particularly plaintive in the light of increasing sectors of building not being designed by architects, although traditionally within their realm of competence. The postwar housing boom, which changed the face of our land, was conceived and put together by "merchandisers." The merchandisers' business is to predict how people will react to certain environmental stimuli. This they learn through observation and testing. *They* know what people want: how many architects do?

S. V.d.R.

An Economic Standard

We have suggested that environmental design implies the creation of rational systems of order. We insist that a valid process of environmental design or basis for architectural synthesis must evolve from continual evaluation of results. We now need to determine what objective standards are best suited to judge how well a specific "place" works.

The making of "places" involves the utilization of resources that have alternative uses. "Economics," according to Lionel Robbins, "is concerned with the relationships between ends conceived as the possible objectives of conduct and the technical and social environment." The concepts of economics provide useful tools in establishing a standard by which to analyze in such a way that program objectives are maximized. This is not simply an additive process but an accelerating one. Measuring a ratio of input to output, of how we may utilize resources to maximize our satisfactions from them, is simply a technical statement of the process that each of us goes through, consciously, on making a decision as to the use of time or money.

It is one of the organizing principles of science. The physicist Ernst Mach defined his work as an attempt to arrange experience in the most economical order. Human action must order "what is"—the experiencing of environment—into an economic system which collectively and individually produces the greatest positive response.

The experience of primitive cultures concerned with satisfying only the most primary needs is important to us. For the making of places which attempt to satisfy these primary needs (the first functional level of ordering and creating community) embodies its own particular process of economizing through an intimate contact with place and its potential. Such economy in creating "place" goes much deeper than the obvious examples of primitive shelters which fulfill their function admirably through a recognition of intrinsically suitable form and material.

We tend to forget that most of what we know as civilization is in a sense economic surplus. It consists of human energy and natural resources not committed to providing basic sustenance. Environmental design decisions cannot neglect the importance of the resource base of our civilization. We should not look for order in the surface array of man-made things, for they are only transformations of our real resources. It is these resources and not their material expressions that we must respect in the design process.

The economizing principle, which synthesizes each unit of human or material resources into an equation to maximize a set of design objectives, should not be confused with cheapness. Cheapness usually means the maximization of dollar return to an individual or group at the expense of significant community values not within the scope of the program. True economy maximizes benefits to the entire community.

The economic standard of objective performance does not absolve us from a professional and individual responsibility of determining what our objectives and values should be. To forfeit our right to influence these decisions is professionally irresponsible. The right democratically to determine the shape of our environment is the real freedom at stake.

S. V.d.R.

The Symbolic Function

The places that man first made were easily identifiable in the midst of natural order and were symbols of his occupation. He needed no state flags, crosses on top, nor wagon wheels on his lawn. As the places, and thus the symbols, multiplied and converged, a hierarchical order emerged, and decorative symbolism was merely an extension of the basic ideas communicated by built form. A man could find his way about a city and return without mental strain. Our streets now have myriad decorative symbols but few that are basic, hence confusion, because they are an extension of nothing. The rapidity and degree of communication of purpose varies with the complexity, and so one may spend ten seconds at a newsstand or ten years in a city to know it. A "newsstand" that hides behind a small sales window in a city wall would have little success, and, if the city equalizes or maximizes everything, one may just close one's eyes and travel by automatic system to one's appointed slot. Yet this is the tendency.

Ed Stone revolted against the dreary urbs and yelled "let's go to bat for beauty," and Yamasaki followed him on a spree in architectural cosmetics applying exotic skin decoration to great cages for men, and some had the gall to call it "New Baroque." As with heroin, the relief was temporary and the aftereffects terrible, with hundreds of less able architects trying to recapture that first emotional thrill of novelty. Elsewhere man was translating the need for "order" into a need for geometric pattern, hence Brasília, a solidified image that holds little respect for the dynamic nature of man's life. Hence, also, many "community centers" which mark the geometric center of arid tracts with forms that ignore the rich possibilities of human interchange that are the basis of communal life.

The accommodation of the dynamic system of human activity demands a fabricated order that has in itself a similar possibility of change; therefore, the elements that must be considered permanent, basic, and continuous are not material, although they influence material development. If we do not seek and find these basic characteristics, a technological repertoire is merely a plaything. Significant buildings evolve from human intercourse and action, and can even evoke them, but if the form derives from some arbitrary, formulist code of aesthetics, out of contact with the client, then it can slowly strangle life.

Eero Saarinen felt that his new CBS building must be the simplest skyscraper in New York, and so it becomes a smooth tower of Euclidean sterility, following all the others into a world that visually eliminates and physically constricts the persons and processes within, while turning a lifeless face to the observer who is awed by its distant immensity. The visiting architect registers awe, notes its meticulous detail, and next year, perhaps, he will build a two-story version in Virginia City. Such image-making is idolatrous. Sir Basil Spence lay entranced in the dentist's chair and dreamt of light coming through a wiggly wall, which looked so nice that he used it in the new Coventry Cathedral. One hardly imagines Chartres originating in a pentatholic coma. "A church," says Peter Hammond, "is shaped by worship," and yet we get "crown of thorns" churches, "fish" churches, "fountain of light" churches, and worse still, "hands in prayer" churches, all striving to look like what they are not.

Let us turn our backs on fantasy and Utopia both, and confront reality. Although we have pretended to let art remarry science, we carefully maintain them in separate corners of the mind, to the detriment of both. We finally accept prestressed concrete and "ultimate design" in concrete, fifty years late, and wave our discovery joyfully in clients' faces. We still question the advantages of mass transportation while trying to abolish the automobiles we love. We flatten magnificently sculpted land for homes, and yet build artificial hills on the roofs of city garages. Clearly we are caught somewhere between the dollar and the dream, each of which is an evasion of the real issue.

Patrick J. Quinn

Dispelling the Mystique

We must first look at the functional problem—not how the building works, but how people work—and derive our notion of economy from the occupation of space rather than its cubic-foot cost. The motivations of human activity and the dynamic movements ensuing must be accommodated, must be anticipated, so people must be regarded as the generators and not just the unfortunate recipients of our brainstorms. This can only be achieved by stripping our architectural thinking of all the peripheral terminological junk with which we have weighed it down. Let's banish from our vocabulary, for a while, such phrases as "expression," "enrichment," "rhythm," "personal style," "scale" (as 3-D size code), "explosion of space," together with all the beautifying devices of imposed order, and seek, instead, the order inherent in a situation, using fundamental values as criteria.

But where does this leave the "art" and "wonder of creation"? The answer is, for a few moments, out in the cold. Architecture is a synthetic act of creativity and cannot be produced by preconception. The elimination of all but essentials is necessary to clarify the vision, by putting one in a position to create. Thereafter it depends on one's talents and one's logic and one's courage.

P.J.Q.

Our Obligation

We have an obligation to make the layman aware of our real objectives by speaking his language, one that he has almost forgotten, and of which he needs to be reminded. His sensitivity must be revived not by encouraging him to join in the jargon of a mystique but by making for him places that are real to him, of which he feels a part because they have grown from his need.

Our teachers of architecture can do well by discouraging young men from imagining themselves as creative geniuses. Genius emerges of itself. The crystallized concepts of three-dimensional compositions should quietly disappear from our curricula, and we must cease to wave before the student such magic phrases as "integration with the site," "integration with the urban scene," "integration and continuity of spaces." Let us instead talk perhaps of "integration with the activities of a place." Students above all need to be confronted with the realities of architecture. They need to be put in a position to create. Only then can we find out who are architects and who are not, and perhaps architecture will be on the way toward recovering its symbolic function.

P.J.Q.

Marginal Quotations

As *scene* is the basic abstraction of pictorial art, and *kinetic volume* of sculpture, that of architecture is an *ethnic domain*. Actually, of course, a domain is not a "thing" among other "things"; it is the sphere of influence of a function, or functions; it may have physical effects on some geographical locality or it may not. Nomadic cultures, or cultural phenomena like the seafaring life, do not inscribe themselves on any fixed place on earth. Yet a ship, constantly changing its location, is none the less a self-contained place, and so is a Gypsy camp, an Indian camp or a circus camp, however often it shifts its geodetic bearings. Literally, we say the camp is *in* a place, culturally, it *is* a place. A Gypsy camp is a different place from an Indian camp though it may be geographically where the Indian camp used to be.

A place, in this non-geographical sense, is a created thing, an ethnic domain made visible, tangible, sensible. As such it is, of course, an illusion. Like any other plastic symbol, it is primarily an illusion of self-contained, self-sufficient, perceptual space. But the principle of organization is its own: for it is organized as a functional realm made visible—the center of a virtual world, the "ethnic domain," and itself a geographic semblance.

Susanne K. Langer, *Feeling and Form*

For 30 years architects have been providing the outside for man, even on the inside. But that is not their job at all. Architecture means providing inside for men even outside.

Aldo van Eyck, Otterlo, 1959

It is my conviction that there is within the human individual a sense of *relatedness to his total environment,* that this relatedness is one of the transcendentally important facts of human living, and that if he tries to ignore its importance to himself he does so at peril to his psychological well-being.

Harold Searles, *Landscape,* Winter 1962

Harrison Brown tells us that we are approaching a time when ores will no longer exist. The deposits of millennia will have been exhausted in a few hundred years.

Aspen Conference, 1962

The physical and social sciences are coming together and finding they have much in common. There is no reason why architecture should not participate in and profoundly benefit from this trend toward unification, but both a broadening and deepening of the current level of architectural discourse will be required.

Joseph Esherick

GIANT FENCES CAN WORK THREE WAYS FOR YOU.

YOU'VE GOT TO BEAT THE DRUM.

GIANT ROADSIDE SIGNS COST PLENTY BUT REALLY STOP TRAF-
FIC.

DO SOMETHING TO START PEOPLE TALKING ABOUT YOUR
HOUSE.

RELAX AND HAVE A LITTLE FUN WITH A GOOD PUBLICITY STUNT.

BUILD YOUR REPUTATION WITH GOOD DEEDS.

GET THEM EMOTIONALLY INVOLVED.

ONCE THEY PICK THEIR LOT THEY'LL ALMOST SELL THEMSELVES
A HOUSE.

YOU CAN ALMOST TIP THE SCALES BY GIVING PROSEPCTS LOTS
OF CHOICES.

GIVE OWNERS A SENSE OF BELONGING AND KEEP SHOWING IN-
TEREST IN THEM.

Captions from photo stories "How to Get the Crowds Out," "How
to Turn Lookers into Buyers," *House and Home,* April 1957

I believe that even philosophers interested in aesthetics find it difficult
to explain the origin of our feelings toward forms which are dictated
by the laws of statics or dynamics, since these laws are not intuitively
understood nor can be explained by the experience of our ancestors.
But there is no doubt that any product of high efficiency is always aes-
thetically satisfying.

Pier Luigi Nervi

Cooped up as we are in the world of common experience, we must endeavor to break away and explore the remoter levels and construct theories befitting not solely the commonplace levels. . . . Those who fail
to explore will naturally construct theories compatible with their restricted experience but entirely out of touch with the wider fields
which they ignore.

A. D'Abro

The present is not a time of style whatsoever, it is a time of groping—
a time of discovery. It is a time, you might say, of realization. Our

problems are all new, our spatial demands are new, and it is a time, therefore, more concerned with trying to create better institutions from those we have already established.

Louis Kahn, Otterlo, 1959

Review of *The Earth, the Temple and the Gods,* by Vincent Scully

Several months ago, four of us collaborated on an article in this magazine arguing that the proper concern of the architect is not chiefly to manipulate materials, form, or space but to contribute to the conscious creation of *place* (of what Susanne Langer has called "ethnic domain"). We went on to suggest that the present parlous state of our environment, the chaotic monotony and the anonymity of our surroundings are at least partly the result of a falling away of human understanding about making, defining, enhancing, annotating, and focusing *place.* It was a thrill to discover *The Earth, the Temple and the Gods,* to know that even if architects were not much concerned with place an eminent art historical heretic is, that Vincent Scully is writing with sensitivity and power about the making of place in ancient Greece, describing some of the most moving places that man has ever made his own—and what's more, describing how he did it. *The Earth, the Temple and the Gods* seems therefore, to me, an immensely important book. (I was pleased to see that another reviewer thought so too: "The most distinguished book of its kind," he called it, "to be published in the English language since . . . Ruskin's *Stones of Venice.*") The sustained power and poetry of Scully's writing are magnificent and moving; his erudition is almost as monumental as some of the temples he describes; and his insights are breathtaking.

All this excellence ought to have produced a book that is itself magnificent, itself a monument gathering up the forces that lie about it. Somehow it did not. The subject is too important and too much alive for the art historical format into which it has been stuffed; the densely printed pages heavy with references and the politely acknowledged opinions of learned colleagues lie remote from an assortment of little fuzzy gray photographs apparently arranged at random, and from more decipherable but maddeningly infrequent plans and diagrams. The form of the book would be fine for the more usual intellectual detective story beloved of art historians, which is an essentially nonvisual undertaking. But here, when the physical participation of the reader is required, when he must be caught up in the rhythm and the thrust and the sweep of the landscape if he is to sense just what it is the temples do, here words and pictures or sketches by Le Corbusier, ideas and diagrams and a sense of the space would have to come together so that the

Originally published in *Landscape,* Autumn 1963, pp. 35–36.

reader who has not stood on the sites could more clearly see what Professor Scully is so eloquently talking about.

And he is (gray photographs or no) marvelously eloquent. Note, for instance, a description of the newer east pediment at Aigina: "The patterns and barriers have burst, and men stride forward in savage pride, fully aware for the first time of the wholeness of their strength. This is the raw material of the classic age, and the fierce moment of its discovery is expressed nowhere so well as in the new east pediment at Aigina. By the time of Olympia, as we have seen, its terrible force was brought into the stillness of early classic order and into the harmonies of the more complex theology of Zeus. But at Aigina the mighty figures of the east pediment broke out of the integrated calm of the old goddess and destroyed forever the residue of human innocence under her sway. They smashed the temple's gentle scale and thundered topheavily from its pediment. Their forms struck and fell across the view toward Salamis, and the slender columns and virginal capitals of the temple now supported not the calm pattern of Aphaia-Athena but the flaunted aegis of a true Athena Polias, protector of the city and instigator of action in men."

The vision of the whole landscape, mountain and temple, is so whole and so new and so poetic and so grand (and so hedged round with art historical and Freudian machinery) that it is easy to become suspicious. The kinetic excitement of Greek landscapes, apparently so thoroughly understood and so skillfully capitalized upon by the designers of the temples, is easy to respond to across the centuries, but the Freudian steam excited by horned land forms and conical hills fails somehow to seem much like Greek steam. It is hard to know just how to react to descriptions of mountains with sleeping-lady silhouettes, just as it is hard to invent responses to people who tell you what they see in the clouds. But more important than how visible is the lady is the much more exciting issue of how visible is the whole; and Scully's magnificent contribution is to look at the whole, not just at some of the forms in it, so that the forms themselves, the Doric temples, instead of emerging, as they usually do in books, as tiresome statistics seeking a norm, emerge as exciting, immensely skillful responses each to a specific problem, that of making coherent the place which has attracted a god. In this light, curvature of the stylobate (or lack of it), a stilted pediment, entasis or none are not statistical annoyances, but are marvelously manipulable devices, capable of making the Greek temples perhaps the most precise and the most potent instrument for making place that the world has yet known.

Moore's second article for Perspecta *was written in 1965 at the beginning of his Yale period. Robert A. M. Stern, a student at the time, edited the double issue, which included pieces by Romaldo Giurgola, Philip Johnson, Louis Kahn, Vincent Scully, H. R. Hitchcock, Paul Rudolph, G. L. Hersey, Peter Millard, and an extract of* Complexity and Contradiction in Architecture *which Robert Venturi would publish in 1966.*

You Have to Pay for the Public Life

This issue of *Perspecta* considers monumental architecture as part of the urban scene. I was asked to ferret out some on the West Coast, especially in California. *Perspecta*'s editors suspected, I presume, that I would discover that in California there is no contemporary monumental architecture, or that there is no urban scene (except in a sector of San Francisco), or more probably, that both monumental architecture and the urban scene are missing. Their suspicions were well founded; any discussion from California in 1964 about monumental urban architecture (as it is coming to exist, for instance, in New Haven) is bound to be less about what we have than about what we have instead.

Any discussion of monumental architecture in its urban setting should proceed from a definition of (or, if you prefer, an airing of prejudice about) what constitutes "monumental," and what "urban" means to us. The two adjectives are closely related: both of them involve the individual's giving up something, space or money or prominence or concern, to the public realm.

Monumentality, I take it, has to do with monuments. And a monument is an object whose function is to mark a place, either at that place's boundary or at its heart. There are, of course, private monuments, over such places as the graves of the obscure, but to merit our attention here, and to be of any interest to most of the people who view it, a monument must make a place of more than private importance or interest. The act of marking is then a public act, and the act of recognition an expectable public act among the members of the society that possesses the place. Monumentality, considered this way, is not a product of compositional techniques (such as symmetry about several axes), of flamboyance of form, or even of conspicuous

Originally published in *Perspecta*, no. 9–10 (1965), pp. 57–97.

consumption of space, time, or money. It is, rather, a function of the society's taking possession of or agreeing upon extraordinarily important places on the earth's surface, and of the society's celebrating their preeminence.

A version of this agreement and this celebration was developed by José Ortega y Gasset, in *The Revolt of the Masses,* into a definition of urbanity itself. "The *urbs* or *polis,*" he says, "starts by being an empty space, the *forum,* the *agora,* and all the rest is just a means of fixing that empty space, of limiting its outlines. . . . The square, thanks to the walls which enclose it, is a portion of the countryside which turns its back on the rest, eliminates the rest, and sets up in opposition to it."

Ortega y Gasset's product is the city, the urban unit based upon the Mediterranean open square, a politically as well as physically comprehensible unit that people used to be willing to die for. The process of achieving an urban focus is the same as that of achieving monumentality: it starts with the selection, by some inhabitants, of a place which is to be of particular importance, and continues when they invest that place with attributes of importance, such as edges or some kind of marker. This process, the establishing of cities and the marking of important places, constitutes most of the physical part of establishing civilization. Charles Eames has made the point that the crux of this civilizing process is the giving up by individuals of something in order that the public realm may be enhanced. In the city, say, urban and monumental places, indeed urbanity and monumentality themselves, can occur when something is given over by people to the public.

Planners have a way of starting every speech by articulating their (private) discovery that the public body's chief concern is *people.* The speech then says unrelatedly that it's too bad the sprawl of metropolis is so formless. It might well be that if the shibboleth about people were turned inside out, if planning efforts went toward enlarging people's concerns—and sacrifices—for the *public* realm, then the urban scene would more closely approach the planners' vision, and the pleasures of the people would be better served.

The most evident thing about Los Angeles, especially, and the other new cities of the West is that, in the terms of any of the traditions we have inherited, hardly anybody gives anything to the public realm. Instead, it is not at all clear what the public realm consists of, or even, for the time being, who needs it. What is clear is that civic amenities of the sort architects think of as "monumental," which were highly regarded earlier in the century, are of much less concern today. A frivolous but pointed example is the small city of Atascadero, which lies in a particularly handsome coastal valley between Los Angeles and San Francisco. It was first developed in the 1920s as a real estate venture with heavy cultural overtones and extensive architectural amplification. Extraordinarily ambitious "monumental" architecture popped up all over the town site. Buildings of a vague Italian Romanesque persuasion with a classic revival touch, symmetrical about several axes, faced onto wide malls punctuated or terminated by Canovaesque sculptural groups. The effect was undeniably grand, if a bit surreal, exploiting wide grassy vistas among the dense California oaks. But there wasn't much of a town until the 1940s. Then, on the major mall, an elaborately sunken panel of irrigated green, there cropped up a peninsula of fill surmounted by a gas station. Later there came another, and more recently an elevated freeway has continued the destruction of the grand design. All this has happened during the very period in which Philadelphians, with staggering energy and expense, have been achieving in their Center City long malls north from Independence Hall and west from a point just off their City Hall, grand vistas at every scale, an architectural expression overwhelmingly serene, all urban desiderata which the Atascaderans did not especially want or need and have been blithely liquidating. Doesn't this liquidation constitute some sort of crime against the public? Before we start proceedings, we should consider what the public realm is, or rather, what it might be in California now and during the decades ahead, so that the "monumentality" and the "urbanity" that we seek may be appropriate as functions of our own society and not of some other one.

In California cities, as in new cities all over the country (and in California just about all cities are new cities), the pattern of buildings on the land is as standard as it is explosive. Everywhere near population centers, new little houses surrounded by incipient lawns appear. They could be said to be at the edge of the city, except that there is no real edge, thanks to the speed of growth, the leapfrogging of rural areas, and the long commercial fingers that follow the highways out farther than the houses have yet reached. Meanwhile, in areas not much older, houses are pulled down as soon as zoning regulations allow, to be replaced with apartments whose only amenity is a location handily near a garage in the basement.

The new houses are separate and private, it has been pointed out: islands, alongside which are moored the automobiles that take the inhabitants off to other places (fig. 26). It might be more useful and more accurate to

26
House in Malibu

note that the houses and the automobiles are very much alike, and that each is very like the mobile homes which share both their characteristics. All are fairly new, and their future is short; all are quite standard, but have allowed their buyers the agonies of choice, demonstrating enough differences so that they can readily be identified during the period of ownership, and so that the sense of privacy is complete, in the car as well as in the house. This is privacy with at least psychic mobility. The houses are not tied down to any *place* much more than the trailer homes are, or the automobiles. They are adrift in the suburban sea, not so mobile as the cars, but just as unattached. They are less islands alongside which the cars are moored than little yachts, dwarfed by the great chrome-trimmed dinghys that seek their lee.

This is, after all, a floating world in which a floating population can island-hop with impunity; one need almost never go ashore. There are the drive-in banks, the drive-in movies, the drive-in shoe repair. There is even, in Marin County, Frank Lloyd Wright's drive-in Civic Center, a structure of major biographical and perhaps historical importance, about whose forms a great deal of surprisingly respectful comment has already appeared in the press. Here, for a county filling up with adjacent and increasingly indistinguishable suburban communities, quite without a major center, was going to be *the* center for civic activities, this public realm, one would have supposed, for which a number of public-spirited leaders in the community had fought long and hard. It might have been, to continue our figure, a sort of dock to which our floating populace might come, monumental in that it marked a special place which was somewhere and which, for its importance, was civic if not urban. But instead of a dock for floating suburbanites, it is just another ship, much larger than most, to be sure, and presently beached (wedged, in fact) between two hills. It demands little of the people who float by, and gives them little back. It allows them to penetrate its interior from a point on its underside next to the delivery entrance, but further relations are discouraged, and lingering is most often the result of inability to find the exit.

A monster of equivalent rootlessness hoves into view from the freeway entrance to California's one established, anchored city, San Francisco. The immense new Federal Building just being completed by John Carl Warnecke and a host of associated architects stands aloof from the city's skyline, out of scale with it, unrelated to anything in the topography, no part even of the grandiose civic center nearby. Slick details, giant fountains, and all, it draws back from the street and just stands there. It is one of the West's largest filing cabinets, and it is unfair, of course, to expect from it any attributes of the public realm. Indeed, if San Francisco, one gathers, had not grudgingly stepped aside for it, some distant bureaucrats would spitefully have removed it to Oakland. So much for the Federal Heart of the city.

Even in the few years of Yankee California's existence, this kind of placelessness has not always been characteristic. During the twenties and into the thirties, with what was doubtless an enormous assist from the Hollywood vision in the days of its greatest splendor, an architectural image of California developed that was exotic but specific, derivative but exhilaratingly free. It had something to do with Helen Hunt Jackson's *Ramona,* with the benign climate, with the splendor of the sites and their floral luxuriance, with the general availability of wood and stucco, and with the assurance supplied by Hollywood that appearances *did* matter, along with the assumption (for which Hollywood was not necessary but to which it gave a boost) that we, the inheritors of a hundred traditions, had our pick. What came of this was an architecture that owed something to Spain, very little to the people who were introducing the International Style, and a great deal to the movie camera's moving eye. It seemed perfectly appropriate to the energetic citi-

27
Santa Barbara
County Courthouse,
William Mooser

zens of Santa Barbara, for instance, that after their city had been devastated by an earthquake, it should rise again Spanish. The railroad roundhouse appeared to become a bullring, the movie house a castle. Everywhere in the town, the act of recalling another quite imaginary civilization created a new and powerful public realm.

Out of this public act came one of the most extraordinary buildings in the United States, probably the most richly complex and extensively rewarding stew of spatial and sculptural excitements west of Le Corbusier's Carpenter Center for the Visual Arts: the Santa Barbara County Courthouse (fig. 27). It was completed in 1929. William Mooser was the architect, and the inspiration, say the guidebooks, was Spanish. But nothing in Spain was ever like this. Instead of setting itself off against the landscape, in Mediterranean fashion, this assemblage of huge white forms opens itself up to it. The landscape is a big and dramatic one in Santa Barbara, where the coastal plain is narrow, the ocean close at hand, and the mountains behind unusually high and startlingly near. The Courthouse takes it all in: it piles around one end of a large open park, whose major forms are sunk into the ground, thus allowing the giant arch, the main feature among the dozens of features visible from the street side, to lead not into the building but through it and immediately out the other side, so that the building minimizes its en-closure function and asserts itself as backdrop—a stage set, if you will—with the power to transform the giant landscape (fig. 28). It is almost too easy to make a comparison with Le Corbusier's new Harvard building, sim-ilarly pierced (in Cambridge, in 1963, by a make-believe freeway ramp) and similarly composed of an immensely rich but strongly ordered concatena-tion of sculptural forms. At Harvard they are twisted enough and powerful enough to dislocate all the polite Georgian buildings around, to wrench them loose and set them whirling. Fewer structures are set whirling by the Courthouse, but a full complement of phantoms is raised up out of the lush landscape.

28
Santa Barbara
County Courthouse

The Santa Barbara County Courthouse did so much about sweeping the whole landscape up and in that one might expect the really large-scale projects of the sixties to catch even more of the grandeur of the place. Whole new college campuses, for instance, which are springing magically out of fields across the state, surely present unparalleled chances to order a public realm, to invest a place of public importance with the physical attributes of that importance. Yet, by any standards, the clearest and strongest campus to be found in the state is still the old campus at Stanford, designed in Boston by Shepley, Rutan and Coolidge and built in the years just after 1887 (fig. 29). The buildings in the old campus are H. H. Richardson warmed over (and cooled off again in the long passage from the architects' Boston kitchens); the gaudy mosaic facade of the chapel, the centerpiece of the composition, is an affront to the soft yellow stone surfaces around. But the play of the fabled local sunshine with the long arcades, the endlessly surprising development of interior spaces from big to small to big again, the excitement of a sensible framework that is strong and supple enough to include the most disparate of academic activities—all combine to make this a complete and memorable place. Even though the surrounding countryside is not swept

29
Stanford University,
Shepley, Rutan and
Coolidge

into the picture, as at Santa Barbara, at least there is an orchestration of spaces varied and complete enough to evoke a complex public use. It is a place, however, that dates from the previous century, and this is a survey of our own times, times that have multiplied opportunities for spatial and functional orchestrations like the ones at Stanford and Santa Barbara. What, then, do we have?

Foothill College in Los Altos, by Ernest J. Kump and Masten and Hurd, comes first to mind, because it has won every prize in sight, and because it is a beguiling place (fig. 30). It sits strong on a pleasant rolling site, on which prodigies of bulldozing have created earthworks worthy of a Vauban, though a bit dulled by a foreground of parking lot. Its nicely detailed buildings share the charm of the best Bay Region domestic architecture, topped by memorable shingle roofs, which have added the glories of old Newport and older Japan to the idiom of the Bay, without ever losing control. Yet I am bound to report that their sensitive and disciplined complex is simply not in the same league as the older campus or the Courthouse. There is no heightening of importance, no beginnings, even, of the establishment of a *place* singled out for special public importance and illuminated

30
Foothill College, Los Altos Hills, Ernest J. Kump, Masten and Hurd

by that recognition—a place, for instance, important enough for an academic procession to occur. The old Stanford campus may not culminate in anything of special beauty or worth, but it works at culminating. Foothill, rather, with great charm, dissipates itself and loses its powers. Sasaki and Walker's landscaping senses well this urge to dissipate, and devotes itself to filling with impenetrable bosques the places where the spaces might have been. Equalitarian it is: every tree and every building is as important as the next.

And so the public realm is made scarcely distinguishable from the private; the college's fortress base of earth does not anchor it, and it floats, as free as the houses in the suburban seas around.

The same firm's newer campus, for Cabrillo College near Santa Cruz, is far less beguiling and floats even more free. The buildings, carefully and sophisticatedly detailed, stick close to the idiom established when California was young and places were Places, but the idiom does not stretch to cover the requirements, and the act of multiplying varying sites of hipped-roof buildings surrounded by porches only serves to confirm the rigidity of a whole campus made of a single verandaed form. A window is a simple thing, and not new. In the cool climate of coastal northern California, the sunshine it can admit is pleasant if there is not a wide veranda in front to reduce north, east, south, and west to shady equality. The citizens of old Monterey built porches like these in the cool fog, lived behind them, and died like flies from tuberculosis; presumably medical science and the mechanical engineer will save us this time.

Meanwhile, the attempt to stuff the functions of a whole college into this rigid domestic idiom puts Cabrillo in strong contrast with the old Stanford campus, where the spaces evoke a wide variety of uses; here everything is not only equalitarian but equal. Impeccable details and all, it makes nothing special, it adds nothing to the public realm.

During the years of California's growth, as its cities have appeared, the extravagances of the settlers upon it have suggested to many that straight opulence might create centers of the public realm. Three city halls, especially, clamor for our attention. The San Francisco City Hall probably heads the list for sheer expensive grandeur. The expensiveness was, one gathers, as much a political as a physical phenomenon, but the grandeur is a manifestation of the highly developed Beaux-Arts compositional skills of architects Bakewell and Brown. These great skills, though, have been curiously ineffectual in commending themselves to public concern. It is a curious experience, for instance, to stand in the towering space under the aggressively magnificent dome and to notice that hardly anyone looks up. And the development of the extensive and very formal civic center outside has had remarkably little effect on the growth of the downtown area, which has remained resolutely separate from all this architectural assertion. Surely a part of the failure to achieve an important public place rests with the entirely abstract nature of the Beaux-Arts' earlier International Style. It takes a major master, like Sir Edwin Lutyens at New Delhi, to lift this idiom out of the abstract to give some point to its being somewhere. San Francisco City Hall demonstrates skill but no such mastery, so the city is not specifically enriched by this building's being here; it could be anywhere.

Or almost anywhere. It could not easily be in Gilroy. A small garlic-farming community of the Salinas region, Gilroy relied on a similar, if more relaxed, show of opulence in the building of its own City Hall in 1905 (fig. 31). An elaborateness of vaguely Flemish antecedent served the town's desires; a truly remarkable array of whirls and volutes was concentrated here to signal the center of the public realm. But, alas, this concentration has not kept its hold on the public mind much more effectively than San Francisco's

31
Gilroy City Hall

City Hall has, and now this fancy pile is leading a precarious life as temporary headquarters for the town's Chamber of Commerce and police station.

The citizens of Los Angeles adopted a slightly different route to achieve importance for their City Hall (fig. 32). In their wide horizontal sprawl of city, they went *up* as far as seemed practical, and organized their statutes so no other buildings could go higher. But economic pressure has mounted, and now commercial structures bulk larger on the skyline than the City Hall. The Angelenos' vertical gesture should get some credit, in any case, for being a gesture, an attempt to make a center for a city which otherwise had none. As a formal gesture, it has even had some little hold on the public mind, although its popular image now involves a familiar tower rising in the smoggy background, while a freeway interchange fills the sharp foreground. Investing it with life, and relating the life behind its windows to the life of the city, may never have been possible; such investment, of course, has never happened.

It is interesting, if not useful, to consider where one would go in Los Angeles to have an effective revolution of the Latin American sort: presumably, that place would be the heart of the city. If one took over some public

32
Los Angeles City Hall,
view from freeway

square, some urban open space in Los Angeles, who would know? A march on City Hall would be equally inconclusive. The heart of the city would have to be sought elsewhere. The only hope would seem to be to take over the freeways, or to emplane for New York to organize sedition on Madison Avenue; word would quickly enough get back.

Thus the opulence and the effort involved in the San Francisco, Gilroy, and Los Angeles city halls seem to come to very little in the public mind, lacking as these buildings all do any activity that elicits public participation or is somewhat related to public participation. Whatever the nature of the welfare state, these public buildings seem to offer far less to the passerby than such typical—and remarkable—California institutions as the Nut Tree, a roadside restaurant on the highway from Sacramento to San Francisco, which offers in the middle of a bucolic area such comforts as a miniature railroad, an airport, an extensive toy shop, highly sophisticated gifts and notions, a small bar serving imported beers and cheeses, a heartily elegant—and expensive—restaurant, exhibitions of paintings and crafts, and even an aviary—all of them surrounded and presented with graphic design of consummate sophistication and great flair. This is entirely a commercial venture, but judging from the crowds, it offers the traveler a gift of great importance. It is an offering of urbanity, of sophistication and chic, a kind of foretaste, for those bound west, of the urban joys of San Francisco.

In the days before television, moving picture theaters afforded one of the clearest and easiest ways for people to participate in the National Dream. In California, especially southern California, where movies came from and where the climate allowed forecourts for theaters to be largely out of doors, some of the most image-filled places for the public to congregate, some of the most important parts of what at least seemed to be the public realm, were these theaters. The Fox in Santa Barbara invites our inspection on many of the same grounds as the Santa Barbara County Courthouse (fig. 33). The idiom is a movieland Spanish (again, like nothing in Spain), the architectural opportunity a double one: First, to make of the immense auditorium, set a block back from the theater's entrance on the main street, one of the city's noblest bastions, with high white walls sprouting turrets and balconies and follies. Only the grandest of the princes of the other hemisphere could have afforded walls this size to stick their balconies onto. Second, and more importantly for the city, to make partly roofed and partly open the block-long passageway from the box office to the ticket taker, thus providing the

opportunity to extend the sidewalks of the city, still outdoors, past gardens
and along a tiled esplanade, where soft lights play at night, and where by day
the sun filters down among the leaves. Santa Barbara's sidewalks are ordinary
enough, but in the mind's eye they merge with the passage to the Fox Theater and other commercial arcades and patios off State Street to form a public realm filled with architectural nuance and, even more importantly, filled
with the public (fig. 34).

Another such public monument, which should not soon be forgotten,
although it has been left isolated by Los Angeles's swiftly changing patterns,
is Grauman's Chinese Theater, on Hollywood Boulevard, which seems more
astonishingly grand today than it did in the days when millions in their
neighborhood theaters watched movie stars immortalizing bits of its wet
concrete with their hands and feet.

More recent years have their monuments as well. Indeed, by almost
any conceivable method of evaluation that does not exclude the public, Disneyland must be regarded as the most important single piece of construction in the West in the past several decades. The assumption inevitably made
by people who have not yet been there—that it is some sort of physical extension of Mickey Mouse—is wildly inaccurate. Instead, singlehanded, it is
engaged in replacing many of those elements of the public realm which have
vanished in the featureless private floating world of southern California,

34
Santa Barbara, paseo

whose only edge is the ocean and whose center is otherwise undiscoverable (unless by our revolution test it turns out to be on Manhattan Island). Curiously, for a public place, Disneyland is not free. You buy tickets at the gate. But then, Versailles cost someone a great deal of money, too. Now, as then, you have to pay for the public life (figs. 35, 36).

Disneyland, it appears, is enormously important and successful just because it recreates all the chances to respond to a public environment, which Los Angeles particularly no longer has. It allows play-acting, both to be watched and to be participated in, in a public sphere. In as unlikely a place as could be conceived, just off the Santa Ana Freeway, a little over an hour from the Los Angeles City Hall, in an unchartable sea of suburbia, Disney has created a place, indeed a whole public world, full of sequential occurrences, of big and little drama, full of hierarchies of importance and excitement, with opportunities to respond at the speed of rocketing bobsleds (or rocketing rockets, for all that) or of horse-drawn streetcars. An American Main Street of about 1910 is the principal theme, against which play fairy-tale fantasies, frontier adventure situations, jungles, and the world

35
Disneyland, Main
Street

36
Disneyland

of tomorrow. And all this diversity, with unerring sensitivity, is keyed to the
kind of participation without embarrassment which apparently at this point
in our history we crave. (This is not the point, nor am I the appropriate
critic, to analyze our society's notions of entertainment, but certainly a civilization whose clearest recent image of feminine desirability involves scant-
ily dressed and extravagantly formed young ladies—occasionally with fur
ears—who disport themselves with wild abandon in gaudily make-believe
bordellos, while they perforce maintain the deportment of vestal virgins—
certainly a civilization which seeks this sort of image is in need of pretty
special entertainment.) No raw edges spoil the picture at Disneyland; everything is as immaculate as in the musical comedy villages that Hollywood
has provided for our viewing pleasure for the last three generations. Nice-
looking, handsomely costumed young people sweep away the gum wrappers
almost before they fall to the spotless pavement. Everything works, the way
it doesn't seem to any more in the world outside. As I write this, Berkeley,
which was the proud recipient not long ago of a set of fountains in the
middle of its main street, where interurbans once had run and cars since had

parked, has announced that the fountains are soon being turned off for good, since the chief public use developed for them so far has been to put detergent in them, and the city cannot afford constantly to clean the pipes. Life is not like that in Disneyland; it is much more real: fountains play, waterfalls splash, tiny bulbs light the trees at night, and everything is clean.

The skill demonstrated here in recalling with thrilling accuracy all sorts of other times and places is of course one which has been developing in Hollywood through this century. Disney's experts are breathtakingly precise when they recall the gingerbread of a turn-of-the-century Main Street or a side-wheeler Mississippi River steamboat, even while they remove the grime and mess, and reduce the scale to the tricky zone between delicacy and make-believe. Curiously, the Mickey Mouse–Snow White sort of thing, which is most memorably Disney's and which figures heavily in an area called Fantasyland, is not nearly so successful as the rest, since it perforce drops all the way over into the world of make-believe. Other occurrences stretch credulity, but somehow avoid snapping it. The single most exciting experience in the place, surely, is that which involves taking a cable car (as above a ski slope) in Fantasyland, soaring above its make-believe castles, then ducking through a large papier-mâché mountain called the Matterhorn, which turns out to be hollow and full of bobsleds darting about in astonishingly vertical directions (fig. 37). Thence one swings out above Tomorrowland. Now nobody thinks that that mountain is the Matterhorn or even a mountain, or that those bobsleds are loose upon its slopes—slopes being on the outsides of mountains. Yet the experience of being in that space is a real one, and an immensely exciting one, like looking at a Piranesi prison or escalating in the London Underground.

Of course Disneyland, in spite of the skill and variety of its enchantments, does not offer the full range of public experience. The political experience, for instance, is not manifested here, and the place would not pass our revolution test. Yet there is a variety of forms and activities great enough to ensure an excellent chance that the individual visitor will find something to identify with. A strong contrast is the poverty or absurdity of single images offered up by architects, presumably as part of an elaborate (and expensive) in-group professional joke. The brown-derby-shaped Brown Derbies of an earlier generation, which at least were recognizable by the general public, have given way to such phenomena as the new Coachella Valley Savings and Loan in Palm Springs which rises out of vacant lots to repeat

37
Disneyland, mountain and cable cars

Niemeyer's Palace of the Dawn in Brasília (fig. 38). Across the street from this, a similar institution pays similar in-group tribute to Ronchamp (fig. 39). The most conspicuous entry in this category of searches after monumentality, though, is architect Edward Durrell Stone's revisitation of Mussolini's Third Rome in Beverly Hills (fig. 40). This one has plants growing out of each aerial arch. Apparently there was a plethora of these arches, for

38
Coachella Valley
Savings and Loan,
Palm Springs

39
Bank of America,
Palm Springs

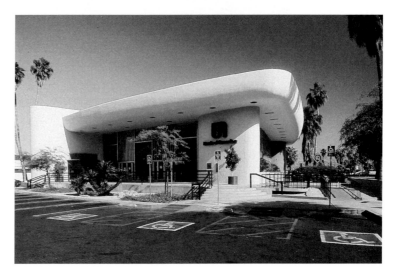

40
Wilshire Boulevard,
Beverly Hills, Edward
Durrell Stone

they crop up, again along Wilshire Boulevard, as far away as Westwood Village, without, however, contributing much continuity to that thoroughfare.

Methods of seeking "character" for buildings in northern California are mostly much less theatrical, and adhere most strictly to a single pattern, an outgrowth of the redwood Bay Region Style in the direction of the standard universal American motel, employing stucco walls, aluminum windows, wooden shakes, and casual, if not cavalier, attitudes toward form. A case in point is a recent competition conducted by Los Gatos, a small and pleasant residential city near San Jose, for its city hall and civic center, to be located on a block near the center of the town, which backs onto a wooded hill and boasts some magnificent trees. Most of the entries were less concerned with responding to the site than with attempting to create a local character from long blocks roofed with widely overhung gables, and roofs covered with thick wood shakes, usually verandaed, and smothered in shrubbery—where there were no parking lots. It really isn't fair to describe this newer shagginess by invoking the Bay Region Style, an appellation devised to describe wooden houses of chaste simplicity, clarity, and economy of means. It is better, perhaps, to cast the blame across the seas and christen the idiom, as an Arizonan of my acquaintance has, "Califuji." The winner of the Los Gatos competition, I hasten to point out, was not at all of this persuasion. The scheme, by Stickney and Hall, is a completely simple and smoothly functioning set of flat-roofed blocks placed around a central space built on the top of the council chamber. The group of buildings fronts on the main street—the buildings relating to each other and to parking—and opens up, thanks to the plaza above the council chamber, to the wooded hill behind.

New monumental buildings in northern California, which sometimes bear firm recollection of the residential Bay Region Style, have achieved varying degrees of architectural and critical success. John Carl Warnecke's post office and bookstore adjoining the old campus at Stanford University uses its materials, masonry walls, and Mediterranean red tile roofs as a point of departure to make, with two large, steep overhanging roofs, a form almost strong enough to take its place beside the old campus. A finely detailed colonnade roofed with hyperbolic paraboloids (presumably the approved late twentieth-century successor to the arcuated colonnade) tucks rather redundantly under the great tile overhang, and fails to measure up to the rest. The care taken in framing its concrete members is, however, heartening assurance that the arts of construction have not yet died out.

At the University of California Student Union, in Berkeley, Vernon De Mars has sought to induce an active public response by devising (in a manner that closely parallels Disney's) astonishing juxtapositions of fragments which, individually, are often exquisitely designed but are left to fend for themselves in a hubbub meant to recall, within a planned environment, the chaos of the city (fig. 41). The forms, like Disney's, sometimes unabashedly recall another time or place: a steel trellis surmounting the major block of the building is said to owe allegiance to Bernard Maybeck's wooden ones of an earlier generation, which generally bore vines; the spaces around

41
Student Union,
University of Cal-
ifornia, Berkeley,
Vernon De Mars

the building are by way of appreciation of the Piazza San Marco; and the carefully developed street furnishings recall Scandinavia. But the scope offered for this collection of occurrences is by no means Disney's, so that the chance to recreate the moods of the city is severely restricted, and the Student Union has just one mood: it is cheerful, unremittingly cheerful. Mostly this is fine, but on the occasions when a sober tone is wanted, something is missing: from the Student Union there is no aerial tramway direct to Tomorrowland, no Disneyland chance to create still another world.

Whatever is missing, however, this collector's approach to enlivening the public realm demonstrates certain advantages over the single-mindedness of, say, the San Francisco City Hall or some of the sober classroom blocks that stand about on the Berkeley campus. The simplicity and anonymity of these high blocks, mostly tile-roofed, set on knolls in groves of oaks and giant eucalypti, are in the spirit of the Bay area, are praiseworthy, and have often been praised. But success eludes most of them, probably because they are set out to recall the area's last two lively idioms, but seldom with enough conviction to rise above the perfunctory. The two local idioms they seek to recall were lively ones, and look lively still.

The first, a high-spirited explosion of classical or other borrowed forms, which break apart to leave voids in astonishing places, so as to create lofty spaces and dark shadows, has left a major monument on the campus, the Hearst Mining Building of 1907. John Galen Howard was its architect, but in it the magnificent mad hand of Bernard Maybeck, the local cultural hero, is evident. The second local idiom, in whose development William W. Wurster has been the central figure, usually comes out best at small scale, since the carefully understated, spare, and almost anonymous efficiency of a well-understood carpenters' constructional system is clearly in evidence here. "No matter how much it costs," Mrs. Wurster points out about her husband's work—and the best of the rest of the vernacular—"it will never show." The new language of buildings on the Berkeley campus of the University of California, where they succeed, succeed because they share either in the exuberance of the first local idiom or in the naturalness of the second. When they fail, they fail from dispiritedly attempting continuity with the first local idiom (their great tile roofs lifted up and out of sight) or from seeking to cash in on the apparent casualness of the second local idiom, without noting that that is a casualness born of an intimate understanding of a constructional system and a way of life.

Not only the university but all of California and the West now face an architectural crisis different in many ways from the problems of the rest of the country. The Boston architects of the nineteenth-century railroad tycoon Leland Stanford had their own clear notions, social and architectural, of the nature of hierarchy, and they manifested them with great success in the old Stanford campus. But twentieth-century California has been equalitarian. As its population grows phenomenally, the people who comprise it, rich and poor, come from all sorts of places and owe no allegiance to any establishment of the sort that exercises at least some control of money and taste in areas less burgeoning. While California was largely rural, this equalitarianism lent special delights to living here. In southern California, from a combination of white-walled story-book Spanish and white-walled International Style, there developed, through Gill and Schindler and Neutra and *Arts and Architecture* magazine, and thanks to the climate and the landscape, a way of building large numbers of private houses of a charm and comfort never before possible anywhere on such a scale. This development was surpassed only in northern California, where, if the climate was a bit moodier, the views of bays and forests were better, and there were architects, first of the generation of Bernard Maybeck, then of the generation of William Wurster, Gardner Dailey, and Hervey Parke Clark, who were willing and eminently able to make the most of the opportunities, to develop a domestic architecture not only esteemed by architects but almost universally accepted and enjoyed by the people for whom it was made. This is the domestic architecture we can call (though the architects who made it don't much like the appellation) the Bay Region Style.

When California was rural, a golden never-never land with plenty of room, with open fields for the public realm, with magnificent scenery for a sharable image, and with Hollywood's grandiose offerings for a publicly sharable experience, nothing could have been more natural than this emphasis on provision for domestic life, nothing more understandable than the gradual atrophying of concern for a public realm that people go to and use. The public weal was being extensively considered in projects built hundreds of miles from Los Angeles and San Francisco to provide those cities with water and electric power; but the kind of monumentality that occurs when the Establishment requires buildings more important than other buildings, in places of special importance, when skilled architects give physical form to this requirement, and when human use and the public imagination confirm this importance, never occurred. It never occurred because the Establishment didn't exist, and because there was no need for it. California during the first four decades of the twentieth century was being developed mostly at a domestic scale, and very well, too; it seemed quite proper that man's impact on the land should be of this cozy, equalitarian, and very pleasant sort.

The process, however, is continuing in 1964, and by now it brings worry. The domestic arrangements of the earlier decades are being reproduced endlessly, no longer in the places that laid some claim to public attention—places like Bel Air, Berkeley, and Sausalito for the view; San Francisco and San Diego for the bay; Hollywood for a very special activity; and Santa Barbara for high mountains coming close to the sea—but in the no-places in between, such as Hayward, Daly City, Inglewood, Manchester, and other municipal fictions even less memorable. The character and the sense of special place that came to the first communities for free, from the oak trees around them and the yellow hills and the mountains and the sea, do not similarly serve the later comers or anyone: the oak trees go and the yellow hills vanish, the smaller mountains are flattened and even portions of the sea are filled in, all to be covered in a most equalitarian way with endless houses. Even the movie studios are being covered up.

It occurs to some, as the gray domestic waves of suburban sea fill in the valleys and the bays, and lap at and erode the hills, that something should be done, and that the something should be urban and monumental. The Bay Region Style, for all its domestic triumphs, offers no architectural framework for making a special celebration; the characteristic Wurster reticence, which has served so well in helping to create the continuous domestic fabric of the Bay cities, is too deeply ingrained to allow that. In southern California a latter-day straightforwardness born mostly of a habit of commercial expediency militates against architectural celebration of a particular place. But even more basic than the absence of a viable architectural idiom for making public centers is the absence of any Establishment ready to shoulder the responsibility for, to take a proprietary interest in, the public realm. So what, as we started out by asking, might we have instead, for an architectural framework and for an opportunity?

The hope exists that the first best chance for differentiation in these floating gray suburbs will come from our developing an interest in and techniques for a much more accurate definition than we seek presently of what the problems really are. If all places and problems are similar (as we might suspect from our endlessly repetitive new cities), then the whole act of marking something special is spurious and futile. If, on the other hand, there is a valid basis for differentiating one place from another and one building from another, and if the differentiation is not now made because techniques for defining a problem are too crude, then the use by architects of other tools already available, among them the tools of mathematics and of operations research, might offer help. We should be able to expect that our developing industrial plant, controlled by electronic devices of incredible sensitivity and complexity, should be able to give us a much wider, rather than a more restricted, range of products. Just so we might expect, as architects, that by using the techniques available to us, from computer and operations research methods to our own underused analytical capacities, in order to discover more accurately and completely than we do now the particularities, even the peculiarities, of the problems we are assigned, we might achieve a much wider, fuller, more differentiated and specific range of solutions than we do now. We should, then, at least have a method. Given the chance, we might rescue the dreary suburban sea from the sameness forced upon it as much by the blindness of our analytical tools and our tendency as architects to generalize on an insufficient base, as by the social and economic restrictions thrust upon us.

A few houses (since it is California, inevitably they are houses) by a few architects, mostly under the immediate influence of Joseph Esherick, are especially concerned with the specific analysis of and response to problems of site, its outlooks and climate, the client and his needs. This is not a revolution, really, away from the attitudes of the second Bay Region idiom; it embodies many of the same methods of direct response to the problem; but it seeks to clarify and extend these methods to cope with the aggravated situation.

Esherick's Cary House in Marin County, for instance, given a wooded view, does not rely on a wall of glass pointed generally in that direction, but has instead a wall with glass openings, each carefully placed to perform a specific function of admitting light, lighting a surface, or exposing a carefully selected portion of the view. The Rubin House in Albany, by George Homsey, though on a less dramatic site, reacts even more specifically to such local delights as the dappled light coming between eucalyptus leaves, and the usually hazy sun of the bay shore sliding through skylights and along white walls. The exterior of the Graham House, by Richard Peters and Peter Dodge, on a steep Berkeley hillside, also demonstrates forms that grow not from a generalized formal impulse but from a specific search for light, air, space, and outlooks. All this extends the simpler idiom of the earlier unformal Bay Region work, toward what promises to be a much fuller vocabulary, generated like its precursor not by restrictive formal systems but by specific response to specific problems. So far these are restricted domestic problems; but there is no reason visible yet why the elusive problems of the public realm should not respond, in an area with hardly a public realm, to sophisticated extensions of the same efforts.

For the opportunity, the actual commission to create a public realm, we must look to other sources than the Establishment of other times or other places, to people or institutions interested at once in public activity and in place. We depend, in part, on more Disneys, on men willing to submerge their own Mickey Mouse visions in a broader vision of greater public interest, and who are nonetheless willing and able to focus their attention on a particular problem and a particular place. Disneyland, however arbitrary its location, is unique, even as Los Angeles is, and much of its power over the imagination comes from the fact.

A chain of Disneylands would have a disquieting effect not unlike that of the new transcontinental chains of identical motels that weigh the tired traveler with the hopelessness of driving all day to arrive at a place just like the one he started from. One can hope, too, for the day when the gradual loss of differentiated place, the gradual emerging of the gray no-places and the inundation of the places of special significance, will cause the slumbering citizenry to awaken, to demand to spend its money to have a public life. But it seems unwise to wait for that.

Right now the largest single patron available to be pressed into the service of the public realm is the State Highway Department. Freeways until now have been one of the most serious generalizers of place in the state, ruthlessly and thoughtlessly severing some communities, congesting others, and obliterating still others, marring, gouging, and wiping out whole landscapes. Yet, for all that, they loom large in the public eye as one of the strongest, most exciting, and most characteristic elements of the new California. If one had to name the center of southern California, it would surely be the place not far from the Los Angeles City Hall where the area's major freeways wrap together in a graceful, strong, and much photographed three-level interchange (in the photographs, the tower of City Hall rises through the distant smog). Much of the public excitement about San Francisco's small dramatic skyline is a function of the capacity to see it, a capacity which is greatly enhanced by the bridges (themselves major California monuments), by the freeways that lead to them, and now by the freeway that comes up from the south and breaks through the hills in the nick of time for a magnificent view of San Francisco. Indeed, in San Francisco as in few places, the view which gives a sense of the whole city is one of the most valuable parts of the public realm, one of the parts that is most frequently attacked and must be most zealously defended. One of the public views' most effective defenders could be the freeway builders, though admittedly they have more often acted as saboteurs, as when they tried and party succeeded, in San Francisco, in building a freeway wall between the city and the bay.

I am writing this in Guanajuato, a middle-sized town in the middle of Mexico, crammed into a narrow canyon, with just two narrow streets (one up and one down) in the bottom of the canyon, and with a maze of stepped pedestrian ways climbing up the canyon's slopes through the most remorselessly picturesque townscape this side of Greece. Under this runs a river, which used to inundate the city from time to time. Ten years ago a suburban portion of the river was still further depressed, and its former bed was lined with a handsome pink stone to serve as a canyon for cars, moving downhill above the river. Now, in a bold project happily called "the urbanization of the river," this development is being continued through the center of the town to let the river run with cars as well as water, sometimes behind buildings, sometimes under the ancient vaults over which the buildings of the town center spanned the river bed. None of the picturesque eighteenth-century delights is being threatened; a whole new twentieth-century layer of visual delights, at the scale of the automobile, is being added instead. The urbanity that results from this enlargement of the public realm is even more striking than the visual charm. The pedestrian spaces remain undefiled, even unattacked, while cars grind below, as in a miniature of a Hugh Ferriss City of the Future that loses, miraculously, none of the delights of the past (figs. 42, 43).

Guanajuato should offer us some lessons. The cities of California are much bigger, broader, and grayer, but then their budgets are larger, too (especially the items for freeway construction). They urgently need attention, before the characteristics that distinguish them at all are obliterated. There is no need and no time to wait for a not-yet-existent Establishment to build us the traditional kind of monuments or for a disaster gripping enough to wake the public conscience to the vanishing Places of the public realm we got for free. Most effectively, we might, as architects, first seek to develop a vocabulary of forms responsive to the marvelously complex and varied functions of our society, instead of continuing to impose the vague generalizations with which we presently add to the grayness of the suburban sea. Then, we might start sorting out for our special attention those things for which the public has to pay, from which we might derive the public life. These things would not be the city halls and equestrian statues of another place and time, but had better be something far bigger and better, and of far more public use. They might, for instance, be freeways: freeways are not for individual people, as living rooms are and as confused planners would have you believe the whole city ought to be; they are for the public use, a part of the public realm; and if the fidgety structures beside them and the deserts for parking—or for nothing—under them don't yet make sense, it is surely because there has so far been too little provision for and contribution to and understanding of the public realm, not too much. The freeways could be the real monuments of the future, the places set aside for special celebration by

42
Guanajuato, Mexico, tunnel

43
Guanajuato

people able to experience space and light and motion and relationships to other people and things at a speed that so far only this century has allowed. Here are structures big enough and strong enough, once they are regarded as a part of the city, to re-excite the public imagination about the city. This is no shame to be covered by suburban bushes or quarantined behind cyclone fences. It is the marker for a place set in motion, transforming itself to another place. The exciting prospects, not surprisingly, show up best at Disneyland. There, from the aerial tramway over the bobsled run on the inside of the plastic mountain, is a vision of a place marked out for the public life, of a kind of rocketing monumentality, more dynamic, bigger, and, who knows? even more useful to people and the public than any the world has seen yet.

Los Angeles is in many ways the antipodes of San Francisco, which is where Moore apprenticed in three architectural offices between 1947 and 1949, for Mario Corbett, Joseph Allen Stein, and Hervey Parke Clark. He went there from the University of Michigan because he wanted to be a "Bay Region" architect, inspired by the work of Maybeck, Howard, and Morgan; he would later grow to admire the work of Wurster and Esherick. The two years of apprenticeship led to Moore's registration as an architect in 1949.

Throughout Moore's Princeton years, he spent summers working in Monterey for Wallace Holm and in San Francisco for Clark & Beutler. When he began teaching at Berkeley in 1959, Moore continued to collaborate with Clark, most notably on the Citizens' Federal Savings Building, and also worked with the landscape architect Lawrence Halprin. Clark offered to make Moore an associate in 1962, which he declined, instead forming his own partnership with Lyndon, Turnbull, and Whitaker, MLTW.

His work in the Bay and surrounding regions is best known, of course, in MLTW's work at Sea Ranch, one hundred miles north of the Golden Gate, in Sonoma County. Moore left San Francisco in 1965 but continued collaborations and work there, primarily with Lyndon and Turnbull. At the end of his life, he completed a major work in the Bay Region tradition, the Haas Business School at UC Berkeley, designed with John Ruble and Buzz Yudell.

The first of the following set examines John Entenza's Case Study Houses in Los Angeles for a Progressive Architecture *review of Esther McCoy's book* Modern California Houses. *The set concludes with analyses of two important San Francisco projects: Ghirardelli Square by Wurster and the Cannery by Esherick.*

Unposed Questions

Review of *Modern California Houses: Case Study Houses, 1945–1962,* by Esther McCoy

Connoisseurship in the arts is high-speed activity these days; a goodly number of critics manage to stay close on the heels of junk artists, pop artists, and other apostles of the new, traveling light and casting off last week's ideas without a backward look. But some heavily laden historians manage to re-

Originally published in *Progressive Architecture* 45, no. 6 (June 1964), pp. 238, 244, 246.

main in the van as well, freighting the products of the season with the significances of a long past.

It is fair to wonder, when a book subtitled *Case Study Houses, 1945–1962* appears, what effect that seventeen-year lapse of time will have on the book's writer—are houses of 1945 a still-integral part of the present, are they far enough past to be charged with historical meaning, or are they merely passé, without point, like the contemporary pages of my high school annual? Miss McCoy plays it cool; she juxtaposes houses of immense importance, already a part of our history, with houses not especially distinguishable from the tract houses they preceded, with houses of the most foppish and evanescent preciousness. What is more, she has selected photographs (mostly exceedingly handsome ones by Julius Shulman) that render it very difficult to tell one level of accomplishment from another.

Modern California Houses, surveying a fascinating phenomenon—editor John Entenza's patronage of the art of architecture in southern California since the Second World War—arrives at the threshold of many interesting questions that are never asked. Perhaps they shouldn't be. Perhaps it is quite enough to regard this volume as the description of a vision, as a celebration of the longevity and importance of Entenza's *Arts and Architecture* Case Study House program. There is reason to be grateful for documentation of this remarkable set of twenty-three houses and eight projects, but it would have been fun to see their juxtaposition animated by a clear point of view (as, for instance, Vincent Scully in *The Earth, the Temple and the Gods* animates the differences among some Greek temples that look to the uninitiated every bit as much alike as these southern California houses do).

The Eames-Saarinen steel houses, finished before 1950, qualify as among the major architectural monuments of our time, in addition to being a fascinating contribution to the art of building in steel. But it would have been interesting to learn why, after 1950, the program regarded steel as morally essential for the short horizontal spans required in houses, in spite of the extra trouble and expense that are extensively described; while on vertical surfaces any old pretechnological material was regarded as good enough—brick or board or block or stone—as long as it didn't hold up the roof it was perfectly capable of supporting. Other interesting questions accompany architect Raphael Soriano's "leap from the particular to the general, from the personal to the impersonal, from the isolated case to the prototype." When is a prototype not a stereotype? And why do these houses on their way from the particular to the general keep getting bigger? Is this in response to some unspecified social shift?

I make a point of these unposed questions because the works described seem to be sufficiently related and sufficiently important to bear questioning. *Modern California Houses: Case Study Houses, 1945–1962* is full of pretty pictures that are nice as reminiscences; but it is on the verge of being much more interesting and useful.

"No matter how much it costs," Catherine Bauer used to say of the work of Wurster, Bernardi and Emmons, her husband's firm, "it will never show." In the North Beach bars in San Francisco these days, there is animated discussion of an attitude called "think rich." The prime architectural exponents of this attitude turn out to be the very same Wurster, Bernardi and Emmons, in their recently completed Ghirardelli Square. Somewhere in the tension between these two attitudes lies the considerable charm and (I suspect) enormous importance of this very San Franciscan undertaking.

A group of red brick factory and office buildings with a large sign over it reading "Ghirardelli" (a brand of chocolate sold in the West) has long dominated the view north over the bay from the swank slopes of Russian Hill. One of the buildings is among the oldest in San Francisco, dating from early in the last half of the nineteenth century. Another, the tower at the corner, was designed in 1907 by William Mooser, who was to be responsible a generation later for that most powerful of all western monuments, the Santa Barbara County Courthouse. But more prominent than these visual delights (and the reason, I suppose, why nobody ever objected to there being a factory in the middle of the view) was the smell of chocolate that lingered around the premises—and still does.

Times changed, and with them came the opportunity to do something else with all this red brick. It would have been easy to tear it down, but a great loss to San Francisco, which highly prizes its short past. It was much more difficult, and certainly must have been far more expensive, to use the old buildings, to play on them, to make a very special place.

The chance to create this kind of place was provided by a single public-spirited citizen. He is William Roth, civic leader and ex-president of the San Francisco Planning and Urban Renewal Association, now serving in the State Department in Washington. Roth bought the landmark without a specific use in mind, but with the sure knowledge that the public interest would be better served by keeping the brick buildings instead of sweeping them away for more high-rise apartments like those crowding the hill behind.

WB&E were retained to do a study on possible uses of the property, and they and Lawrence Halprin came up with a scheme very much like the

Originally published in *Architectural Forum* 122, no. 3 (June 1965), pp. 53–56.

present one (but with a motel where the winding entry steps are now). Half of it was executed: Ghirardelli still makes chocolate on the western portion of the site, but one day soon will move out for the Square's expansion.

There was courage in the execution, as well as in Roth's initial investment. The layout of the square flies in the face of everything that shopping center proprietors hold dear. It is not just a matter of not being led inexorably past every shop in the place on the way to every other. There is high adventure in even *finding* some of the upper-floor enterprises.

It is mostly here that the opulence lies, the "think rich." This is a particularly impressive kind of opulence, rising above those economic urgencies which have boxed in every other recent structure in San Francisco, of whatever level of elegance.

Happily, the details, though they must have cost plenty, never let it show. More happily still, for Roth and the Square's designers, it all seems to be working. Ghirardelli Square has what William Wurster calls "the aura of success."

The success of Ghirardelli Square is partly due to the San Franciscan's urban self-consciousness. This corner of the urban scene seems mostly to be filled with San Franciscans and not tourists. (Tourists wear sport shirts and thin print dresses and talk loudly.)

The rest of the credit is widely distributed. Much of it goes to the designers, who walked the thin line between gaiety and coyness; to WB&E for their buildings; to Barbara Stauffacher for her graphics; to Halprin, who was instrumental in the invention of the whole project, for his bright and cheerful plants and lights and surfaces and fountain.

A minimum amount of credit might be begrudged to the ten-level garage which underlies the whole and adds economic feasibility to it, but introduces tensions of its own less pleasurable than those above ground. Far more goes to the distinguished merchandise that is to be seen in the shops, and to the supporting activities that are most carefully and unspontaneously arranged (such as Cinco de Mayo celebrations).

Finally, perhaps the largest share of all should go to the San Francisco Bay. The great triumph of Ghirardelli Square is that it makes the most of being on it.

The Cannery: How It Looks to a Critic

San Francisco's Ghirardelli Square probably got as far as you can go in the sunny realm of urban design. The Cannery goes a step further.

The idea originated with a lawyer, Leonard Martin, who conceived of the giant Del Monte Cannery just behind Fisherman's Wharf as a natural setting for swank merchandisers. Martin's idea, in turn, was transmuted by Joseph Esherick into a phenomenon that seems to have a closer relationship to the Japanese tea ceremony (in its high period) than it does to Ghirardelli Square's blandishments.

The notions of wabi and sabi are central to the ceremonial art of the Japanese tea masters during the last 400 years (and locked tight, I submit, into the Cannery). These notions are based on the expectation that the humblest details of common life, and the objects that pertain to it, can, after serious-minded study, undergo a transfiguration which lifts them into the highest and purest levels of Art as Religion or Religion as Art. (This is almost the opposite of current pop doctrine, which holds that "if you can't beat 'em, join 'em.") In seventeenth-century Japan, objects useful for the tea ceremony (like pots) might seem pretty ordinary to the uninitiated. If they had transmuted the quintessence of commonness, these objects were so prized by connoisseurs that they might bring a fortune in the marketplace, before taking a central role in a highly developed, highly esoteric, and certainly not popular ritual.

I don't think it is altogether ridiculous to regard the transfiguration of Leonard Martin's Cannery in rather the same light. In this case, Joseph Esherick is the tea master who presses the super-aristocratic ritual of understatement, while the many-wallpapered kitsch of an apparel shop called Splendiferous fills a role like that of the teapot.

To be sure, the pioneer tea master can occasionally be detected tripping over the stepping stones—or was he being pushed? The block-sized, brick-walled ruins of the old Del Monte Cannery started to have a narrative unraveling of white-walled pedestrian streets inside, where Esherick, who is the past master of light slipping over white walls, could manipulate his magic; but then someone decided that all the plaster walls should be painted a spine-chilling, purply, almost brick color which soaks up the light. This is a bit like burying the teapot.

Originally published in *Architectural Forum* 128, no. 6 (June 1968), pp. 27–79.

It is very difficult to describe. It is so resolutely discursive (roughly like a Norse saga written by S. J. Perelman) that one comes away not exactly certain where he has been.

The old Del Monte Cannery was a brick-walled structure with repetitive gabled ends, occupying half a large block with railroad sidings separating it from a warehouse.

The warehouse is now being transformed into a transportation museum, and Thomas Church is turning the sidings into an olive grove. The Cannery itself has been gutted, and only the old walls have been left; inside these walls have been placed three stories of brand-new phenomena, split by a zigzag pedestrian space. This space seems to shrug off the spatial crescendo one has been led to anticipate at this point in the plan. Instead, the people busily buying expensive things on three levels are the center of concern, forcing their powerful suggestion on the newcomer who has not yet spent his money.

A curiously underplayed escalator and a dazzling elevator, as well as many stairs, entice people upward to where extraordinary architectural wonders lie.

The best things are the most nimbly flat-footed, like the plain pipe racks, sort of, in the elegant men's shop or the lighting fixtures illuminating the sausages. The uninitiated architect-observer (to return to the tea ceremony) might feel the same queasiness that he would in front of a $1,000 common teapot as he views the straight-faced ritual combination of three hideous wallpapers in that very successful space called Splendiferous. He might or might not take solace on learning that the success of the establishment is precipitated on the advent of another apparel shop called Very Very Terry Jerry.

If the observer digs the ceremony though, even if he doesn't get with the statues, he certainly ought to be good for the Mies corner play on the San Francisco warehouse idiom, with giant pipe rails, or the mock-Corbusian downspout, or the damnedest stair rail this side of Giulio Romano.

But it is, of course, the brick walls themselves that form the real Book of Tea, describing the game while they spin a narrative at once so dewy-eyed and so mad that a giant Byzantine fantasy becomes an elegant ingratiation. What is this tale that the walls are telling? Will the sardines ever come back to be canned?

It's wrong if this makes the Cannery seem at all like a joke. This is serious play, as the tea ceremony was, and the very survival of the spirit of our cities, the transmutation of the local and the particular, the common, to some sort of useful universal, is the prize. The ceremony is in the hands of a master; we can only hope no one drops his cup.

Moore's third article for Perspecta *was written to explore the emergence of technological society and its impact on architecture.*

Plug It In, Rameses, and See if It Lights Up, Because We Aren't Going to Keep It Unless It Works

If architects are to continue to do useful work on this planet, then surely their proper concern must be, as it has always been, the creation of place, the ordered extension of man's idea about himself in specific locations on the face of the earth to make what Susanne Langer has called "ethnic domain." This, supposedly, will be useful to help people know where they are, which will aid, by extension, in helping people know who they are.

The most powerful and effective places which our forebears made for themselves, and left for us, exist in contiguous space. They work on an organized hierarchy of importances, first dividing what is inside from what is outside, then in some way arranging things in order of their importance, so that objects give importance to a location, and location gives importance to objects, as at Peking, where an axis penetrates from outside through layer after layer of increasing importance (like the skins of an onion) to the seat of the emperor himself, or as in Hindu towns where caste determined location from clean to dirty along the flow of water which served everyone. The visible order of these hierarchical places was buttressed by the confidence that they shared the order which made comprehensible the world, as the temple of Angkor Wat provides with its cross axes and its concentric rings of temples a diagram of heaven recalling the concentric rings of mountains around the seven seas which center on the sacred Buddhist mountain.

Our own places, however, like our lives, are not bound up in one contiguous space. Our order is not made in one discrete inside neatly separated from a hostile outside, in which we are free to structure a visible simulation of our vision of the world. The world that means the most to us, as everyone from Bucky Fuller to Marshall McLuhan has already pointed out, has for the past half-century not really been very visible anyway.

Many of us have strong stamping grounds that exist in separate places ending at one airport (in my own case Kennedy) to pick up again in some other airport (in my case San Francisco's). At both ends of my territory I

Originally published in *Perspecta,* no. 11 (1967), pp. 32–43.

know the street names and have even established ownership of some real estate. Even more important, independently of where we move our bodies at any moment, we have, as we all know, instant anywhere, as we enjoy our capacity to make immediate electronic contact with people anywhere on the face of the globe and revel in the vicarious pleasure we get from shooting people off the face of the globe in order to make contact with them in outer space.

Our new places, that is, are given form with electronic, not visual glue. Now this electronic glue, as people nervously joke, has some limitations. It is still argued, for instance, about courtship that although a great deal of preliminary maneuvering can occur over the telephone, face-to-face contact is still required for any real consummation of the activity. It is conceivable that before long this may be an antiquated argument; one could have supposed not many years ago, for instance, that dancing required face-to-face contact, but clearly that notion is passé, and one's partner now in the frug (or the successor to the frug) could as well be under another strobe light in Los Angeles, say, while one is oneself gyrating in a discotheque in New York.

About the time that architects and planners started to bleat about "human scale" as though it had to do, for the first time since Cheops, entirely with man's body and not at all with his mind or his ideas, and to rhapsodize about the Piazza San Marco, the heart of Venice and "the finest drawing room in Europe" (fig. 44), people were everywhere changing their effective bodies, electronically extending themselves in whole new ways. And while the Piazza San Marco has been repeated on urban renewal sites across the United States (complete with everything but inhabitants), the hierarchy of importances from private to monumental has vanished.

Industry went first; the pyramidal hierarchic organization of the corporation of the 1920s has been replaced by networks much better suited to the instant communication and instant feedback possible today, which allows immediate response to daily market demands over enormous distribution systems, and forces the early retirement of executives who can't flexibly cope. The image of the pyramidal hierarchy with someone or something clearly on top, and other successive layers of someone or something else below that, sending their information to the apex and receiving orders back from on high, has vanished everywhere except in the military, in government agencies, and in the minds of people looking for some contiguous hierarchic visual order. The pyramids of business, like the pyramids of Gizeh,

44
Piazza San Marco,
Venice

were built to last without any further help from anybody. The network, on the contrary, needs help. It needs to be plugged in, into the right markets to make money, into electricity in order to light up, into a sewage system in order to drain, into a working social framework in order to avoid immediately being torn down.

For some time the modern city, like the modern corporation, has been a model of the new unhierarchy; Los Angeles for instance has poured itself unhierarchically across the landscape, demonstrating that you can do in a city almost anything you need to do in a city almost anywhere (including rioting: an article of mine in a pre-Watts issue of *Perspecta* had announced erroneously that Los Angeles was a poor place for that). It is curious to note with what consistency architects, and especially architecture students, continue to fly in the face of all the available facts, with the breathless announcement that the only problem worth their consideration is the super-high-density pedestrian urban core of the sort which continues to exist in New York, Calcutta, Provincetown, Carmel, and a diminishing list of other places (all as though problems, too, were neatly ordered in a pyramidal hierarchy).

A current British version of this old-fashioned systematizing collected under the appellation "plug-in" and garnished with handsome drawings deserves, I suppose, special mention because it comes across, thanks to those drawings, as an arrangement really quite up-to-the-minute in spite of the clear difficulties of giving credulity to an array of late Victorian linear piping systems which would have put new gleam in the eye of Captain Nemo as he twiddled the valves of the *Nautilus.* All right, it's very dense, but it seems to be based on the stage of the industrial revolution which even Detroit seems to have gotten through, so that those pretty lumpy things seem odd survivors in an aspatial electronic world.

Where, then, does this leave us? What might architect place-makers do, if anything? In an electronic world where space and location have so little functional meaning, there seems little point in defining cities spatially even in the negative terms devised by those scholars who postulate hollow honeycombs with crowded edges after center cities are deserted. In a world which has lately witnessed the death of the old hierarchies, except in the aforementioned curious holdout areas, it seems less than germane to consider new environments in terms of hierarchy. It seems less than essential, either, to expose for demolition all the false ideologies to leave on its feet only the one true architecture, the electric architecture (of which there probably aren't any good examples).

Even at this early point in the new age, however, we can note that the architecture of the past several decades, architecture that could, I think, accurately be called the architecture of exclusion, has not gained control of the physical environment, to make place. The perfectly natural attempts of the last several decades to find order by excluding disorder and confusion and organizing whatever fragment remains into a system is the order which characterizes, for instance, Frank Lloyd Wright's Hanna House, where everything is thrown out that does not fit the "organic" geometry of the hexagon, into whose shape even bedsheets are somehow folded (fig. 45). If we can presume that the point in "organic" order is to make something with life which somehow grows, reproduces itself, and spreads into other aspects of life, then we have sadly to admit that the Hanna House has spawned no legitimate progeny. The very specialness and difficulty of twisting and shoving everything into a geometry so natural for bees and so awkward for our own

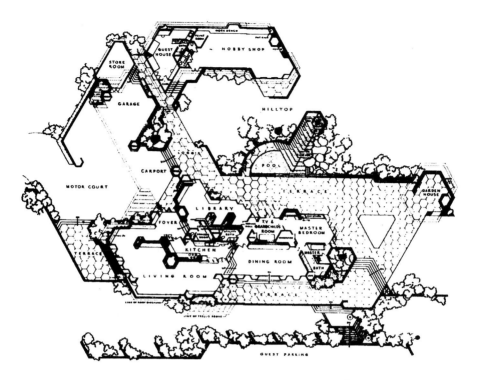

45
Hanna House, plan,
Frank Lloyd Wright

techniques leave the architect with a lovely geometry which stands apart from everything else, and everything else seems to have the edge. Mies's geometry at the Illinois Institute of Technology excluded the possibilities not inherent in the 18-by-24-foot rectangular grid from which his campus plan started; this plan geometry has the unusual extra attribute of being almost undiscoverable by anyone on the ground who is not simultaneously looking at a plan drawing.

Palladio's designs, which sought by the employment of dimensions based in musical intervals to achieve with geometric order the harmony of the spheres, were more than empty games; they were central to the thought of their generation in all the arts, from logic to music. The same geometries applied to achieve four-way axialities in Connecticut suburban residences seem to have failed to bring the whole culture around. The enigma in any revelation that plane and solid geometry together have not solved the environmental problems of the twentieth century must be Louis Kahn, whose geometries begin as formally as Wright's or Mies's or even Palladio's, whose happiest moments with materials seem to occur in primitive mass masonry technologies of Pakistan or India, whose formal enthusiasms appear to be contemporary with those of Caracalla (or Caracalla made magic), but who has cleared the way and served as a guide for most of the includers about whom I now propose to speak (and he stays ahead of them). (Maybe the geometry of the Philadelphia Museum School will turn out, after all, to be alive, and will reproduce itself.)

Architects of exclusion have for generations perfected their art, and built their buildings on plots assigned them. But somehow the special strip which they abhor has arrogated to itself more vitality, more power of growth, indeed more inevitability of growth, than the whole of their tidy output put together.

The manifestation of all this vitality must have some message for us, even as the enormously successful sales of suburban tract houses must be saying something about what people want to live in. I doubt that the message is that the architect who produces at enormous expense a replica of the commercial strip which could have been done as well without him is about to save the world; but it does seem reasonable, after generations of failure on the part of the architecture of exclusion to come to grips with our civilization and to establish a vitality of its own, that the chance should now be given to, or seized by, some architects of inclusion, the includers who, like some playwrights, make their order with as much of life as they can include, rather than as little, who welcome redundancy and depend on it even as the electronic information networks do, and who are willing to accept into their systems of organization those ambiguities and conflicts of which life is made.

Robert Venturi's search for ambiguity is paradoxically probably the clearest instance of a conscious architecture of inclusion. His interests range from the history of architectural composition (with an encyclopedic knowledge of its hallowed monuments) to the popular roadside manifestations of our own time. His Guild House in Philadelphia for the elderly calls at once upon the intricacies of apartment floor planning of the 1920s and the simple palette of materials of nineteenth-century Philadelphia, to which is added a kind of commercial formalism with a row of white subway tile which makes a gesture toward the grandest of historic composition—making, dividing the whole big lump of a building into base (of white tile), shaft (of brick) and capital (of brick as well, but divided from the shaft by the course of white tile) without ever departing from homely matter-of-factness, so that a

gold anodized television antenna on the pediment above the entrance provides a sculptural flourish at once fiercely ingenious and pathetic (we know
how cheap they are). Directly below this flourish the conflicting requirements of entrance and central support fight it out. Behind it, on the back,
the unadorned bricks and apparently regular holes state confidently that this
is an ordinary housing project.

    A set of stores and offices attributable mostly to Donlyn Lyndon on a
strip commercial street on the Monterey Peninsula in California demonstrates some of the same sympathies for the vitality of the commercial strip
vernacular, with the desire to embrace rather than to exclude its life, while its
naive forms function in rather sophisticated ways to control the sun's entry.

    The Whitney Avenue firehouse of Peter Millard, with its meticulously
toilet-trained pipes and conduits, appears at first to have little in common
with its gaudier sisters of the strip (fig. 46); yet the architect's attempt to include things, to worry about more conflicts which need to be demonstrated,

46
Fire station, New
Haven, Peter Millard

and more problems which need to be solved, from the relation of the fire station, for instance, to its clapboarded neighbors on a residential street, to the relation of the little rooms to the garage for the large fire engines, all involved him in the complexities of his problem with the same immediacy as Lyndon's and Venturi's buildings take on the problems which beset them.

Five of Millard's students (Golding, Ives, Mackall, Michels, Ryan) matched his involvement when they produced for a real client (for a site which vanished after working drawings were made) a clubhouse for teenage dropouts in New Haven, where a concern for the common materials of an industrial slum, the block walls and the pipes and the grilles and the conduit, was joined by a concern for the life and the movement of the teenage user, whose entrance into the club and his saunter down the steps in full view of all his confreres is as carefully considered as the entrance of his girl from the lady's room down a miniatured flight of stairs which forces a recall of the Ziegfield Follies of 1933.

That the idiom does not matter all that much to an architecture of inclusion is demonstrated by the Santa Barbara County Courthouse of 1929, one of the century's great monuments of the architecture of inclusion. The courthouse, after decades of critical abuse, still attracts streams of tourists who come to see it as architecture, to revel not only in its Hollywood extrapolation of certain vaguely Spanish themes (in what Osbert Lancaster calls Spanish Supercolonial) but also in its syncopated orchestration of window openings, door shapes, and arcade in the white walls which respond as much to the Chicago jazz of the year it was built as to any far-away clicking of castanets. People and activities are included here, from horseback rides reenacting an almost nonexistent Spanish past to passersby for whom the building opens up the grandeur of the site and the thrill of the place, whose history may be ephemeral but whose presence is nonetheless real.

Santa Barbara's inclusion into its fabric after an earthquake of 1925 of an almost mythical Spanish history has been as clear a source of vitality for that particular place as the hopped-up forms of the commercial strip. Our Faculty Club for the University of California at Santa Barbara seeks to include this special vitality as Lyndon's Fashion Fabrics building sought to pick up the vitality of Monterey Peninsula's commercial strip, not to borrow from a set of forms, but rather to take for our own its dizzily vigorous way of flinging up simple (but lofty) white walls whose crashing incongruities of scale will, we hope, seem eerily comforting in the soft white sunlight, without letting go for a moment of the place's crazy made-up past, but rather collecting the memory of it, even as Le Corbusier's Carpenter Center for the Visual Arts is, I think, meant not to be built around a pokey little pedestrian ramp but rather around a form made to collect the image of motion on a freeway, which simply had to be reduced and symbolized in order to get it onto the lot.

That is a sly device, juxtaposing one's own yet unbuilt work with a Corbusier masterwork. It is, however, even more of a pleasure to give notice to a new building with no architect of record which is a moving example of this architecture of inclusion. The Madonna Inn, on the highway south of San Luis Obispo, California, would never get a passing grade in a school of architecture where tastefulness was prized. It was built (and keeps being built) by a family of highway contractors whose involvement with bulldozers and enormous pieces of earthmoving equipment puts them in close touch with huge boulders, which they have, with enormous feeling, piled together to make a gas station and a motel. Entry into this motel, past a rock and down a stair into a dining room upholstered in purple velvet, is one of the most surprising and surprisingly full experiences to be found along an American highway (fig. 47). It may be beside the point, but I don't think so, that in the men's room, next to a giant shell with gold faucets, the approach to a rock grotto, which serves as a urinal, interrupts the beam of an electric eye and sets

47
Madonna Inn, near
San Luis Obispo

going a waterfall down over that grotto. It is disquieting in another sort of way to note that the armies of Italian craftsmen are even today meticulously carving grapes into wooden column capitals and beating sheets of copper into shape over tables in the coffee shop. It is not at all disquieting, but rather exhilarating, to note that here there is everything instead of nothing. A kind of immediate involvement with the site, with the user and his movements, indeed with everything all at once, with the vitality and the vulgarity of real commerce, quivers at a pitch of excitement which presages, more clearly than any tidy sparse geometry, an architecture for the electric present.

Throughout the late 1960s and early 1970s, years of tumultuous social up-heaval and then economic recession, Moore struggled to lead students within a fragmented educational culture, and to fill his offices with work. "Eleven Ago-nies and One Euphoria" lists the challenges Moore encountered as an educator during this time at Yale, in the face of student demonstrations, the burning of the Yale Art and Architecture building, and student rejection of the educational establishment. John Cook and Heinrich Klotz (Klotz would later write The History of Postmodern Architecture*) interviewed Moore in New Haven while urban projects such as Church Street South and the Jewish Community Center were being designed. In "Edifice Rex," Moore distinguishes between the hori-zontal model and the vertical model of architecture, later to be defined as the difference between being "vulnerable" and "invulnerable," which he used to ex-plain the work of Rudolph Schindler. The frustrations of this time may have made him particularly sympathetic to Schindler's work, whose own brilliant ac-complishments were made despite professional struggles and modest commissions, as David Gebhard recounted in his biography, here reviewed by Moore.*

"In Similar States of Undress" is a review of Five Architects, *a book that documented the work of Michael Graves, Peter Eisenman, John Hejduk, Charles Gwathmey, and Richard Meier. "Learning from Adam's House" is Moore's re-view of* Learning from Las Vegas, *the book resulting from Robert Venturi, Denise Scott Brown, and Steven Izenour's design studio conducted at Yale Uni-versity during this time, and Joseph Rykwert's* On Adam's House in Paradise.

Last is Moore's introduction to his own book, The Yale Mathematics Building Competition, *with Nicholas Pyle. This competition, organized from the start as an attempt to find a "non-monumental" building design for the Yale campus, resulted in a monumental flap, involving Moore, Venturi, Colin Rowe, and Vincent Scully. The winner of the competition, Robert Venturi, was seen to have been selected by the jury in an act of insider favoritism. When Moore chron-icled the competition and its outcome (itself a disappointment since it ultimately produced no building), he asked Colin Rowe to critique the competition method and the winning entry, but Yale University Press did not include Rowe's essay in the book. In 1976 Peter Eisenman reassembled the volume as an issue of* Op-positions. *Rowe's essay was published once again in volume 2 of* As I Was Say-ing *(Cambridge: MIT Press, 1996).*

Architects in practice, enjoying until lately an era of unprecedented prosperity, have come in increasing numbers to the schools of architecture, seeking recruits interested in joining them for fun and profit. Increasingly, they have gone away dismayed. They have encountered schools tottering in the grip of undifferentiated agonies, and students either indifferent to, utterly hostile to, or planning an instant takeover of the profession. If they went to the most prestigious schools, they will have noticed that "nobody designs things anymore" and "nobody even makes any drawings," though they might, if they stayed long enough, have been shown some very competent movies or some surprisingly slovenly posters developing a social theme. The visitor will in any case almost certainly be baffled and will in all probability be deeply offended.

It is not my purpose here to soothe away the hurts. It is, rather, to contend that the Agonies are real, but susceptible of being overcome; that if they are overcome, architectural schools won't be the same any more; and if they are not overcome, then there probably won't be very many architecture schools. My qualifications to make sweeping contentions are extensive (twenty years in a variety of architecture schools, and frequent visits to an even wider variety) but incomplete. (I'm simply too old, for instance, and too much a historian to understand the prevalent willingness to destroy all imperfect institutions.) So my contentions are incomplete too, and a panacea absent, but hopefully it will be useful to enumerate the Agonies.

Agony 1: Architecture students are generally members of the younger generation, therefore on the other side of the rapidly forming barricades recently described by the Scranton Commission. That report says better than I could why the young are alienated, and what next to be done about it.

Agony 2: "Relevance" is demanded by students and sought by schools in self-destructive frenzy. Since it is the nature and strength of the University that it is basically irrelevant, at least so far as relevance is viewed in the narrow and immediate way it is meant in the current rhetoric, our main hope is that the frenzy will die down before destruction is complete. The whole point in having an architecture school in a university, instead of in a low-

Originally published in *Michigan Society of Architects Monthly Bulletin*, February 1971.

rent loft, I should think, is precisely that it does free it from immediate practical and professional concerns and grants it the distance (the irrelevance) to develop constructs useful for the long range; if so far we haven't succeeded, removing the opportunity is not likely to help much.

Agony 3: The search for "relevance," of course, is made more frantic by the general knowledge that the architect is responsible for only about ten (or five, in other accounts) percent of the building in our country, though the profession has noisily claimed responsibility for the whole physical environment, or at least the post of "leader of the team." Some candor, or at least modesty, is in order: if the architect can improve (and the schools could lead the way) the speed and cost and efficiency of his service so that most of the other ninety percent want it, fine. If, on the other hand, he can parlay his role as artist (who gives a view of order *in* reality, so as to give the viewer some perception) so that the physical environment will be reformed by his example, then fine, too. But the casual assumption that environmental success cannot help but crown our present efforts has to go.

Agony 4: In the confusion and frustration about what the architects' job is, the ancient hierarchy which put the shape-making designer on top and demeaned the role of nearly everyone else maintains a curious hold. Architectural educators frequently confer to note the Flexner report which revolutionized medical education half a century ago (not entirely successfully, it will be quickly pointed out, but impressively) by devising a system which distributed the kudos and the tasks among researchers, biologists, and others as well as among practitioners. A parallel distribution, the educators agree, among researchers and specialists as well as "form-givers" is needed if the architectural profession is to have the strength to take on the total-environmental task it has set for itself; but since the distribution is lubricated by money, it hasn't yet proceeded very far.

Agony 5: In the absence of that pecuniary lubrication which might better develop a complete service for architects to render to society, the fright among students about the arrogance of the designer's solution, especially for the poor and the other new kinds of clients, has become explosive. "Advocacy" planning became an escape from this fright which briefly assumed most of the aspects of a panacea, until it turned out that advocacy, like other design techniques, required more than just goodwill and that "holding a mirror up to the community" might have some of the effect it had on Snow White's aging adversary. The need persists for the architect himself to plan, with real facts for and with real people, not as form-giver but as form-finder.

As the architecture schools seek to respond to this need, they leave behind the time-honored design problem, which is just too simple to cope with the complexity of real situations and produces a too-easy sense of accomplishment. The alternatives, as teachers and students try to make problems "real," are not yet altogether worked out; the attempt, for instance, to pretend to do something with a real community standardly founders on the community's unwillingness thus to be played with, and the attempt really to do something with a real community introduces a time dimension dramatically at odds with the student's expectations about his own action-packed education. A better answer, I suspect, will put students in close touch with those places where a useful service is being rendered to talk and even draw and put their thoughts in order.

Agony 6: At almost every meeting of architects and architecture students, someone gets up to observe that everything said so far is meaningless because architects have no power and only design what they are told to, and that architecture schools are criminally negligent for not training students to be mayors or governors, and the hell with all this physical environment. I take these outbursts to be related to the same megalomania rooted in frustration that I noted in my second Agony: it is not clear to me why architects have any more right than anyone else (though they have as much) to political office. It is clear though that if we could more demonstrably improve the world with our works, we would have less cause to pine for other glories.

Agony 7: An undeniable hindrance to architects' present effectiveness is the historic exclusiveness of our peer group, and the almost complete absence from it of blacks or other members of minority groups. Would-be black architects have been discouraged, overtly and because the profession hasn't promised all that much, either in social accomplishment or in personal success. (If you think architects are well off, just try fund-raising among architecture school alumni.) Clearly, we must welcome minorities into the field, right now. It helps, I think, that we are at the edge of the verbal culture, making things, and are therefore able to attract minority group members traditionally excluded from the nuances of a largely verbal education. And the rest of us might be nudged by the vocal unionites into greater usefulness, if we are not panicked by the cries for instant relevance.

Agony 8: The nature of the kind of progress that attends the improvement of our material standard of living is that it involves the development of continually improving tools, extending the individual's capacity to produce. Our field must be unique in the naivete of its assumption that six or seven years of college fit one to be a draftsman, whose tools have been extended in this century largely by the introduction of the electric pencil sharpener, and whose beginning salary is one of the few authentic reminiscences of 1910 left around. The meaninglessness of most of the draftsman's tasks are recognized, and some alternatives are already in sight from computers and component manufacturers. Schools cannot persist in training people for a vanishing role, and students are already indicating dramatic resistance to any such emasculation. They should be heeded.

Agony 9: Any modern theory of design has, I believe, to be founded on a way to translate our well-known capacity to endow an individual product with love (to produce something correct and beautiful) into a capacity to endow the multiplied product with the same qualities. As we lavish out attention on individual works, we underemploy our draftsmen, fail to perform the task we have so noisily arrogated to ourselves, of improving the whole environment, and cast real doubts on our usefulness. This has been noticed by some students.

Agony 10: The need for students to take on the complex world grows more dramatic, and the opportunity to see it grows apace; but little advantage has yet been taken of that. For instance, since man has so often built well all over the world, surely the most potent teachers of architects are the buildings and cities that have succeeded. Increasingly, airplanes can take us, teachers and students, quickly and cheaply to anywhere; but we still depend on magic lantern shows. One of the most urgently needed architectural educational reforms, I submit (and one much worth supporting, with money), is the introduction of the real world, to work in and to see.

Agony 11: When education focuses on certification, educators note it has reached a dead end. The emphasis on the architecture school as an agent for certifying one's professional legitimacy can be found in the voices of such disparate groups as the NCARB (who want the architectural degree to be the key to registration as an architect) and militant black students (who sometimes demand quick professional degrees as a lever of power). The connection between a university degree in architecture, irrelevant in its detachment, and vital to our future because of that, and professional certification, relevant and legal and basically conservative, should now loudly be dropped.

Euphoria: With all the absurdities of a strict professional education in architecture in a changing world, we have in our province the process of *design,* that combination of research and understanding and intuition and improvisation which tries out solutions to problems in too many unknowns to be susceptible of solution by the disciplines based on logic and words. The complicated work is in desperate need of the ministrations of the designer, not the arrogant visionary who slaps his preconceptions onto the unwilling, but the solver of the loosely structured problem, the visionary who dares to destroy constructive preconceptions to come to solutions he has to invent (and which he is willing to test, with the people with whom and for whom the solutions are made). The world needs this, desperately. If we can lose the agonies attending our professional hang-ups about revolution, relevance, ineffectiveness, hierarchy, advocacy or arrogance, divine right, racism, inefficiency, failure to reproduce, isolation, and certification, we will have left in our province one of the key tools for the solution of the world: design. And from this we can take heart.

CHARLES MOORE: Our office is especially interested in solving problems that are normally not considered elegant. Our biggest interest, right now, is housing. We've grown very interested in trailers—well, industry doesn't like to call it that—*modular* housing.

JOHN COOK: You're talking about architecture as the purchase of a package deal.

CM: Well, it isn't exactly a package deal, it is a process. The modular manufacturers have production lines which turn out their awful products. They could revise their production lines to turn out what they regard as *our* awful product: I found myself insisting on more windows than they had because I wanted to avoid the cramped spaces that are characteristic of that sort of modular housing. I am not interested in making an issue of the baseboards, or the trim, or the wall.

JC: Traditionally, an architect likes to design down to the ashtrays.

CM: I care more, in this instance, about the plan configuration.

JC: Must the architect be an artist?

CM: I think he must. I lectured about this recently in a course called Advanced Fenestration. It was based on a T. S. Eliot quote about art and artists. He was talking about playwrights, and making the point that the artist's function is to give the listener or looker a look at order in reality, in order that he might have the chance to develop for himself some perception of the order of reality. That seems to me an interesting place to start, because it talks about *order* the way architects are endlessly doing, but it also talks about *reality,* which architects almost never mention. My claim is that simply to make order, the way architects did in the first half of the century, is to run the danger of being as irrelevant as a playwright who deals in drawing room comedies at a time of social crisis. The order is not very interesting by itself, unless it has to do with the order of some kind of reality that seems important. I extrapolate from that to note that buildings are like plays, narrative objects which can have the same variety of roles that plays have. Buildings, that is, can make comments about the situation, about their site, about the problem of holding the outside out and the inside in, and the

Originally published in John W. Cook and Heinrich Klotz, *Conversations with Architects* (New York: Praeger, 1973), pp. 218–246.

problem of getting themselves built, about the people who use them or the people who made them—all sorts of things that can be funny, or sad, or stupid, or silent, or dumb. I maintain that all those things are legitimate things for buildings to do, and that architects who have tried to make everything sublime, however stupid its purpose, have done the same thing as the drawing-room-comedy playwright, and, by doing it, have lost the attention of the public.

HEINRICH KLOTZ: For instance, in the International Style, the building lost its character, became neutral. Man's desire to live in a varied environment was ignored.

CM: That's very accurate. The things our buildings have spoken of have often been folksy, or crude, or dumb, or irrelevant, which is all right with me. I think that's the right way to do them, when that is what's indicated. Our commissions, so far, have not been the kind which have given us the opportunity to make a "keynote speech." Our most controversial job at this point, for instance, is the Church Street South housing project in New Haven, Connecticut.

JC: How did that come about?

CM: Where's the best place to start? Mies van der Rohe had been the architect. He didn't even bother to quit, he just went away. There was left a model, which I responded to in a very negative way—a sort of green field rendered in phlox, with little buildings standing far apart and a few towers. He had done a school in the middle of the site—kindergarten through fourth grade, which had come in something like 100 percent over the budget, and he had thrown up his hands and said it was hopeless. The Redevelopment Agency changed their signals, and we got into the act with an opposite set of attitudes about it. The former mayor, Dick Lee, was brokenhearted about this project more than once. He was sad about losing Mies, but he was also sad when we got under way, because of what it looked like, because it wasn't elegant, it wasn't a beautiful monument to anything. We wanted to weave it into the fabric of New Haven, but here the "fabric" was a set of giant monuments by Kevin Roche, an expressway, and wide boulevards. Vincent Scully had been pushing very hard for respecting the street. That's pretty hard to do in this instance, which we discovered as we tried. I thought that we ought to be thinking about tying into the city, and since, for fabric, at this place in the city, all we have is streets, we ought to be responding directly to the streets. The apartment blocks flank the streets, and at one end there is an 8-story elderly housing building. The city planners hate it. The say it looks like the worst architecture in Bridgeport.

HK: How much per square foot will the project cost?

CM: About $18.

JC: Including the towers?

CM: No, the towers are approximately $22. We were able to allocate some of the land for city parks. There are meant to be a whole series of things that couldn't have been afforded on a housing budget: walks, lights, pine trees, stairs up and a bridge over the connecting street, concrete walls with holes that give a controlled view, fountains, and fancy paving. We managed to persuade the FHA to build up the commercial area from something like 1,000 square feet to 8,000.

JC: The commercial area doesn't flank the street, but actually fits into the complex.

CM: Yes. The commercial area is visible from the street, but it's really pulled into the complex. We have used billboards as big, colorful decoration. I hope to have art students paint them. The large, decorated walls will go in a little bit later than the completion of the apartments.

In the meantime, I'm awfully afraid of the negative image. Originally, the apartment blocks were to be made of precast concrete, in bigger scale than is normally used in the United States. There were, and still are, 4-foot-wide, 31-foot-long concrete planks, spanning from front to back wall. Originally, in our design, we were using one-story-high, 9-foot by 31-foot-long precast concrete panels for the outside walls. In Massachusetts, they had been used transversely in buildings as the partitions by the same builders, who were then able to do fancier architecture along the facades. We had the idea of reversing the use—turning the system inside out so that the ordinary dumb piece, the unchangeable panel, was the architecture. We had devised two basic panels to be used throughout the project, one with four windows, and one with two doors and four windows, and one with two doors and two windows. It turned out very late in the design stage that the concrete precast panels in Connecticut are controlled by a single company and cost too much money, so we had to go to concrete block. The change was very sudden. We got as much pleasure as we could out of contrasting ordinary concrete block with one designed with a very rough texture, but the buildings have come out to look much more barracks-like so far than we hope they will when we're finished; this, I think, is because of the wide, fast boulevards around; as you drive by, you're more aware of the project as lump than you are of it as something that is helping to make a series of spaces. We think these spaces, properly landscaped, will have a positive, memorable identity. We've been very interested in establishing the identity of places, and in establishing a chain of events that hook them together. One is supposed to think of where he lives as being at such-and-such a place. Hopefully, he will think of the way to get there and the place itself as memorable. This, obviously, is bought at the expense of the identity of the single unit. We had to say that it was the green court or park rather than the single unit that was memorable, though we're furnishing one apartment in as wild a manner as we can manage.

It was, for me, a new and very interesting act, to submerge the individual identity of the unit in order to strengthen the identity of this as a project. We could have been erasing its identity at all the edges, and concretizing the memorable or the imageable place were one lived. Now, that's where I think we went at least partially wrong. There is a sameness about all the buildings there, which started out for good structural reasons that don't exist any more. What I wanted was to have no project identity and no single home identity, but to have a sort of street identity.

JC: When you changed to concrete block, could you have avoided the awful sameness of the buildings?

CM: Yes, if we'd *begun* with the concrete block instead of the precast panels. By hindsight, it now seems to me that we should have linked some of the buildings together. We should not have separated the building blocks, so that one would not have the chance he now has to keep an image of the blocks in mind as he drives around, like so many sausages.

HK: But, on the other hand, by separating the blocks, and facing them as they are, there are always views opening up.

CM: There are lots of interesting little vistas.

JC: The emphasis in the whole area is placed upon those things which are normally considered superfluous. The addition of ornament makes the place more human. If you don't have it, it would remain bleak.

CM: If you didn't have it, it would be just awful. It is central to our philosophy that there should be this applied ornament—that we depend on it to make the identity. We're not depending on the integral beauty of the buildings.

HK: You kept most of the buildings more or less on the same level. In Europe, there's a very strong tendency to vary the height of the different buildings to get a more lively . . .

CM: We tried to do that once, for the mayor especially, who came by and said it looked like Fort Dix. We couldn't find the money. Three and four stories is the highest we can get. We couldn't go lower than that because of the density we needed, and we couldn't go higher than that because we would have needed elevators.

HK: Even with all the "pretty" ornaments, you still have the horrible sound insulation problem. You have cardboard walls. You can hear every . . .

CM: You're supposed to call them gypsum board, not cardboard.

HK: You can stick a knife into the wall.

CM: We have just the FHA requirement of 51-decibel sound reduction.

HK: It's again minimal . . .

CM: Well, as is usual with the FHA, the minimum equals the maximum. You can't afford to do any more than that, and you're not allowed to do any less. You should not hear a neighbor dropping a shoe or a mattress squeaking. What tempted me to take the job, 51 decibels and all, was the possibility to do something with nothing. It depends on a lot of old-fashioned artistic things.

HK: Like placing two boring blocks in a perspective foreshortening, in order to have the Knights of Columbus Building right in the center of a view (fig. 48).

CM: The whole sequence has alternate views of our towers and of the Knights of Columbus. These are considerations which our revolutionary students would regard as flat bullshit. They don't see any relevance to that outmoded idea.

48
Church Street South
housing, New
Haven, drawing,
MLTW/Moore-
Turnbull

HK: Visual composition doesn't count?

CM: Apparently not. I think they are wrong. As someone involved in their concerns, I feel very much the villain, and often hopelessly trapped. In some lectures in Denmark last year, I tried to put it in terms of order and reality from the Eliot quote I mentioned. It seems to me that our predecessors and the elegant people—the establishment architects practicing now, like Philip Johnson—are interested in order. People like me are interested in order and reality. The students are really interested in the middle—going to the values of one side and then the values of the other, back and forth.

The students are against shapes and say that people who make shapes are bad. I still don't see how you can make something that doesn't have any shape. It has to have shape, even if it's dull and stupid. However, I do agree with the students that most of the shape-making by architects has been irrelevant and unreal. I think I would agree with the students that to spend a lot of money to make shapes when other needs are not being met is folly and criminal and piggish, and maybe people who do it should be considered criminal.

JC: The whole concept in Church Street South might collapse without shape-making, and the addition of ornament.

CM: Yes. Now, that's very different from Mies's attitude, say, for he wouldn't have been able to do this within the limits which were set, because the requirements were so hopelessly impure and full of cheapness.

HK: As soon as you accept the FHA program, you become a member of the establishment.

CM: Right. That's what I damn well am—I'm the dean of an establishment, East Coast, Ivy League school, I am an architect in the AIA, and have been for quite a while, and I have spent a lot of time at Ivy League establishments like Princeton, learning how to manipulate shapes, in order to achieve effects that are considered desirable by somebody, and I damn well mean to ply my trade. I choose to put the emphases in different places from where Philip Johnson puts them, but I am being an architect in the full, establishment-pig sense of being an architect. It takes the energy of other people; what you're doing is making a scheme for directing the energies of other people, so that they build something instead of something else. And just how that's done in an altogether communal and nonhierarchical way, I can't imagine.

JC: Wouldn't it help to try to change the program of the Federal Housing Administration?

CM: Yes, it would help to change it. It comes down to gathering experience about how far one can go, the same way a naughty child (or any bright child) does. This was my first big housing; I didn't know how far I could go. I never went as far as I dared without losing the job, because once I started, I couldn't afford to lose the job. That was another part of my inexperience. I didn't have the kind of contract that left me ready to back out at any moment, without going to jail. I was trapped in several ways. I pushed the commercial area from 1,000 to 8,000 square feet. We probably should have pushed to 30,000, but 8,000 was as far as we got. Next time, I'd know enough to have a better contract, and could push harder.

JC: The better you are established, the more you can try for changes.

CM: Yes. Another trap, of course, was that the whole thing was designed for one level of technology, and then was built on another. We thought our principles in the project were good, despite the traps. The principles included the regarding of the making of place as the important thing we were doing, and the use of reality, which in our terms meant commonplace things that people were used to, as a kind of hook onto the ideas we would be at any time trying to develop.

JC: In other words, architecture belongs to existing reality. That means not just building your buildings and ignoring others.

CM: Yes—it means it should adjust itself to existing reality—which includes the kind of imponderables in the souls of clients and users, as well as the more obvious environmental realities.

HK: I think we can illustrate with one of your earlier projects, the Citizens Federal Savings Bank in San Francisco. You had an existing late nineteenth-century, classicizing, Beaux-Arts building, and built an extension. I think this can illustrate how you use an existing physical reality (fig. 49).

49
Citizens Federal Savings,
San Francisco, remodeled
and extended by Clark and
Beuttler

CM: Yes. I was an associate in the office of Clark and Beuttler in San Francisco, in charge of the design. We all had to fight hard to get that to happen, because the bankers were interested in tearing the building down, or facing it over to make it look modern. It was one of the few buildings left from the 1906 fire—as they call the earthquake there. It wasn't a great building, but it was a legitimate piece of 1904.

HK: What was your argument?

CM: It was a fine building, it was old, part of San Francisco; what could you gain by defacing it or tearing it down? We had the chance, because the clients had bought the corner as well, to do all the code stuff, elevators, stairs, toilets, in the new spaces, and to get . . .

HK: You cleaned it out.

CM: Cleaned out the inside of each floor. It was much more interesting to me to design the little corner piece that made it all happen than to design an ordinary office building. On the ground floor, we opened it to the corner. It was important to them to get a Kearney Street address in San Francisco, so we put a door over there. And, as far as I was concerned, that was as real a reality as anything else.

HK: It now turns out that your corner extension gives the existing building a new value. You didn't hesitate to use forms which were not fashionable.

CM: That's right. I'd been at Princeton in the years before that, an assistant to Enrico Peressutti, who would come every year from Milan. He and I would work out the previous year what the graduate class would do, and I would lay the groundwork. We had a series of problems in the three years I helped him, in which old things were looked at and new things were added to them. Each time it was, in Peressutti's words, an exercise in learning to live with old things, and to complement them and to make them exciting. Like being a friend of somebody's, he kept saying, making the thing that was there more special than it had been before. So this was quite a simple outgrowth of those attempts in graduate classes at Princeton.

HK: All the old centers of Europe are really in danger of being torn down. You are much more aware, apparently, of the few old things you have. We Europeans take the tradition for granted. We think we have so much, it doesn't matter if we tear down one more building: finally, there's nothing left. You Americans have also made some horrendous mistakes in the area of preservation, but some good attempts are being made.

CM: In this part of the country, the eighteenth century is beloved, and the nineteenth is ill-regarded. Great buildings in Philadelphia were torn down in the name of restoration—a Furness bank, for instance. Some wonderful buildings were laid low to make greensward around some stupid little eighteenth-century shanties. Gradually, though, the prejudice against great gutsy stuff is being overcome. My problem as a practicing architect is that I don't get enough of those restoration jobs.

JC: Your new Jewish Community Center tower in New Haven is built directly across the connector from the Knights of Columbus Building. How do you relate to it? Do you compete with it?

CM: Inevitably, we compete with it. We thought a great deal about our building's relation to the Knights of Columbus. There are differences which are very strong. Roche's cost $11 million, ours cost about $2½ million. His has about the same number of square feet, but they are far more elegant square feet than ours, and therefore more expensive. Our floor-to-floor height is less than his, so our building is going to be much lower—only 60 percent as high. And we're down in a slight hole anyway—his is on higher ground. I'm worried about how ours will look in relation to his, just because it's a lot smaller, so it may look like some baby brother tagging along behind. It is, like his, a square, and it's self-consciously turned back on the New Haven grid, instead of 45 degrees from it, like his is, although that makes ours 45 degrees from the new grid in our part of town. We wanted to face our flat corners with the same tile he was using on his round corners, but we couldn't afford it.

There are a number of curious optical things that happen. His is remarkably transparent in the middle, and I think it will stay that way, because I don't think they're going to program any partitions. Because of the towers, it looks very wide, whereas ours, with the corners chopped off, is going to be, from almost any angle, quite slender. They'll come off, in perceptual terms, quite opposite.

JC: Are there commissions you would not accept for sociological, political, or moral reasons?

CM: Yes, we turned down one, not long ago, to design housing on the People's Park in Berkeley, California. We were asked by the University of California if we would be interested in being on a panel of three architects to look at the job; they didn't say in what capacity. I went very carefully, because the people who offered it were friends of mine from the old days, and I looked at the history of that whole scene, with tear gas and helicopters, and concluded that anything that was done was not going to be socially acceptable. It was to have been a $5.5 million . . .

JC: How much money would you have lost?

CM: The fee would have been about $300,000. We wouldn't have made much, however. It was an exciting chance to do something, and our office in San Francisco needed work. But I couldn't accept it because I didn't believe in the good will of the Regents and the governor. It's not much of a park; it never was. But the fact that people had been pushed out of it by troopers and tear gas was the major issue.

JC: Did any sociological theory influence your work at Church Street South?

CM: Very little. One of the things of importance to us is that our solutions should be specific. Even those few great buildings that there are in the world which rise above the specific into some eternal realm had to start from a need to respond to a particular program, place, time, climate, and set of people. A good deal of what makes modern architecture terrible is that it is so often an attempt to get the universal solution to what isn't the universal problem. I found it very difficult when we started on Church Street South, because we had no real specifics about who was to live there. That was sort of numbing for us. We decided that, since it was the late 1960s, most of the people who were going to live there would be black. We needed someone who was knowledgeable about lower- and lower-middle-class black lifestyles in order to get some specific insights. We went to the New Haven Redevelopment Agency, and they climbed right up on the desk, because it's a political issue that more black people are coming into a city which has a long tradition of Italian rule. That is, the sort of people who think Italians are better than anybody else seem to be in the slight majority in New Haven. The people in the agency didn't much like the idea that we, as knowledgeable WASP architects, would try to find out what black lifestyles were and thereby admit that a sizable number of black people would live in this project.

JC: They didn't want to admit to this?

CM: No, sir! Everything must be as "American" as mom's apple pie, and everybody's alike. We would have welcomed any specific input we could have gotten about anyone's lifestyle, but the official vision doesn't allow for any differences. None of my designs for anything, from one-family houses to the Community Center, could be said to have been consciously influenced by sociology. The influences have been consciously specific and individual, and never consciously general and normative—except, of course, where normative documents like the FHA Minimum Property Standards have touched us.

HK: The one-family house is still a standard building type in America. It is usually the first commission an architect gets; this is true in your case.

CM: Yes, I still have strong feelings in favor of one-family houses as legitimate architecture, even in the late twentieth century. I've taken a lot of gas from students about still doing one-family houses, because they are considered to be antiurban and, therefore, antiblack and antipoor.

HK: You spread the suburbs. Greater Los Angeles, for example, is nearly as large as Denmark.

CM: It's true, but we still have a long way to spread. There's Nevada, hardly even touched yet. That could be suburbanized. Still, it has to be said that the single-family house, or semidetached house, the dwelling on the ground made out of wood, and made simply, is still, for almost everybody in the United States, the only really economic thing to build, the only thing that people can actually afford with their own money.

HK: It may be the only hope to get privacy.

CM: The amount of money it costs to build high-rise, and to build with fireproof materials, and to make stairs and elevators in the inner city, is simply far more that almost anybody can afford. Just to pay for what it costs to cart the junk around, and get the wrong things out of the way, and assemble the materials, and pay the wages, and build it in New York City, brings the cost to a ridiculous amount of money for a public housing unit that still doesn't have any privacy, and doesn't have any outdoor space attached, and doesn't have any of the standardly presumed amenities. For half that, you can build a pleasant house in the suburbs, with a backyard, and a frontyard, and a place for the bicycle, and sunshine. Although granted that a unit in the suburbs takes up more space, at this point it seems to me to be the only possible way of getting decent housing. Let me show you what I am working on. This is about a 17-acre site in Orono, Maine, next to the University of Maine. It is divided into two areas. One has 40 units on it and the other has 160 units. The site for the 160 is really quite beautiful, with big old trees and a young pine forest, so there's a chance to wiggle the buildings in among the trees and have something like the simpler Finnish housing projects, whose pleasures come from simple, well-considered buildings on a handsome site. I've been working harder on this than on anything else lately. The units are very simple and inexpensive. They are modular pieces that are made by a trailer company and trucked to the site; they can be delivered for $9.50 per square foot, which is cheap, and they will be put on regular foundations, which will be built on the site. The funny little vestibules we mean to paint up like guardhouses or candy boxes. With a few special pieces for the laundry building, with the painted vestibules and some fences, with a couple of sort of triumphal archways—things that can be painted fancily—with a landscaping scheme, and the trees already there, and, finally, with some luck, we can get this to look good, and to be a very pleasant place. There is a local art council which is talking about making a set of pieces of sculpture and play yards, or maybe painting some crazy designs on the asphalt, by which people can orient themselves.

Though it looks very picturesque, the whole village is composed of standard units (fig. 50). The limit to these units is that they can only be eleven feet eight inches wide in order to be transported on the highway. They can be up to 60 feet long. In order to make them feel like something other than trailers, we have to have big windows. Each apartment opens directly to the outdoors, and everybody has a garden. Three trailers, or modules, make one four-bedroom apartment. The idea is to avoid the standard trailer appearance, and also to avoid having a lot of rooms lined up along a hallway; we put them together so that a shorter hallway gives access to more spaces. The units will probably have a plastic roof and masonite with a plastic coat on the outside. Our scheme is to have the walls white and roofs white and the snow white and then . . .

JC: The White Charger!

CM: Yes—and very New England. These vestibules will be painted brightly in curious shapes, except in the section for the elderly people, where we thought they could be dark green, in the manner traditional to New England. The vestibules where the swinging "now" type students will live we felt should have huge purple and orange diagonal stripes, and other appropriate signs.

HK: Most of the interest is focused on the porches. They provide variety, not only because they are painted, but also because they shoot up beyond the roof line.

CM: We leave them up high for no good reason, except a visual one.

JC: Is there uniform fenestration?

CM: Yes, of two types. I think in the kind of jumbled complexity of these things there's a considerable advantage in having some things sort of stupidly simple. Church Street South, for instance, has only one size window, and it bugs some people, but I think it's a discipline which saves us from pure chaos.

JC: The interesting thing about this, more than the single unit, is the total layout of the project. The site is strangely shaped.

CM: Yes. They bought up different pieces—which happened to turn out that shape. I wasn't sorry it was strange. There were times when I was a little depressed with its complexity. Our notion was to have a pedestrian street: simple, cheap houses, with their own outdoor spaces and their own gardens, that could be linked together with other houses and put along a pedestrian-scaled, highly imageable, picturesque circulation spine. Old people, especially, and students, as well, would not be isolated in a parking lot, but were somewhere where they could get to other people and still have privacy. In the site plan, the pedestrian street is the shaded area. It is to be graveled. At points along the way, there will be art, or something brightly colored, or a place to sit, or something else special. The rest of the idea of the plan is simply that there should be a driveway that rings the whole thing and lets you park your car in your own place, near your back door. Every unit faces onto the pedestrian street on one side, and the parking area at its back door.

HK: There is a strong differentiation between the interior pedestrian area and the exterior driveway.

CM: Yes, and I've worked very hard at it. You can imagine the FHA and others not being too excited about that. Somebody at the FHA wants to run a 50-foot street down the middle of the pedestrian walkway. We have had some turmoil about it. Part of the problem is to keep the pedestrian walkway strong enough, useful enough, so that it really matters.

HK: It's not just a passageway. It links a sequence of little places, then stretches out, and opens up again. It's very lively.

CM: I think so, though I'm sure that people like Venturi, with his anti-piazza, pro-street attitude, would regard it as screamingly picturesque and dubious. We expect to push the natural forest cover back with a bulldozer while the units are being built and then slip it back into place, so that it is as undisturbed as possible. Everything is going to be homemade; even these pieces of so-called art in the pedestrian area are not going to be somebody's Frank Stella thrown on the ground, but are probably going to be mounds of asphalt with stripes and arrows painted on them.

JC: Can the children play on them?

CM: Yes, that's the way we planned it.

JC: It integrates the playground.

CM: I'd like to have some fountains, too. Not basins, with all the troubles that a basin has, but something like four giant showers with a tile floor, so that kids in the summertime can play in it. A play fountain.

JC: Is your plan for Orono, Maine, only a local solution, or does it have a more general significance?

CM: I think it's worth making a set of distinctions. One of the things which I find myself rallying against is the standard picturesque site planning of a suburban nature that keeps being applied, no matter what the site: resorts in Colorado, for instance, that look like pages from an Alpine tour guide.

JC: Vail, Colorado.

CM: Vail is a most beautiful example of this. And, it seems to me, dead wrong. I'm urging some students of mine, who are doing a thesis on Copper Mountain, Colorado, to make their little valley have a main street straight with a grid crossing it. I wish they would make a false-front facade on both sides of the street to create a piece of man-made order in the great jumble of the mountains. It's much more useful, I think, than the picturesque, phony attempts at an Alpine village.

It is always a matter of balancing and making some tension between the pieces and the whole. In this project in Maine, the pieces are just dead simple. The only thing we can play with is the space between the units. So we have a highly disciplined beginning (the module), which we had to break out of. I can imagine, in other circumstances, with a more interesting unit, that it would seem to me perfectly legitimate to have a simple, rigid site plan. Now, this is a small place. It's very limited in its narrative scope and power. It's playing the same note over and over again in ways that try to sound different, but it's not a diagram of a way of life. It's a very low-key, small thing, that tries very simply to make decent housing look pleasant. This scheme certainly is not susceptible of infinite expansion. Even though we are using identical units, we attempt to let somebody know when he is home, to make his own place special without its screaming at all the others.

It is interesting to compare it, I think, with Albertslund in Denmark, a very recent housing project in the suburbs of Copenhagen, a new town, really. There are some very nice patio apartments there at fairly low cost, and some garden apartments. But it has an absolutely rigid site plan, straight out of the 1920s, with every street the same, and every street straight, bam, bam,

bam, across the flat fields of Denmark. The units are lovely, really very pretty, but the project has the standard bugaboo: How do you know when you are home? There's a Kafkaesque atmosphere, desperately oppressive.

HK: Your description sounds like someplace in New Jersey.

CM: Right. Which is what makes me think people should abandon New Jersey. I suspect it will be the first American state to be asphalted over from border to border.

HK: The Coronado project in California was your first large housing project (fig. 51).

51
Coronado
condominium, Moore
Lyndon Turnbull
Whitaker

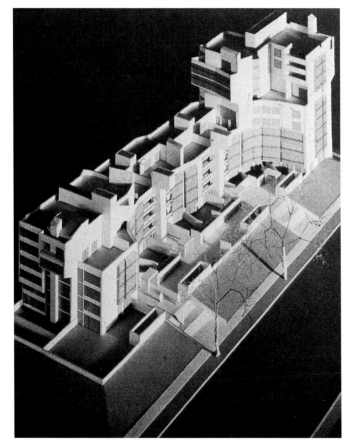

CM: Don Lyndon and I worked on this in 1961. The problem was an interesting one. Coronado is an island that separates San Diego Bay from the Pacific Ocean. It is flat, and completely settled with a lot of retired Navy people. The whole island is laid out on a grid. There's a magnificent hotel, the Del Coronado; it was built in 1888, a huge wooden structure—very high, very picturesque, glorious, and goofy. Then the rest of the town is one-, two-, and three-story houses. So, the whole visual atmosphere here made us attempt to take the scale of three-story buildings and pile it up, to get a high building that was still not a monolith, or of such a scale that it was hostile to the surroundings. The various city boards liked it and gave it zoning approval. But it never happened, for a long series of reasons. It was a condominium that came too soon.

HK: This project is very interesting historically. These years around 1960, of course, are very important because of the big change that came about when architects began to break away from the box shape of the International Style. There are three different designs for that project. The second one interests me especially because you suddenly introduce a rather unusual movement into the whole body of the building. That was not common at that time.

CM: It's more exciting than the first one, which did revel in great tensions among its more or less simple spaces; but the latter shows a great deal of pushing and pulling among the elements, and that, I think, makes it more interesting.

HK: In the first plan, you stick to the traditional Bauhaus concept of arranging geometric blocks irregularly. In the second, there is a significant change. You now have blocks which incorporate the play of elements in the body of the building; a flat rear wall and a concave sweep in the front facade. By reinterpreting your project, you reflect at the same time the change in the history of modern architecture.

CM: I was talking to Don Lyndon recently about what we were both doing then. I think that what we did together there had quite different effects on both of us, and I think it's accurate, for both of us, to say that what was true then would not be true now—the kind of naughtiness of that scheme. We were doing very dangerous things. On the one hand, we had to make something that appealed to a fairly conservative town; on the other hand, we wanted to make a statement against things we felt were wrong, a revolutionary statement.

HK: You considered that as a revolutionary statement?

CM: Yes, but a kind of *sub rosa* revolutionary statement, since it couldn't be so revolutionary that the retired admirals would tell us to get lost, so that's why I use the word "naughty" to describe it.

HK: The facade has an irregular broken sweep, and, within that, many things happen.

CM: It would have been awful to have a flat facade. Within something which kept us pretty heavily constrained, we found ourselves pushing and pulling and trying to make something that was varied and special and did the other things. The reason that it is any good is probably that it was very hard to do. We had to press hard just to get a fairly taut curve. That is why it is as disciplined as it is.

JC: Yet you introduce variety and original shapes.

CM: We didn't *have* to have the elevator equipment dangling out in space at great expense, but it seemed important to us for that sort of thing to be there. Today, many architects automatically do it. I just couldn't do it now, but it seemed important to do it then.

JC: Did you know the work of Aalto at that time?

CM: From the books and magazines.

JC: Aalto had achieved similar qualities earlier, for different reasons. His concern for acoustics in large spaces led him to curving walls which break in angles, specifically in his famous church in Finland in 1956.

CM: Of course, we knew of Aalto, but I'd never seen Aalto's work until this last summer.

HK: At that time, there were just a few mavericks, notably the late Hugo Häring, Scharoun, and Aalto, who didn't fit into the general International Style concept. It was much later, around 1961, that their ideas became more and more accepted as a reaction against the rectangular box.

CM: I have a different background. I graduated from the University of Michigan and got my first job in 1947, in San Francisco. There, the wildest and most wonderful work belonged to the past. Bernard Maybeck and other splendidly crazy people were still very much alive in 1947. The Greene brothers (Charles and Henry) were among us, and the work of Willis Polk. There were a lot of shingle fantasies, very Beaux-Arts. In northern California, there was still a sort of more or less controlled goofiness in the Bay region. The ones who followed after William Wurster, for instance, had brought it to a sensible, carpenter level. But the previous generation had been altogether crazy in a wonderful way.

HK: Maybeck generation?

CM: Yes. The Christian Science Church in Berkeley is a wonderful building across from the People's Park. I think it is an infinitely better building than Wright's Unity Temple of the same time, much more rich and exciting, with a lot of just nutty details, like Gothic tracery upside down (fig. 52). Maybeck was really a kind of declaration of independence. He said that the rules

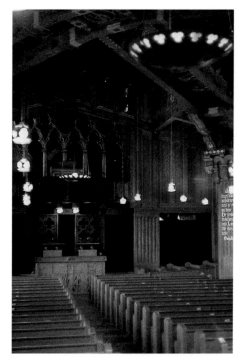

52
Christian Science church, Berkeley,
Bernard Maybeck

which might obtain elsewhere didn't really obtain in California, and he wanted to do what he felt was right. In our Coronado project, there was a good deal of conscious revolt against what was thought to be right. By 1960, there was a sort of John Carl Warnecke successful-practitioner syndrome which pretty much dominated things in San Francisco, as well as everywhere else, and it was no longer nice to do things that weren't altogether straight and square. Right now, Don Lyndon and I are having a great controversy about the Pembroke dormitories (at Brown University). Because he has an eye for differentiating and specializing—he has pages and pages of window details, which seem of great importance to him. But I managed to persuade the people who are making the working drawings to put all those pages at the end of the set, so we can lose them when we have to.

JC: Yet you are very interested in fenestration, yourself. You simply play with the window shapes and use them as an ornament.

CM: That is a major difference between Lyndon and me. I think the most interesting way of doing fenestration is to do it with very simple, ordinary units, to use one size window next to another size standard window. I normally use a minimum amount of effort on each of the windows by using the kind you can order by the numbers. It seems to me a very important part of concentrating effort in those places which really matter.

HK: You achieve variety with standard units.

CM: Yes. Don is much more anxious to make each window special.

JC: He tends to overwork?

CM: In my terms, yes. In his terms, I tend to underwork.

JC: Of course, you don't limit yourself to standard windows. One of your special characteristics is shape-making, cutting interesting holes into thin walls, outside and inside.

CM: I think possibly the first time we did that was in the Santa Barbara Faculty Club, although there are some private houses that were finished earlier where we did the same thing. In the Johnson House, these cutouts simply derived from the situation (fig. 53). The roof goes down and makes different-height walls, and you can either poke a wide window into it, or a high, narrow window into it. If you want something more complicated than just

53
Johnson House, Sea
Ranch, MLTW

the windows you can order by telephone, you grab a saber saw and saw some holes, preferably inside, where you don't have to fit glass into the openings. In the Santa Barbara Faculty Club, the chance to play with those things became, for the first time, an exciting possibility for me. The front wall of the club, which faces the lagoon, is partially the result of a controversy with the campus architect, Charles Luckman. When he saw our building, he said it was unacceptable, looked terrible, didn't look like his stuff, and had to have a *brise-soleil*. He thought that would cause us to put a screen over it which would hide this awful building that we had done, and he wouldn't have to worry about it any more. It swept over me, in the middle of the night, that all we would have to do is have another wall in front of our opening, with other holes in it. Thanks to Charles Luckman, then, came the first of our freestanding walls (fig. 54).

JC: Your freestanding walls are very thin. They never gain the massiveness of present-day "brutalism." But, by overlapping the screen walls, you gain a plasticity which the brutalists try to achieve with massiveness. It's a three-dimensional juxtaposition of shapes.

CM: To do this was especially effective in a place like Santa Barbara, where the light is very elusive and beautiful and comes shooting down in beams that make other patterns on the inner walls. It's easy to take a freestanding wall that doesn't have the problems of climate and cut holes in it, and do whatever you want, let the rain come on in, if that's what it's going to do. I find it simpler and more pleasant to juxtapose fairly simple elements, in such a way that the relationships get complicated, instead of making one thing that is complicated within itself.

JC: Of course, one thinks right away of Louis Kahn's grand screen shields at Dacca, which are different, yet somewhat similar.

CM: Louis Kahn is right there from the beginning in the Santa Barbara Faculty Club walls, which are a dead steal from Kahn's Luanda consulate in Angola, which was very carefully worked out by him. There, he developed the idea of having white walls in front of the windows, screen shield walls, as you call them. They were bright, but not nearly so bright as the sky, so you could look out a window and see an intermediately bright surface which broke the glare. Ever since Kahn described that to me and others, in the late 1950s, we had been waiting to use it. It is of great importance to play with the light in

54
Faculty Club,
University of
California, Santa
Barbara, MLTW/
Moore-Turnbull

such a way that it is possible to look out of a window without it being simply a glaring hole. In the Santa Barbara situation, it got to be interesting just in terms of the shapes. I thought it would be fun, too.

JC: At the same time, the critics admire you for building ordinary architecture. It seems to me a certain contradiction to admire you for your ordinariness as well as for your fancy fun, your shape-making pop holes.

CM: The whole business is fraught with contradiction. It is not an act of ordinariness, but the building is meant to do what it does by very ordinary means, with a minimum of strain in the areas in which strain would be inappropriate. One does it with cheap materials or with standard forms or with minimum budget. I have some Scotch-Irish moral compunction about spending very much of a client's money when we don't have to, and it seems to me not particularly nice to engage in the kind of structural or shape-making gymnastics that require a great deal of huffing and puffing, and the spending of lots of money.

HK: You are often compared with Robert Venturi.

CM: Venturi says, and I guess he means it, that Main Street is almost all right. If he means that great revolutionary cataclysmic changes in the environment are not sensible, suitable things to seek, I agree. If he wants to maintain Main Street as it was, I don't agree. I think that the environment is lousy, and there is hardly any place in North America that the hand of man has touched that it hasn't ruined. Anything we do has to be a great deal different from anything we have done before, if it's going to begin to meet the human needs attached to it. I think that to be ordinary, in the sense of simply continuing what is already known to people, is wrong. I get very upset at the standard student approach now which supposes that, if you interview enough housewives in a housing project, and write down what they like best about where they live, you'll know what the solution ought to be. This can't be true. However, I think it would be a mistake to tear everything down in order to arrive at some new environment, even though what is there isn't any good. It is a mistake to throw away everything that's familiar. My particular interest is in using familiar pieces, mostly cheap pieces, putting them together in ways that they have never been before, so as to get something that's strange and revolutionary and mind-boggling and often uncomfortable, but only using the ordinary pieces. I think that's a better way of making a revolution than just inventing a whole new crazy set of shapes. That is, I'm not really, for instance, moved by Bruce Goff or Paolo Soleri. I'm astonished sometimes, but it doesn't help me.

HK: Mr. Moore, what you described here is identical with what Mr. Venturi wants to do. There is no apparent antagonism between your theories and Venturi's. The results, though, the buildings, may be very different.

CM: I know that, and I know that Venturi is often misunderstood. We both put existing pieces in a new light, so that you notice them. The semipop musicians, like Dave Brubeck, do something very similar: they take ordinary themes and mess with them just enough, so that you can still recognize the themes but you notice them for the first time, because something, maybe something awful, is happening to them, they're being kicked around in a way you didn't expect.

JC: Even though you use common elements, you aggressively deny anonymity. To the common materials, you are adding a certain pop art vocabulary.

CM: I think the only way to do commonplace things so that people will look at them is to drive them right to the edge of disaster, without, hopefully, their falling off. My hope of their not falling off is based on the pleasantness, the cheerfulness that we mean to surround almost all of our stuff. We try to make it happy, which is different from Venturi. Vince Scully contends that Venturi is virtually the only American tragic architect since Louis Sullivan, and he says that I am not in his league because I am not tragic. So be it. I think that it is all right if Venturi is tragic, but the special importance of it is lost on me.

HK: Of course, there is always the danger of sliding away into ordinary ordinariness. Things become ordinary in your work even if you don't want it. Because it needs to be cheap, it stays cheap. Then all the theorizing about the values of ordinariness sounds like an excuse.

CM: Yes. That's certainly my main danger, and a very present trap. Church Street South is the most vivid example of the danger, it is the most dangerous piece of work we have done.

JC: If you don't get the money for the little pretties on which the whole environment depends, Church Street South is going to be a new boring zero. Are you afraid of being banal?

CM: We are on the edge of banality, whether we want to be or not. That's just the nature of our work. It has something to do with the tiny margin of leeway between just doing a really stupid job and doing something that has elements in it that make it all right, make it worth having done.

JC: Clients are still not used to adding on the jewelry, there's always a tendency to withhold that little bit of money you need to make it pretty.

CM: Right. If it's a house we have done, the client says, "To hell with you, Charles Moore, we've spent all our money, all $59,000 of it, and here's the house, and it's all ugly, so go away." And I say I will not go away. I will come with a paintbrush and I will do a picture, transform it, or reveal its worth.

We did a house once in Bedford, New York, a nice house, but very conservative, with a sloped, gabled roof to fit a "colonial" neighborhood. It was turned down by the developers because it wasn't colonial. Though I had thought it was colonial, in that it was congenial in colors and materials. They didn't mean that, they meant "colonial," Cape Cod. So we decided to do a double-scale Cape Cod cottage, in which the chimney in the middle of the building was 15 feet square, and actually had a fireplace at each corner and a skylight in the middle so the space went up, and it was all kind of like a Piranesi prison inside of a double-scale Cape Cod cottage. We figured these developers were stupid enough not to read the scale off the drawings, so they would only see the nice standard Cape Cod elevations. We lost the client somewhere along the line; it cost too much money.

HK: It is actually a Roy Lichtenstein idea to blow up comic strips, and thus make them suddenly frightening.

CM: Yes.

HK: Architects have the tendency to dress up their drawings in order to make them look full of life. They add a couple of nice little trees, a young lady with a child walking down the street, and all the other devices to make one overlook the architecture. To count on trees, to count on grass which finally will never grow, to count on nice stairs which sometimes don't get built, you know what I mean . . .

CM: I remember Ernie Kump came to school when I was at Michigan and told us to do that. He said, "Now, when you make a drawing, be vague about everything you are building, but draw in their dog."

HK: In one of your presentations, you have some people riding on horseback. It gives it the touch of New England aristocracy, of course. That's cheating.

CM: I confess to getting very scared of those pretty drawings. As a matter of presentation, I like much more the rough cardboard model rather than scenery full of cheat. It's going to be the late twenty-first century before most of those trees are there.

JC: You accent the elements of irony in your architecture. Do you ever give in to a self-conscious seriousness?

CM: I think it's very important for people to take the work in the spirit in which it's offered, which is often one of some levity, but often quite straight. I confess that I'm made less uneasy by triviality than by portentousness.

HK: You don't want to overinflate the client's ego?

CM: I like them to feel as though they're undergoing an adventure. I think that the dining room in the Santa Barbara Faculty Club is perhaps our most successful space in this respect. It is an exciting, even breathtaking place to be, but not ostentatious—it's too goofy to be ostentatious (fig. 55). It's damn strange in a way that is not unpleasant. It can be thought of as a medieval banquet room in the shape of a piece of pie. People in there may get a kind of vicarious enjoyment out of all the historical precedent, without supposing for a minute that they are living it. This kind of playing with reality is often taken with great seriousness by people as a personal attack on them. Their lives are so important that anybody who is screwing around with their environment in this fashion is suspect; they take it as laughing straight at them for being such pompous fools. I'm not laughing at them for being such pompous fools. They can laugh at themselves, if they want to, but I am interested in laughing at their environment. They may be pompous fools, but they have that right.

HK: What would you do if you had to build a bank?

CM: We are now remodeling a bank. We have invented a magnificent neon sign for a little bank in Westport. It is a recent, very handsome Davis Brody

building which we're remodeling about two years after it was finished, because the bank had been enlarged and everything was wrong. We're doing the graphics, as well as the revised interiors and front. It is called County Federal Savings, and we invented a sign that says "County" in elegant letters, with a star inside the "o" of County. "County" is blue, and the star is red, a sort of Texaco sign. The "o" is neon.

HK: And this is the sacrosanct place where people bring their dollars? Don't you need some big, impressive, heavy columns and walls?

CM: Davis Brody gave us all the heavy walls we need. We were going to have an enormous blown-up $5 bill over one of those heavy walls, but the bank president doesn't want it. In fact, he doesn't want anything we've suggested so far. He seems quite negative.

HK: He certainly wants to have a serious building that people can trust.

CM: He's got a serious building. It is a very trustworthy building, but needs one simple little neon sign to help it.

I find myself in the paradoxical role of at once designing and undesigning. I function as a designer, using the elements I have in hand very carefully, within my capacities. But I also have to speak as an undesigner, saying that what's wrong with us architects has been a narrow concern with composition that doesn't allow for the importance of people. On the one hand, there are still the designers, the Philip Johnsons and the Paul Rudolphs, who are actively composing. On the other hand, there are the students, announcing that the architect should devote his life to a service in which people are led to decide for themselves what they want to live in. I don't believe in either of these extremes. I find myself in the middle, like any liberal. I think there is still a role for the composer to compose something, if it is sufficiently uninsistent, so that people's lives can go on unencumbered by it. I also suspect that, when it comes to practice, much of the rhetoric of the students is going to turn into the same kind of solid arrogance that the Rudolph-Johnson way of doing things already includes.

JC: Do people want the superficial decorative treatment you give to the brutal basic elements?

CM: Let me throw in some pseudohistorical terms. We have been led to believe, by functionalists of the twentieth century, that the ridiculously expensive building and the pompous monumentality of the nineteenth century was all done with the outlay of needless amounts of money. If buildings were stripped down to their essentials, they would be pure and true and wonderful. It turned out that, when they were stripped down to their essentials and were hence so wonderful, they cost more than they ever had. It had not followed that it was the ornament that was making the building unavailable to the people. The ornament disappeared in favor of secret ornament. When Mies van der Rohe glued bronze mullions on the skeleton, it was as much ornament as some Greek-inspired anthemion of the generation previous.

The issue is that that generation built beyond its needs, and our problem is that we build beyond our means. Most apartments cost more than the people who live in them can afford. Many economists say it's just because people aren't prepared to commit enough resources to the place they live. But I think the whole method of building is too high-priced. In a healthy situation, people would have a wide choice within their economic range. They can have that in selecting their automobiles. The means of building houses is beyond people's control and imagination. You sort of take what you can get.

HK: Take the cheap FHA units and look at the insulation problem, for example. The noise level is unbearably high. In fact, there is essentially no privacy. I was not even surprised that you accepted the 51-decibel minimum FHA standard at Church Street. I am now living in a 51-decibel cardboard apartment, not living in it, but controlled by it. I'm entirely dependent on the neighbors who live up above. They go to bed and get up at different times than I want to. Their schedule now determines when I wake up and when I go to sleep.

CM: That's really what I'm trying to get at. You, as an inhabitor of something that's given to you, live at the mercy of these forces. We're all wrapped up in an altogether artificial scene, in which people get what's built according to a set of standards that have all been codified. If you were a southern European peasant of some time ago who lived in a house that was too small, you would simply build another room on it, and you would build it with mud from your fields or the rocks from your fences. In our situation, hardly anybody has that kind of freedom. Even the middle-class suburban dweller discovers that to add a room is going to cost him $10,000 or so. In this situation, we as architects have to depend on something that *is* under control, something very superficial, like paint and trivia, in order to make this anonymous housing special.

JC: You count on the trivia as an essential part of the architecture.

CM: I do, really. Our contribution is in two parts. One, the functional point, is independent of art or understanding of society or anything, it's like solving a puzzle. And the second is to take a perfectly trivial margin of money and involvement in order to make at least a token claim on these places on behalf of the people who live in them. It is a simple response to an almost futile situation.

JC: Or maybe also intelligent.

CM: Maybe also intelligent. But you have to have the options of saving all those other things in order to have the chance to say something intelligent. And, indeed, you wouldn't know if something was intelligent, unless it were somehow in doubt and jumping up out at you from the masses of stupidity that surround it. The basic freedom and lightheartedness of that opportunity is the critical point. It seems to me that in Venturi's recent writings, for instance, the whole opportunity for expression is taken as a burden, and it becomes a dreary need to be profound and serious and meaningful—and all of that is to be done with the "ordinary." I am interested in getting the freedom from seriousness to mess around, so as to allow a chance to have something exciting and unexpected and wonderful happen. I'm really very heavily distressed by this sanctification of ordinary that begins to make it as difficult to kick as the elegances of the Johnsons and the Rudolphs. I attempt to deal with things that are not so ponderous that they can't be lifted, and to keep a certain silliness afloat so that results can also come out of circumstance and out of accident.

JC: When do you call a building "narrative"?

CM: The chief element of narration is usually what is said about the trouble it's gotten into and is struggling to get out of. A building that is a pure cube is not saying anything you don't know already.

JC: Could the narrative element be a billboard?

CM: Yes. Tim Vreeland has a beautiful slide of a gas station near Albuquerque which is an old cinderblock box building. Separate from it, and very high, at the scale of the desert, is a sign that tells you what it is.

JC: The sign is important, the architecture is not.

CM: It means that men put most of their energy into the sign, which becomes the architecture, really. The sign draws the business, not the building.

HK: I would like to know more about the background of the ideas which led into what we might call "pop architecture." I think it's important to give the right people the right credit.

CM: I don't know where it started. Venturi was the first one to do what has come to be called "supergraphics"—in his Grand's Restaurant in Philadelphia (fig. 56). As far as I know, the whole business of paintings and flat-footed messages on the exterior and interior walls started with that restaurant, destroyed seven or eight years ago. In the Santa Barbara Faculty Club, we have made comments, however abstract, about what was going on in the more permanent materials that lay under the paint. In the simplest case, on a water pipe, we might paint "water pipe." We all owe so much to Lou Kahn that he has to be taken as a source of it, too.

56
Grand's Restaurant,
Philadelphia, Robert
Venturi

HK: Where is the connection? When we talked with him, he would not accept Venturi's or your ideas. He would not have anything to do with pure decoration, just painting on words.

CM: That's true.

HK: Were there any narrative elements in Louis Kahn's architecture which you picked up?

CM: I started to say that much of the narrative aspect of buildings comes from the building's trying to say what it wants to be, not from flat-footed separation of functions. For instance, one takes a difficult detail which has an awkward solution; the detail could have been thrown out, or covered up in favor of something slick. There I say no; take it, show it, emphasize it. The dining room of the Santa Barbara club has an absurd beam, a great big beam, which cuts the pie-shaped room. It goes whaling off to some other wall, where it finally comes to rest. I make a great deal of it and hang lots of lights on it.

HK: You emphasize the awkwardness.

CM: You emphasize the awkwardness and *then* try to solve the problem.

HK: You emphasize what other people hide.

CM: I emphasize the trouble, yes. If you're being eaten alive, you don't stand there pretending everything is all right. You dramatize your plight. Then solve your plight as neatly and completely and elegantly as you can.

HK: The functionalists also claim that they don't cover up—by showing the function, they show the truth.

CM: What they showed was the structure and the system. They showed the front organs, the things they wanted to show as being important in the hierarchy. And what they didn't show was the stuff which didn't fit, the oddball stuff, the functional misfits, the things which were unsymmetrical. I am interested in the other sort of backdoor stuff that didn't fit in that earlier kind of formal statement of the truth.

HK: Why do you want to get away from the slickness of the International Style?

CM: Because I don't think it is a very useful, interesting, meaningful, worthwhile description of what's going on. It's like the prepared statement of a politician. It's very important to spend a lot of time preparing a statement, as the Bauhaus did preparing a building. But I'm also interested in what the politician really thinks. I want to know what lies behind the statement, or what incredibly sordid deals are made in the smoke-filled back rooms. The private asides are a legitimate part of the whole. Looking at the building, I would like to know all of this as well as the Bauhaus-approved face. I don't mean that the Bauhaus is putting on a false face. They were against that. I would be perfectly happy to accept a false face, if I could know that behind it was something else, also available. This puts me in absolute opposition to something like the Paul Rudolph parking garage in New Haven. The last thing in the world you need to do is make a sculptural statement out of a place where you put cars. Why not just put the cars there? It is not appropriate to its use, which is storing cars. Cars don't need sculptural storage. If the sculpture gets in the way of the tops of the Volkswagen buses, then it's worse than useless. It seems to me out of control. It is not an interesting piece of narration, because it is not talking about anything which has to do with anything. If it would just shut up and house cars, or talk about something interesting, then that would be much more to the point.

JC: What would be interesting about a garage? What if you had a large block in the center of town to build a garage on? Rudolph says that even a garage can give character to the town and can help organize the urban chaos. Therefore, he doesn't want to make an ordinary garage like millions of others.

CM: He and I would disagree about whether a soft, sculptural thing would do it. If you want to have a strong statement in town, you make a strong statement in terms of the town, you don't flossy it up. This is like having a police force in drag, it seems to me.

JC: The question is still what you would do.

CM: When you drive into a garage and park your car, the car is dead, and you become a pedestrian. The place where you get out of your car and start to walk should become a place of great importance, and a place where a good deal of environmental excitement could happen. In Rudolph's garage, no excitement comes from driving the car in, and no excitement comes from walking away from it. When you drive in, you are too concerned about whether your aerial will be ripped off. When you walk away from your car, your only excitement is whether you're going to survive. There are no sidewalks, you have to walk in the traffic. All of the excitement there is solely in that giant ashtray shape, not in you as somebody using it. That, I believe, is the wrong way to get excitement. There's plenty of excitement potential in the whole set of actions one goes through, if one only looks at it from the viewpoint of the user. But there's not much potential excitement if you look at it as a statement of "parkingness" or "urban automobileness."

To me, this narrative function that we have been talking about is all of these together, the building being as descriptive as it can about what is interesting about it—either the way it's built or the way people use it; the message is either shouting, or being quiet, or hiding, or pretending to hide but letting you know what is going on. I think Louis Kahn would say that this is trivial in the extreme. But it certainly stems from his idea of having the building be what it wants to be.

JC: This seems to be the point where, by having been built right or wrong or mute or noisy, to be what it wants to be, to say what it wants to *say*, which starts us looking at buildings for what they're saying, rather than just accepting their pure existence in the Corbusian manner . . .

HK: In the International Style, a church could look like a factory—like Oud's church at Rotterdam. The meaning was no longer important, because functionalist purity was all-important. When a Beaux-Arts architect wanted to build a bank, he just took a marble colonnade with a pediment, and it was a temple, "The Bank." When you build a bank, it has a neon sign on it. The whole value context of estimating what a bank is is changing. A bank may not need to narrate security and stability any longer, the building doesn't need to look safe, but the alarm system has to function. Nowadays, a bank could even look like a gambling house.

CM: Yes, it depends on the value system of the society. Our bank looked, to some of the directors, perfect and wonderful, and they were very excited. To some of the others, it looked like a Texaco station, so they killed it. Now, we're doing it over so it doesn't look so much like a Texaco station.

HK: Don't you often run into the difficulty that the client wants the building to have a different message than what you want to give it?

CM: Indeed, that is a problem which I shall probably face if I ever get large enough commissions. We just don't have very many institutional clients who have such an elevated notion of themselves. As soon as we get that kind of client, we will at least pretend to listen.

JC: Morris Lapidus is one who listens. He designed his Hollywood movie set hotels in order to give people what they want.

CM: I think a lot of Morris Lapidus. To me, what he and his son Alan are doing is even more correct than what Venturi is doing. It's a little more real. I think their illusions are not so extensive.

JC: Yet, is that architecture or merchandising?

CM: I don't really know what is meant by architecture, I guess. If architecture consists of building pyramids, then clearly we don't need it. If you march through history and look at the central preoccupation of every civilization, one by one, in order to see what architecture is, I doubt if you'd come up with enough common denominators to let you know.

JC: Listening to you, it seems that everything that happens, from the foundation to the play mound in the piazza, is architecture.

CM: As far as I'm concerned, it's all architecture. I don't have any way of cutting off anywhere and saying that it's somebody else's province, or irrelevant to mine. I'm not concerned about refining a definition of architecture, but about the fact that architecture has remained too pure. My criticism of previous arrangements would mostly be based not on what architects *did* say, which is fine in almost every case, but on what their language left out. It is important to make architecture talkative again.

JC: When the narrative aspect takes over, and the jewelry, the billboards, and the asphalt mounds become essential, then architecture is the making of an environment.

CM: The environment has to become architecture, because if it doesn't nothing is going to be. You can say that there was a time when a certain aristocratic fringe of what was built was "architecture," and the rest was vernacular trash. If you say that fifteenth-century Florence consisted of some palaces and churches, and left out all the rest that didn't make it into the history books, then you haven't adequately described the nature of Florence.

JC: In other words, you care about the shacks, too.

CM: Yes. Florence looked the way it did because of the important edifices which had something special about them, as well as all the other buildings which made up the urban milieu that made palaces possible. It is just as useful to take them together as to separate them. We have standardly separated them for the purpose of identifying the important ones in the first category . . .

JC: In order to write a neat history of styles. Most of your architecture fits into the category of the vernacular. Would you have built a Boston City Hall?

CM: It seems to me that one of the neglected aspects of the American city is the public realm. There have to be buildings that are identifiable as belonging to a lot of people and used by everyone. A hospital, for instance, is not a very good public symbol because it belongs to the sick. But a city hall is still in a position of being a public symbol. It still has to say what it is in ways that are honest and appropriate.

HK: Would you use marble on a city hall?

CM: No. I probably wouldn't, it's too expensive. Even in a public building, I think I'd feel uneasy about spending money which might be better used for policemen's uniforms or something equally trivial. I just don't see any reason in our society to put on the dog in such an everlasting fashion.

HK: How would you make it stand out as a public monument?

CM: It probably should be a monument, it should be an identifiable place, a monument in the sense of a *marker*. It should not just be a building like a lot of others in a street.

HK: What if you had to build a city hall next to Paul Rudolph's Art and Architecture Building?

CM: The only thing I would do would be to withdraw from the competition, make a little park with the building underground. Power by contrast.

HK: Your little house in New Haven was in a rather ordinary neighborhood (fig 57). What made you buy this place?

57
Moore House, New
Haven

cm: It was very cheap, and I was sick of driving into the city. The house had been lived in by a little old lady who died, and the price was very low, so I bought it.

hk: When you bought it, did you always have in mind what you were going to do to it?

cm: No, I bought it because it was pleasant the way it was. I wasn't at all sure that I would do very much to it. I didn't want to gut it and make a Mies van der Rohe out of it. I wanted to have that funny little old house and play with it. I bought it in December and didn't touch it until May. Just came over and sort of looked at it, wondered what to do with it. In May, I started tearing into it. When I did the first layer of remodeling—moving the bathroom and putting in the stairs and cutting the holes—I still didn't know what I was going to do with the plywood.

HK: Did many things come by accident?

CM: Yes, it was done piece by piece. When I started in the entrance hall, I had no idea what the rest would be like.

Bob Rosenblum came when it was first being finished and announced that it was a piece of contemporary sculpture and not architecture at all. I like to think of it as furniture design.

It is also important to my way of thinking that those plywood walls, with all kinds of shapes and colors, are not very serious (fig. 58). They're made fairly cheaply and very quickly. We just opened them up with a saber saw. They are not travertine, they're not pigskin like Philip Johnson's bathroom, they don't represent any eternal investment. They are a statement of

58
Moore House
interior, New Haven

pleasure and prejudice. It really becomes important just in terms of my style and pocketbook. They don't represent a big investment of concern, but are a response to fleeting things, light and air. And when they don't seem to be accurate responses any more, they can be torn down and replaced easily. I like to think that this house is, in the best sense, trivial.

These interior spaces have different names. The first one, at the entrance with silver-painted plywood surfaces, is named "Howard," after a dog in New Orleans. I thought it would be better not to try to put functional names on them, since they had no functions. You walk around in what was originally the very tiny living room of the house, which is now just a sort of foyer, a set of cutout sliding numbers in it for lack of anything else. And, from that, you come into what was originally the main dining room. When you walk into one end of that room, you're in a space that goes all the way up to the roof, where there's a skylight. That space is named "Berengaria," who was the wife of Richard the Lion-Hearted. It's a name I like, and I've had cats named that. And then you go downstairs and into the lower level of the house, that is, if you didn't take the stairs which go up into the bedrooms. Down there is the dining room and the kitchen. Indeed, it's a sort of nowhere, not in an uncomfortable way, but you're just not on stage, whereas Howard is a more difficult place to be. The hammock is downstairs in Howard. I seldom use it; it looks very attractive, but I hardly ever find myself lying in it because it is "on stage."

HK: You actually apply forms used in modern sculpture, but you make an environment out of them that people can live in.

CM: I think that's true. I'm baffled by going to the Museum of Modern Art. I am baffled when I go into a dark room and have it called "art" for me, or when I go and confront a room that's painted white and has a fluorescent light leaning against one wall. I'm not affronted by it, or moved by it, or anything. I may think that's a nice thing to do, but I'm always astonished that it has taken a sizable part of the energy of somebody to have done it. If you wanted one, it would cost you a lot of money, which I also think is strange. I think that what lies behind all that ardent sculptural effort is very much worth messing with, but only in a very casual way. I would find it very hard, for instance, to do this house in travertine, or even stainless steel, because it would make it serious, like those rooms in the Museum of Modern Art. And that would really upset me. There are things that a sculptor does than an architect can't, of course. But many of them turn out things which are not in scale with the effort. For them, making that statement honestly becomes a principle as legitimate as the structural honesty of a generation or two ago. I have the opposite problem; I get lots of crank mail from people who announce that it's all a giant put-on.

HK: Architecture very rarely has been ironic. It is serious because it affirms the existing society.

CM: One of the great paradoxes is that art appears to be, by its very nature, revolutionary, but architecture, at the same time, is also establishmentarian art. And I find that very puzzling. Those architects who are most affirmatively doing the affirming of the status quo are the ones who will most loudly tell you that they are dealing with art. I don't see how that can be.

Edifice Rex

Our past holds for us, so far as I know, two workable models for the thoughtful practice of architecture. They are very different from each other, but both have served us well. Then there is a variety of partial models (which have seemed whole to some) and false ones (which have seemed true) which have done disservice, and contributed to the rather low esteem in which our profession is sometimes held. The workable models share one urgent requirement which distinguishes them from others: that they be complete.

One model can be called vertical. George Hersey has devised a vivid description of it for his Renaissance studies, though it is still in use. It starts with a lofty idea, an abstraction, which brings new order or new meaning to the world. A system of harmonic numbers once qualified admirably as a lofty starting place; more recently, permutations of set theory or aspects of linguistics have seemed an appropriate beginning. Then there comes (if it is to be architecture) the trip down from this height, through the realms of politics and showmanship, the establishing and continuous paying of an organization and the retention of consultants and insurance men and accountants and lawyers, all to cause there to appear, out of the ooze and slime of some squalid site, an edifice. The physical structure, it must be noted, lies not at the apogee but at the nadir of this model. It is subject to cracking and peeling, and liens from unpaid subcontractors, and suits from visitors who claim to have sprained their ankles on the unaccountably lurching steps.

This vertical model, then, must increase without undue delay the upward voyage, out of the mud and back into the stars, aloft on wings of criticism and collection and appreciation and further theorizing and the development of such talismans as photographs and movies and books. Some of us take particular pleasure in this part of the model, and I think it was not at all surprising that while the student rhetoric of the late sixties was concentrated altogether on responsiveness and immediate service to the poor, and the downward plunge part of this model was held in serious disrepute, great enthusiasm was maintained for this lofting, the ascent to the abstract through photographs and movies.

Upon arrival then, again, on top, back in the realm of theory, our vertical model is complete. That completion, of course, does not build it, which is

Previously unpublished; written 1973.

why this is such a good model. The initial theory, standing as it was or modified by the experiences of the voyage, is capable of repeated reuse for as long as its tenets hold any fascination for us. And building after building can at some point reflect the patterns of thought and order where we find meaning.

The other model which I think works is the horizontal or craftsmen's or Gothic or democratic or American model. This starts with an image, rather than with an idea, and sets about making a building. Much of the pleasure comes in the act, the fixing of board to board, or the laying of block on block. Each building is not the nadir, nor even on a separate pinnacle. It's rather a part of some material or urban fabric, and of someone's continuing experience of building and inhabiting.

This mode has hideous organizational problems. The requirement, I believe, is that buildings be receptacles of human energy, able to repay in satisfaction the energy and care that has gone into them. This means that the care must have been invested in the first place, and suitably focused. Even these days, individual care focused on an individual place can make splendid reflections. But the problems of the architect trying to focus his energies on 4 or 40 or 400 dwellings at once, for instance, seem to me unsolvable unless the energies of others—the inhabitants, for instance—can be enlisted as well. The task at hand, as this model is used, is formidable, involving as it does the encrustation of our concerns with those same batteries of lawyers and accountants who render lurid the descent in the theoretical model. A key ingredient, here, is the accumulation of experience from the built world and remaining aware of it. I mean more than just experience of profit; I think there can still be experience which includes some pleasure. I can't believe, for instance, that a civilization which so recently produced the Château Frontenac and the Ahwahnee and the Lodge at Old Faithful and the Plaza and the Old Coronado and the Bel Air and the Camino Real is now stuck for good with the Marriott and Howard Johnson's and the Holiday Inn.

So the second model is a continuous one, featuring the absorption of influences, building, investing structures with energy, looking at the results (our own and others) and learning from them, and building some more. This might foster our notice that some very unarchitectonic places (like the aforementioned Bel Air Hotel, and lots of cottages we all know) are very nice places to be, and worth having some more of.

The characteristic of both these models is that each has many moving parts, and they won't work without all of them. There are numbers of partial models that have been mistaken for the real thing. Many architecture schools, for instance, seem to me to confuse prescription with theory, to start at the top of the vertical model with a bureaucratized version of what Lou Kahn used to call a "white and gold vision," then descend though layers of tracing paper almost (but not quite) to the ooze and slime of the building site; the journey is generally timed to arrive at that nadir (the jury) at the last possible moment, so the process ends there, with no soaring.

Then there is the process, also induced by some schools, of employing the horizontal model, while (1) putting so many strictures on what are legitimate sources of images and inspiration that the joy of building is altogether constipated and (2) forgetting to look at the products to see whether they work and whether it would be a service to do them that way again.

That last seems reasonable enough, but is almost always, in our society, defeated by our propensity for half-baked abstraction, for rules too soon frozen, or frozen at all. A little psychodrama that is presently being played out in Stonington, Connecticut, is a standard example. Stonington is a delightful village on a narrow peninsula in Long Island Sound. It has some elegant and some bizarre houses, mostly of the early nineteenth century very close together and tight to the streets, and it has every criterion of success. It is loved and sought after, and the real estate values are astronomical. We are involved with a piece of land fairly near the village, where the program suggests a similar clustering. But the zoning is set up to equate laziness of setback with laziness of income, and of spirit. Twenty-foot front setbacks (more than in the village), seven and a half feet on the side, are for neighboring Pawcatuck known to be less wonderful. Therefore thirty feet in front and ten on each side on giant lots will be required, and another suburb will be achieved. They say they hate the suburb and want the village, but they have those numbers! And I harbor the suspicion that a great many of the sacred precepts of zoning and planning and modern design and even preservation are as obstructive to our having the world we really want.

I describe my two models because they are, I believe, dramatically different from each other, and architects waste a lot of time confusing two quite different things, building as manifestation of an idea and building as an act of building, building as noun, if you will, and building as verb. I don't think they reflect each other (Lou Kahn seemed comfortable, at various times, in both those arrangements), but I think they are distinguishable from those efforts without theory and without love which clog our cities and countryside.

Review of *Schindler,* by David Gebhard

David Gebhard's book about Rudolph Schindler was, for me, the most moving story of an architect that I have read since I was astonished at an early age by Frank Lloyd Wright's *Autobiography.* Being moved, of course, can include a lot more than transport on the wings of the dove; and it is this book's special quality that the bittersweet victories (or were they defeats?) of a fine flawed career are brought so close and made so tense that for paragraphs at a time I imagined I was Schindler or he I.

The method of the book contributes to this power. David Gebhard has brought to it art historical scholarship, a fine feeling for southern California, and especially the perceptions of Esther McCoy, who worked for and knew Schindler. He has used all these to tell the story of the young man born in Vienna and trained there, who continued his training after 1914 in Chicago and then with Frank Lloyd Wright, on whose business he went to Los Angeles in 1920. From then until he died in 1953, Schindler's story was part of the exotic development of southern California, bizarre then but later the model for most of the rest of the world. It is this part of the story that Gebhard tells with special insight, from which he extracts the full poignancy of the recent past in a sunny place now engulfed as surely as the lost Atlantis, buried under itself, submerged in the people and their wholesome constructions and their noxious fumes. Schindler's renown in southern California was engulfed, even as he practiced, by the far more slickly packaged reputation of his Viennese contemporary Richard Neutra, and by his failure ever to get any really substantial commissions. It is one of the sympathetic wonders of Gebhard's work that he perceives Schindler's ideas, even the little ideas, even when they were aborted, and makes clear how these saved Schindler from the despair that so small a set of opportunities might have included.

The format of the book is a delight. There are many photographs and drawings of Schindler's own work, also a good many of contemporary works by others, illustrative of Schindler's enthusiasms and the author's. The plates are interspersed with the text, and their numbers are in the margin, so that it is easy to leaf backward and ahead with a minimum of frustration.

Originally published in *Progressive Architecture* 54, no. 1 (January 1973), pp. 132, 136.

A possible role for the reviewer is to consider the basic question: Why in the world read a book about Rudolph Schindler? There are, happily, an impressive number of books around today about architects too soon forgotten, especially the contemporaries of Richardson and Wright. It turns out that many of them did large, handsome, and inspiring buildings. Why then Schindler, whose *oeuvre* was small and inexpensive and (to my eyes) wildly erratic in quality? The answer, for me, was voiced in a radio interview I lately heard, in which a famous actor was praising a young actress with whom he had worked, and whom he much admired. He searched for a word to describe her, and came up with "vulnerable," that is to say, open to all kinds of things (nobody is open to everything) in the world around. Rudolph Schindler, at least in Gebhard's book, comes off as vulnerable, too, and I like to think I am. His vulnerability caused him pain, and lost him work, and created some terrible-looking buildings as well as some of lasting power. But it makes this book about him fascinating reading, in which he stands not only for himself bur for a great many other vulnerable architects, most of them summarily dismissed by historians as derivative.

Bona fide vulnerability, as I see it, involves caring about the specific things you find and find out about so much that you will change your position to accommodate them: invulnerable architects see and learn things too, but they have a position, or a sense of mission, early arrived at, to which the learned and seen things contribute, without the power to change it. Vulnerable and invulnerable is not good and bad. Moshe Safdie's *Habitat* is the proud story of an invulnerable who has seen and known and felt a great deal, to the greater glory of his steady vision. Maybe there could be a historical game: I like to think that Bernini was invulnerable and that Borromini was vulnerable. Some architects are perhaps vulnerable to a point, and then fix their positions. I'm willing to believe that Lou Kahn's AFL-CIO Medical Center in Philadelphia was the work of a vulnerable, his Exeter Library of an invulnerable. (This excuses me for preferring the former.) Walter Gropius was the thoughtful arch-invulnerable; the International Style the temple of invulnerability.

I prefer distinctions, like this, that have good and bad on both hands. The one David Gebhard uses, to some of the same ends, is between high and low art, and he sees Schindler's translations from the one to the other, either way, as contributing to his strength. I don't really dispute the existence of the chasm between high art and low, or the tense drama of the leap over it, but

I do think the distinction is more useful to the gallery world of painting and sculpture, where some things deemed to be high art acquire very special attributes and price tags, than to architecture, where buildings submitted for our periodic ritual premiation generally have much in common with and only some distinction from the "folk" work of our rich contractor friends. Schindler's work is common but very special in ways which make reading about it, as I've said, tense and bittersweet, and more than a little unnerving.

Reading the book, I kept being reminded of my first trip to Japan, when I was aspiring to be a Bay Region architect. I had been to Europe, and had been transported by the presence of Chartres and the Parthenon and the Alhambra and Batalha; but I wasn't threatened by them. They were made of beautiful alien stuff. Now here in Japan were people who had taken boards—just what I used, though theirs appeared to be of better quality—and had made with them things more wonderful than I had ever dreamed of. That was threatening. And, of course, it was moving too.

Rudolph Schindler, as he comes alive in David Gebhard's book, did things I try to do, and did some of them thrillingly well, and was never a success really, but kept responding all the while. I'm moved by that.

In Similar States of Undress

Review of *Five Architects*

New buildings are numerous across our century, built to just about every conceivable configuration. Architectural ideas, on the other hand, or even polemics, are dismayingly scarce, and people or groups of people who care about them and make them are, I think, desperately to be praised.

The five architects in the book at hand are such a group and a potent one. As the "Cardboard Corbu" people, they have strong (and I think generally benign) influence in many architecture schools, and some of them, by all odds, are the biggest news in the shelter magazines since Shibui. A whole book by and about them should have constituted an important event. But I don't think it did.

I can't tell whether the book's authors are being shy or spiteful (either one a negative state for polemicists), but I can report that by the time I had penetrated the Preface, the Introduction, the Criticism, and then the initial explanation, I felt very much like a confirmed nudist at an incredibly elaborate presentation of the Emperor's New Clothes. So they're naked (unclothed, that is, in social redemption). Fine, but I had gotten from Colin Rowe's Introduction the impression that this was deliciously naughty. Or maybe trivial. Or perhaps, refined in its triviality. Very Significant, and therefore possibly not naughty after all. Just naked.

The evanescent fibers of the Introduction contrast with the stuff of the Kenneth Frampton criticism (their Majesties' well-tailored hairshirt, I should think), which I enjoyed reading and found helpful in trying to figure out what the collection meant. I was also pleased to find Frampton examining parallels between the work at hand and Shingle Style houses (how could there not be?), since the Introduction had been pretty chilly about any such possibility.

The invisible thread is by all odds most intricately loomed in Peter Eisenman's descriptions of his two houses. (One of the complexities about this reenactment is that the Emperor(s) and the tailor keep changing the roles.) He describes in words and axonometrics a process (I think) for unloading meaning and then dealing with two concurrent structures, the real nature of which you can't see, in order, through the unseen part (called "deep structure"), to arrive at a much more important understanding—so subtle

Originally published in *Architectural Forum* (1973), pp. 53–54.

you don't know you have it—of the real meaning of the architecture, or of life. My characterization is certainly unfair; it is based on my complete failure after several readings of the text to understand what it's all about and why anybody would want to do that. I can certainly understand why any artist would follow a quirky and exacting regimen if it produced works of surpassing wonder, and I enthusiastically endorse Stravinsky's proposition that an artist must seek always to tighten the limitations on himself; but except for some meticulously fine drawings the reader is presented with surprisingly skimpy evidence about the outcome. Or maybe I've missed it again and the real meaning is not in the buildings at all.

I confess to an unfailing surliness when I'm confronted with the rather standard architectural historical trick of puffing up a contemporary building (of one's own, or a friend's) by seeing in it a striking kinship with an older building of undisputed importance, then building the gossamer bridge through time so that the near abutment (our friend's building, or our own) seems perforce as substantial as the far one. The visible extent to which this self service could go was exemplified, when I studied at Princeton, by the description of someone's vacation house as the modern equivalent of the Athenian Acropolis, with a conveniently sited woodshed as Nike Apteros and the two-bedroom manse as the you-know-what. So imagine my orange and black apoplexy in reading a deadpan announcement by William La Riche (a lecturer at Princeton) that "organization of the Hanselmann design of Michael Graves is intended to recall, more than anything else, the procession from the sacred profane to the sacred spaces of the Athenian Acropolis. Among the historical artifacts that have most influenced Graves, the Propylaea holds a predominant position. Like the Propylaea, the Hanselmann Residence imparts a precise spatial and temporal dimension to the activity of transition. . . . The similarity extends to a locational correspondence between the Studio house and the Temple of the Nike Apteros." All this bearing out his statement: "The architecture of Michael Graves embodies the most extensive and provocative recent exploration of these themes." Bad form. Especially since the two houses of Graves are, I think from the photographs, interesting work, in no need of all that puffing up.

Charles Gwathmey is represented with two sets of houses on Long Island. No text. The houses seem beautifully put together. They are "pure," if that means sharing Le Corbusier's enthusiasm for cubes and spheres and cylinders and combining them in ways which maintain their clarity. In photographs (for me) the full "purity" of the Gwathmey Residence and Studio of 1967 comes across stronger than the subtleties of the Steel Residences of 1970.

The complementarities between Gwathmey's work and John Hejduk's are (as I guess they are meant to be) arresting, though curiously the designs occupy altogether different realms. Gwathmey's, that is, are buildings: they occupy real space and stand in the weather and the sun shines on them. And they are built to endure, and to change when the sun moves through the sky. The photographs show us some of that. It is also the case that some of the plan forms are fragments of giant circles. John Hejduk's One-Half House has plans with half a circle, half a square, and half a diamond. In them are fireplaces and other plan forms which play on the three shapes. It was not built, apparently, since there are no photographs. Not many of the world's great designs were ever built, God knows, but this house looks as though it wasn't intended to be, that the sun wasn't meant to shine on it, or you weren't meant to wedge into the laundry room. It appears, that is, to be not architecture at all, but some other art form closer to painting. Which is all right, too, except that it was otherwise advertised.

The concluding section, two houses of Richard Meier, was by far the most accessible to me. A whole range of architectural considerations (site, program circulation, entrance, structure, and enclosures) is described in words and photographs and plans and elevations and the curious slaunchwise axonometrics the Five seem to favor.

We are told little of the people who live in Meier's houses and nothing of the interesting problems which must have attached to building that way, yet almost for the first time in the book I get the sense that these are, however coolly they accomplished their mission, for human habitation. Also, I happen to like the shapes. That may be simple conservatism on my part, since these houses look rather like some few houses have for half a century and there's comfort in that. (How can you, Colin Rowe had asked, be intelligible without involving retrospection?) Or perhaps I finally caught a point the book had all along been seeking to make. The one about how good the Emperor looked.

I'm sorry I caught so few points, and rather angry about it, since I test well for this sort of thing. The book contains some buildings I admire, but I'd seen them published before, and had counted on the weighty phenomenon of a book to clarify my understanding of what the group is about. I want urgently for such a group to speak, since I think, as I started out by saying, that the need for polemics (and hopefully attendant architectural theories and ideas) is desperate and that few are interested enough or able to provide it. I thought these five had a very good chance. And now I'm not even sure they're a group.

Review of *Learning from Las Vegas,* by Robert Venturi, Denise Scott Brown, and Steven Izenour, and *On Adam's House in Paradise,* by Joseph Rykwert

When I read Robert Venturi's book *Complexity and Contradiction in Architecture* I found it helpful and interesting to be reading Tom Wolfe's *Kandy-Kolored Tangerine-Flaked Streamline Baby* concurrently. This time I coupled Venturi, Scott Brown, and Izenour's *Learning from Las Vegas* and Joseph Rykwert's *On Adam's House in Paradise,* with effects symmetrical and equally illuminating to me.

First I should declare myself. I am a contemporary of Robert Venturi, but went after he did to the same graduate school of architecture. While I was there, in the mid-fifties, one of the major revelations was a talk by Venturi describing a house he had designed in terms of the contrast in attitudes between Palladio and Frank Lloyd Wright—Wright, as he viewed it, the designer of forms specific to their use, Palladio the maker of forms unspecific (Venturi's house followed Palladio). I thought his house was exciting, but what excited me even more was the concurrent exposition of two irreconcilable points of view without the condemnation of either. I had never heard an architect do that before, and I have been, for that and an accumulating variety of other reasons, an ardent fan of Robert Venturi (and later of both Venturis) ever since.

I take this ability to tolerate and accept opposing points of view, to include nuances, and to ennoble reconciliation by removing its urgency as a sign of a high level of civilization. For me a statement like "Main Street is almost all right" is downright thrilling for its relaxed and tolerant inclusiveness. My reaction is not shared by everyone, and for reasons I only partly understand such tolerance brings on particularly virulent attack.

Repeated attack brings on war, causing the highly civilized and the broadly fervent to grow embattled. *Learning from Las Vegas,* it seems to me, is an embattled book. Which brings me back to the symmetrical readings of *Complexity and Contradiction* with Tom Wolfe and *Learning from Las Vegas* with Mr. Rykwert. *Complexity and Contradiction* was complex and contradictory, inclusive and tolerant, reveling in ambiguity, but delightedly revealing new sources for enthusiasm. Tom Wolfe's book was a splendid

Originally published in *Architectural Record* 154, no. 2 (August 1973), p. 43.

supplement because it made pointed and extraordinarily vivid the new-found Pop enthusiasms.

Now *Learning from Las Vegas* is embattled. I respect the authors' enthusiasms still, though I do not share them all, and naturally I have some others of my own. But I grow especially uneasy at the barricades that have been thrown up between Ugly and Ordinary on the one side and Heroic and Original on the other. I do this partly because, to me, much of Las Vegas seems to be on the Heroic and Original side, and, too, because as I read the book, with some paranoid twinges, I find myself there occasionally. I grow most uneasy because the dialectic seems contrary to that inclusive tolerance of new and old things and of different points of view that illuminates Venturi and Rauch's work and makes it, in my opinion, so extraordinarily important.

So, at the barricades, we come to the symmetrical piece of collateral reading, *On Adam's House in Paradise*. I thought it was fascinating in its rich and unembattled security. It is secure, of course, because no one that I know of is attacking it—in fact, it is so little advertised that I'm afraid no one will ever read it. But it is secure as well in its scholarship, and gently devastating. It is not, let me hasten to say, easy reading; it is far too rich and beautiful. Like *Learning from Las Vegas* it exalts symbols. It takes off backward through history hunting for Adam's house, the original image. En route, with wit and charm, Rykwert singes every generation of architectural theoreticians back to Vitruvius, but he manages to illuminate their efforts at their immolations. Each irrelevant architectural theory shows up as a human enough reaction against the theories of the theoreticians' teachers. Somehow, in the general destruction, they all survive, included in the millennia-long parade. So the tolerance and inclusive catholicity hidden in *Learning from Las Vegas* by scar tissue is glowingly present in *Adam's House*. You should read them both.

From *The Yale Mathematics Building Competition*

There is a special twentieth-century pattern for memorable architectural competitions: the winner is conservative but highly competent; among the runners-up are designers of buildings of revolutionary importance for modern architecture (in the Chicago Tribune Tower competition these included Eliel Saarinen and Walter Gropius; in the League of Nations competition, Le Corbusier). This pattern has pleased almost everyone, producing safe buildings for the users and sources of wonder for historians. The Yale Mathematics Building Competition upset this arrangement; the winner was at once the "safe" solution, in the users' terms, and perhaps the most vividly iconoclastic of the entries to the historians. Some of us thought that a splendid confluence; others across the country were noisily put off by what seemed at worst a put-up job, at least an arcane put-on.

But describing that late-in-the-century inversion is not the chief reason for assembling this volume. The reason is that the collection of 468 serious attempts to solve a complicated design problem provides an extraordinarily illuminating look at where we are, fifty years into modern architecture. It lets one see which "twentieth-century" canons are holding up and which have already dissolved. The jurors of the Yale Mathematics Building Competition had to look at something over 4,500 sheets of illustration board. Some 300 of these are reproduced here in the hope that they will effectively show where we seem to be.

A point which surfaces frequently in this volume and which ought to be stated clearly at the outset is that this competition did not occur casually, or in a vacuum. It had been advocated for some time and with some spirit by Edward L. Barnes, myself, and a number of others who thought that Yale could make an important contribution to architecture by having an open competition for a nonmonumental, economical *working* building. This is, I believe, a rare phenomenon; most competitions and most competition techniques are based on fixing the jurors' eyes with a striking gesture. Here the Mathematics Department's requirements and my codification of them into a program were developed to thwart the striking gesture, to require instead a more delicate resolution of forces, visual and functional; our bias, we hoped, was clear.

Originally published as "Introduction" and "The Scene," in Charles W. Moore and Nicholas Pyle, eds., *The Yale Mathematics Building Competition: Architecture for a Time of Questioning* (New Haven: Yale University Press, 1974), pp. viii, 1–3.

The nature and point of any architectural competition deserves a word as well. A competition fixes, in a sense, a program, so it is important that the program be well developed; but it does not, so far as I know, ever achieve a final design. Rather, by way of selecting a point of departure, a schematic design, a competition jury is picking an architect with the competence and the approach to work with the client to achieve the final design, and with the ability to make construction documents and get the building built. The competition, that is to say, is for picking the architect. Once he is selected, he has the same responsibilities any other architect would have to make the building responsive in full detail to the client's demands.

The architect selected also has to wait, in some cases—including this one—while his scheme is used to help raise funds to construct the building, since the initial design is an important tool of the fund-raisers. Alas for the speedy realization of the Yale Mathematics Building, its design appeared at just about the point when money was becoming very difficult for universities to raise. So at this time there is still no definite date for construction to begin, though the new facilities are still ardently anticipated by the Mathematics Department (fig. 59). . . .

59
Yale Mathematics
Building Competition
project, Robert
Venturi

Yale's campus has focused architectural controversy for decades, from the time when the opulent Gothicizing of architect James Gamble Rogers angered populists across the country. The university's decision in the 1930s to make Gothic the street face of Davenport College (to match other buildings on the street) and Georgian its courtyard face (for assumable reasons of taste, in the wake of the Williamsburg restoration, and of economy as the Depression deepened) drew the angry fire of modern architects everywhere. Then in the years from the mid-fifties to the mid-sixties, the Yale campus sported enough freestanding new monuments to be called the greatest open-air museum of modern architecture on the continent.

As the preface to the program of the Yale Mathematics Building Competition noted,

> The architecture of Louis Kahn, Eero Saarinen, Philip Johnson, Paul Rudolph, Gordon Bunshaft and others, which has focused international attention on the campus, mostly stands in strong contrast to the buildings and courts of the years around 1930 in the Gothic and Georgian styles which form a superbly integrated fabric unifying the central part of the campus.
>
> Not surprisingly, Yale, proud as it is of its modern monuments, now finds itself looking again toward the integration of new buildings into the strong existing fabric and to the provision of workable, economical, generally monumental space for the conduct of its teaching and its research.

Most of the modern monuments were built during the presidency of Whitney Griswold. Though it was an era still much admired, I think it is accurate to note that nobody, not President Kingman Brewster nor his planner Edward L. Barnes nor the Mathematics Department nor Yale's Office of Building and Grounds Planning nor anyone in the Architecture Department, had any interest years later in the restoration of an era of building individual monuments.

But the question of how to get good, even great architecture for the university is as important in an era when great architecture is expected to be economical and functional and unheroic as it is in a period when grand gestures are sought. All of us involved with Yale's architecture were desperately trying to make clear the distinction between unheroic buildings and unimportant ones. When the whole fabric of the campus is being considered (perhaps especially then), the most modest buildings are important.

To dramatize that and to get good buildings, Edward L. Barnes had been advocating an architectural competition. Both he and I were especially excited at the prospect of conducting a competition for a complex program on a restricted budget on a tight and demanding site; a new building required for the Mathematics Department was a natural. What was needed was really an addition to an old building, Leet Oliver Memorial Hall, on a tiny site at a critical junction between one campus fabric and another. As the preface to the program said:

> Hillhouse Avenue provides a particularly challenging setting in which to integrate a new building. In the late Nineteenth Century it must have been one of the most elegant residential streets anywhere. Now the first of its two blocks contains a number of larger Twentieth Century buildings; the second block, bereft of its elms, still has its fine old piles, mostly of the Tuscan villa persuasion, with frequent Egyptian overtones. They house University officials and some University offices. The Mathematics Building will stand between the newer larger buildings and the fine old houses.

The President and Provost agreed in 1969 to a competition for the Mathematics Building, though the problems typical of a competition in a large country created some concern: Suppose the winner was not professionally equipped to do the job to the university's exacting specifications? Or suppose he came from too far away to work effectively in New Haven? The building is scarcely large enough or the fee for its design sufficient to enable a distant architect to establish an office in New England. These concerns seemed to indicate a limited competition or a regional one. I spoke against that, arguing that what we were looking for was so unusual that there would be no advantage in limiting the entrants to ones already well known to us. I argued, too, that a regional competition seemed inappropriate to a university of more than a regional range, and that in these mobile days a realistic test of an architect's availability to do the job might be a required visit to the site during the period of the competition. The chief effect of this innovation was to fill my mailbox later with sarcastic letters from those very people (West Coast and Hawaiian architects, chiefly) whose exclusion was meant to be obviated by this device, if indeed they could keep track of a small building in New Haven. It was seen in their letters as a facet of an exclusionist plot by the famous Eastern Establishment (to whose meetings I have to admit I have never been invited). To minimize the uncertainties attendant on the winner's having shown too little of his professional prowess, a two-stage competition was decided on, though it is more expensive than just one stage. To minimize the time required of the first-stage entrants, a very short time was allotted for that.

It had been decided that I would serve as professional adviser, because I was chairman of the Yale Architecture Department. That meant I wrote the program around an impressively careful and complete set of requirements developed by the Mathematics Department, the American Institute of Architects, and Yale's Office of Building and Grounds Planning for the extraordinarily difficult site assigned by the planning office. It meant too that I selected the jury. I picked mostly people concerned with Yale, since I believed this especially qualified them to view the delicately balanced task at hand, and I saw no advantage in innocence of our problems or a point of view at odds with what we were trying to achieve. The jurors' names appeared of course in the program, and I counted on their reputations further to convey to contestants what we were seeking.

By the rules of the AIA four of seven jurors for such a competition are required to be architects. Our non-architects included (of course) the chairman of the Mathematics Department, Charles E. Rickart, the Director of Building and Grounds Planning for Yale, Edward Dunn, and Yale architectural historian Vincent Scully.

In 1969 at Yale, the presence of a student on any such body was essential. The AIA rules, though, demanded that the fourth jury member be an architect. Fortunately John Christiansen, a Yale architecture student, had come to school with architectural registration. Edward Larabee Barnes serves as planning consultant to Yale. Kevin Roche, whose office is near New Haven, and Romaldo Giurgola, of New York and Philadelphia, have both designed buildings for college and university campuses. The seven composed the jury.

The professional adviser's efforts after the program has been announced and distributed include receiving registrations and answering questions to clarify the program. Attracted by the realistic size of the second-stage prizes and by the Yale name, there was what I think is a record number of registrations, over 1,600. There were numerous questions, most of them easily answerable.

One difficult question arose, as it always does with an architecture school in a university: Were faculty eligible to compete, or were they in fact employees of the university trustees or associates of the professional adviser? Clearly they were not the latter, any more than other fellow professionals. For the former, there are precedents on both sides. I ruled in the first set of "Questions and Answers" in December 1969 that they would not be considered "employees" of the trustees and were thus eligible, as I have found myself arguing for decades when the opposite ruling has been used to deprive faculty of university work, in ways I think are unjust. Again, some who disagreed posted letters dismayed, sarcastic, or furious.

After the rulings are made and the correspondence braved, the professional adviser's role becomes vaster, but routine: to handle the flood of cardboard, to have the sheets put in a visible location, and to be sure the jurors and their coffee and sandwiches arrive on time. This is the moment to wonder about overkill. By the due date, in January 1970, we had received 468 projects, averaging almost ten boards each: well over 4,000 large talismanic objects, each bearing nuances highly prized by its creators, and bearing, too, the expectation that all would be sensitively examined by each juror during two days of judging. Happily for the professional adviser, that is the jurors' problem. Mine was to remain as innocent as I could of which project belonged to whom, since dozens were from friends and former students and fellow professionals I have dealings with, and it would have been dangerous to know enough so that a lift of the eyebrow could betray forbidden sympathies.

The real work of those days involved larger muscles than those in the eyebrows: the jurors elected a chairman, then decided to look at all the projects independently and to check the ones they wanted to retain for further consideration. My assistants and I removed the ones with no support, and segregated those with the support of more than one juror. Then there ensued a series of individual searches and group discussions until two dozen projects survived and could be viewed at once, and the jurors could sit down to consider them. Finally, five were picked.

The jurors then learned the names of the five finalists, though there was no identification of the projects with the authors. There were sandwiches, and then dispersal. During the second stage, from late January to April 15, 1970, these five finalists developed their schemes. The Yale Divisions of Engineering and New Construction analyzed the second-stage schemes for the performance of their component systems, and the George A. Fuller Company was retained to check the cost estimates of the finalists. The jury met again, studied the five schemes, and decided to vote. I of course knew by now whose scheme was whose, since so much information had been assembled for each team. And I listened attentively. Venturi and Rauch's scheme was number five. Votes were asked for scheme one; there were none. Then scheme two was called, with still no votes. None for three or four; and a shower of votes for five.

The whole sequence was scrupulously, painstakingly anonymous and fair. My most urgent questions about its worth came when the tons of cardboard were jettisoned. The ratio between the time it took to delimit all those subtleties and inventions, and the time there was to study them, calls to mind the ancient Egyptian practice of carrying statues to place in tombs rather more than it suggests any conservation of energy particularly suited to the twentieth century.

Just after the second-stage jury, I asked those jurors whose schedules allowed it to come with me to the storage company where the first-stage entries were expensively occupying large bins. (Contestants had been warned not to send originals, since we could not return any designs.) We reviewed all the first-stage entrants and selected twenty-six which seemed particularly representative or interesting ("typical," in the language of travel folders) to hold onto in case a book such as the present one became possible. It is these which we assess in "The Entries."

Charles Moore wrote "Southernness" for Perspecta's *issue on "Backgrounds for an American Architecture."*

Southernness

If John F. Kennedy did indeed call Washington, D.C., a city of Southern efficiency and Northern charm, it was a statement characterized less by its deadly accuracy and double-edged sharpness than by the startling lack of ambiguity which went with it. The American North is prized for its efficiency and the opulence of its progress. The American South is seen to lack those qualities and to rely instead on more leisurely (and more charming) ways. There is, of course, across the world (or at least much of the northern hemisphere) a continuing distinction between the north (of Italy, say), and the south, rural and poor. Even when big cities are found in the south the differences are still often noted: I have lately heard a careful distinction between the north of Louisiana, sharp and dour, and the south, around New Orleans, more leisured and gracious—and urbane.

It is, in fact, a kind of scaled-down urbanity that seems to me, a northerner, the most powerful southern image. My affection for that quality of that part of the country, and the fact that I have been designing buildings there, led me to write about the South's contribution to American architecture. The only parallel discussion I could remember was Lewis Mumford's in 1941. He had looked at the South mostly through two great architects: Thomas Jefferson (who came, as we all know, from Virginia) and Henry Hobson Richardson (who came from Louisiana but did his work from Boston). I, on the other hand, saw merit in starting from a collection of buildings and towns in the South that had maintained their hold on me and trying to discern what they have in common. That is the plan for the present assembly.

One thing the works in my collection do *not* have in common is local authorship. The architects came from England and France and later from Rhode Island and New York, as well as from Charlottesville and Charleston. Many only visited the South. And many, of course, were not professional architects at all, but engineers like l'Enfant, gentlemen explorers like Oglethorpe, or Renaissance men like Thomas Jefferson.

Originally published in *Perspecta,* no. 15 (1975), pp. 9–17.

The South as it is generally taken (from the Mason-Dixon line to the Gulf of Mexico and from the Atlantic to Texas) has a variety of climates, from the sharp seasonal differences of the Blue Ridge mountains and the Smokies to the almost tropical Gulf coast. But almost all of the South has long hot summers which induce the tempo some of us connect with charm, and others link with indolence and poverty. All of the area, too (except for a corner north of Washington), shares a past which includes the institution of black slavery, secession from the Union, a bloody and debilitating war, and (mostly) a slow and painful recovery. The sense of local autonomy which prompted the secession is now generally well regarded across the country, but black slavery, of course, is not. (You may ask at Mount Vernon where the slaves' quarters are, but you will be shown the "dependencies.") So the climate and the institutional inheritance may provide direction in our search for architectural southernness, even if the backgrounds of the architects do not.

But it is the collection itself that will provide most of the clues. It includes places I find especially memorable and think are especially special. It leaves out other places I like very much but which I felt were already more or less well represented. (Some splendid plantations upriver from New Orleans are omitted, perhaps unjustifiably, as already more or less represented by Bremo in faraway Virginia.) It leaves out gardens, which deserve a separate study, and humble rural dwellings which do too. It also leaves out examples from the present century, at least partly because buildings built during the heyday of the energy blowout have been air-conditioned by refrigeration and so have lost some reason for specialness and come closely to resemble buildings elsewhere. If I could have exhumed that magic moment in the thirties when Miami Beach became perhaps the first place in the world to resemble, albeit in miniature, Le Corbusier's Ville Radieuse, I should have done that as well.

The fifteen places I remembered and chose are, alphabetically:

1.   Biltmore House, near Asheville, North Carolina, designed for George Washington Vanderbilt in 1890 by Richard Morris Hunt of New York.

2.   Bremo plantation in Virginia, designed by its owner General John Hartwell Cocke after 1817 with strong Jeffersonian influence.

3.   Charleston, South Carolina, the city, developed after 1730; including especially St. Michael's Church, built 1752–1761 and designed by a Mr.

Samuel Cardy, an Irishman, or perhaps James Gibson of South Carolina, or possibly even the English James Gibbs; the Nathaniel Russell House, built by 1811 and designed by Russell Warren of Rhode Island; and the Pringle House of 1774 whose designer is not known.

4.   Gunston Hall, south of Alexandria, Virginia, designed in 1758 by Thomas Buckland who had been indentured from England for the purpose.

5.   Homeplace Plantation, in St. Charles Parish, Louisiana, from the hand of an unknown designer at the turn of the nineteenth century.

6.   Monticello, near Charlottesville, Virginia, designed in several stages between 1770 and 1808 by its owner Thomas Jefferson, a Virginian with books from Italy and England and strong memories of France.

7.   Mount Vernon, south of Alexandria; a short ride from Gunston Hall but more casually put together and expanded in the late eighteenth century by its owner, General George Washington.

8.   Another city in a coastal swamp, New Orleans, founded by the French and expanded thereafter under Spanish and American regimes.

9.   The Ponce de Leon Hotel in St. Augustine, Florida, of 1889, for which Carrere and Hastings were the architects and Bernard Maybeck was the designer.

10.   The city of Savannah, Georgia, as it was laid out in 1733 by the plan of James Oglethorpe, an aristocratic English entrepreneur, perhaps after a scheme described in Venice by Pietro di Giacomo Cataneo in 1567.

11.   Stratford Hall, in Westmoreland County, Virginia, designed for the Lee family by a strong unknown hand about 1725.

12.   The Tampa Bay Hotel, more recently the University of Tampa, designed in 1891 by J. A. Wood of New York.

13.   The University of Virginia, a work of Thomas Jefferson accomplished in the years after 1810.

14.   The city of Washington in the District of Columbia, an overlay of baroque radial patterns developed by Major Pierre L'Enfant of France, and classical rational grid proposed by Thomas Jefferson.

15.   Williamsburg, the capitol of Virginia until the end of the eighteenth century, put together by its English governors.

These places, both cities and buildings, with the eventual exception of Washington, D.C., are mostly quite small, mostly possessed of a high degree of geometric order, and must have been, through most of their existence, swarming with inhabitants. Therein lies their special quality and the essential paradox of this collection: although the heavily populated industrial cities of this country have been mostly in the North (where attitudes, as Vincent Scully has pointed out, were non- or even anti-urban and the life of the imagination was focused on the limitless frontier), the much more rural South, at once small-scaled and monumental, hyped up by the ferocity of its summers achieved a pitch of public inhabitation describable only as urban, and urbane.

Even the great houses in the collection must have been extraordinarily different in the days of their inhabitation from the hushed delicacy of their twentieth-century selves. The ladies at Stratford Hall, as they show off the bedrooms (with one bed each), describe a variety of eighteenth-century Lees and their attendants and guests whose simultaneous tenancy must have caused Stratford Hall to approach the residential density of Hong Kong. Their togetherness on a sultry summer afternoon must have been an altogether different phenomenon from the mid-twentieth-century solution to the heat, far more precisely effective and far more deadly, which organizes the population into individual refrigerators for the long summer months.

Whole cities, too, especially coastal ones like Charleston and New Orleans, pressed by the swampy ground into quite restricted compass, then opened up internally to catch any summer breeze, must have been models of pell-mell urban vivacity, with life in the streets at an almost Venetian intensity. In the Vieux Carré, the original part of New Orleans, the density of urban life was intensified in the early nineteenth century as the narrow streets were lined with buildings whose grilled balconies overhung the sidewalks. In such a fine-grained urban scene, acts of geometric formality, even gentle ones, can exert enormous power: just so the Baroness Pontalbo's twin apartment blocks, altogether simple with just three generous stories and continuous balconies along the upper floors, grant in their symmetry a real sense of the center of things (an urban sense) to Jackson Square which they flank (fig. 60). The rather unprepossessingly spiky cathedral in the center of the composition, flanked by government buildings of simple elegance (the Cabildo and Presbytère) along the end of the square opposite the levee, is then thrust into a position of much increased importance by the Pontalbo

60
Jackson Square, New
Orleans

apartments along the square's sides. For contrast, one might consider a typical twentieth-century new town and wonder where in, say, Columbia,
Maryland, one might place two three-story apartment blocks to have any
effect on the urban scene at all.

The urban fabric of Charleston, South Carolina, which also had eighteenth-century beginnings, is, as the plan suggests, somewhat less formal. It
incorporates, however, a number of house types, at least one of them invented for this very site, which sought quite specifically to improve the quality of comfort along this steamy coast and in doing that established the
pattern for an altogether memorable city. The special house form, the
Charleston "single" house, is illustrated by the Pringle house and many others like it (fig. 61). In an incident of urban cooperation by now regulated out
of existence, the system places long, one-room-wide houses at right angles
to the offset, with a two- or three-story "piazza," off of which all the rooms
open, and which runs along the narrow garden. The windows of the house
next door pick up air from this same garden but no valuable space is wasted
on setback; all the lot is rendered habitable, all the rooms have natural
through ventilation and adjacent space on a shared piazza, and every house
has a garden. Entrance is generally right off the street, often highly elaborated to celebrate the passage from the public sidewalk outdoors to the private realm (still outdoors) which begins just inside the door.

Smaller Charleston houses relegate the garden to the rear and adjoin
their neighbors in rows along the street, or more grandly face the street in
a format which allows generous vertical spaces inside, as in the Nathaniel
Russell House, to induce a chimney of air and set the stage for gracious

61
Single house,
Charleston

sweeping movements by ladies in expensive finery (fig. 62). All these building types are set within the limits (disciplined by the climate and the scarcity
of land) of a dense urban fabric which allows a nuance like the thrust forward of the porch and spire of St. Michael's Church ahead of the building
line of adjacent houses to have powerful visual consequences, assuring the
importance of St. Michael's (fig. 63).

By all odds, however, the most highly developed urban geometry in
the South (or the country) is that of Savannah, Georgia, which was planned
around an expandable series of squares by James Oglethorpe, the English
gentleman who founded the place on a bluff above the Savannah River. The
most remarkable qualities of the plan are the great variety of building sites it
provides within such an apparently simple framework and the alternate
traffic patterns it allows. At each square are four monumental building sites,
visible across the width of the square and each public on three sides (fig. 64).
Along the sides of each square, more modest building plots share their
amenity with the neighboring buildings which slip off in an unbroken row
down the block, not actually facing the square but, on the other hand, not
really cut off from it. The most memorable streets, meanwhile, those per-
pendicular to the river, have been spared from heavy through traffic by the

62
Nathaniel Russell House, Charleston

63
St. Michael's Church, Charleston

64
Savannah, Georgia

squares themselves, which provide monuments on axis that require slow-speed circumnavigation each time. Major traffic is thus relegated to the alternate straight streets which harbor commerce, while pockets of residential peace are left around almost all the squares. Streets parallel to the river slip alongside the squares uninterrupted and generally not congested landward of the pair of commercial streets closest to the river. The houses, which are generally row houses in this dense fabric, usually have their main rooms raised one floor off the street for improved circulation of air under the elegantly high ceilings. The drawing is a composite of the kinds of buildings which can happen on a Savannah square.

The Williamsburg, Virginia, that we see today restored to a cinematic purity and elegance was evidently a much more casual collection of buildings than its counterparts farther south came to be. But even the short and very wide main street named for the Duke of Gloucester has a collegiate building (perhaps by Christopher Wren) on axis at one end and a capitol at the other, and passes a long baroque allee which leads to a Governor's Palace as well as bisecting a courthouse square. The buildings of the town, not subject to the densifying pressures of Charleston, New Orleans, or Savannah, are mostly freestanding in gardens, but along Duke of Gloucester Street they almost touch and face directly on the sidewalk, and in the shops and ateliers on the ground floors of these houses there is a strong hint left of the mixed uses which must have contributed to the bustle of life in this small but important city.

Thomas Jefferson, who went to school there, thought that Williamsburg was an architectural disaster area and thought it mandatory in the new republic he was helping to establish that architecture and planning function in a much more sophisticated way than they had in the fairly casual aggregation of tiny monumental buildings in Williamsburg. So although he had in mind a gridded plan for the new national capitol as the rational available format, philosophically perfect as well as convenient (for which reasons he was trying as well to establish the metric system in the new country), he could not have been altogether displeased with Major L'Enfant's baroque allees, especially since they were laid out with extraordinary sensitivity to the natural features of the site, from the hills (like Capitol Hill) to the waterways, which would have put the Washington Monument almost on the shore and allowed a splendid cascade down the hill west of the capitol, even to the irregular landward boundary of the Piedmont, now Florida Avenue.

If these southern cities were like houses, sensitive to their sites, dense, formally coherent, and full of shared life in the streets, an even more evident source of southern urbanity is the houses like cities, jammed with a complexity of people but ordered, with architectural devices establishing a formal dignity that makes these achieved places, not gateways to somewhere else in the way accepted in much of the rest of the country. Even Mount Vernon, the most disorderly plan of the great houses in the collection, makes a single grand public gesture with its portico toward the Potomac, the chief entrance when the house was new, then with its flanking galleries quite gently embraces a whole village of one-story "dependencies."

Thomas Jefferson spent the happiest hours of a whole long lifetime making his house at Monticello into a city, fitting it onto and into his mountaintop and crowning the hill with a monumental house-pavilion, memorable and symbolic enough for the country he was helping form that its picture graces one of the country's coins. Here the theme "house" is stated in the one-room flanking buildings to the first of which Jefferson brought his bride, then gets elaborated through the complex workings of a vast establishment, mostly tucked into the hill and subordinated to it in a highly organized set of galleries. The whole is surmounted by the monumental pavilion, capitol, place of welcome, and sign.

Jefferson's influence on Bremo in Virginia must have contributed to making it, on an only slightly more modest scale, the same kind of ordered miniature complex as Monticello itself (fig. 65). It is worth noting that as far as away in Louisiana, only a cut less ambitious and more coherent, an even more modestly vernacular country house like Homeplace Plantation manages, in a single surviving building far less sophisticated, the same concurrence of geometric order and of life.

But the quintessential house-city monument of them all, with qualities of invention and reflection and passion for architecture and the life lived in it clearer, I think, than in any other buildings on this continent, is Thomas Jefferson's part of the University of Virginia; a plan for a university education made manifest in buildings on a site, with a place for reading and assembly at its head and professors' houses flanked by places for students' residence, with a chance to embody in the houses everything from the most solid Palladian architectural models to the latest from Ledoux, the whole democratized, socialized, and linked by a continuing colonnade. It is the world of the mind in microcosm and a splendid place to sit and work, or talk, or entertain friends.

65
Bremo, Virginia

One last quality of the South began to show up late in the last century: its exoticism. Its Transylvanian sense of separateness from a rapidly changing world, especially evident after the Civil War, prompted northern architects not just to import exotic styles, which they would have done anywhere, but to pursue them all the way to fairyland and create a complex exotic world: French in the Smoky Mountains (fig. 66), Spanish (with more evident local reason) in St. Augustine, Florida (fig. 67), Moorish, somehow, in Tampa (fig. 68), or Spanish on the east coast of Florida.

There is nothing newer in this collection not because nothing has been built, but because the advent of air conditioning by refrigeration has hastened the loss of that special set of challenges of climate and site that provided the lively, urbane, and, withal, charming cities and buildings in the collection.

66
Biltmore House,
Asheville, Richard
Morris Hunt

67
Ponce de Leon Hotel,
St. Augustine, Carrere
and Hastings, Bernard
Maybeck

68
Tampa Bay Hotel,
J. A. Wood

This next set of essays was written during Moore's southern California period, when he was teaching at the University of California, Los Angeles, establishing Moore Ruble Yudell with John Ruble and Buzz Yudell, and working with the Urban Innovations Group, a teaching practice connected with the university.

Moore delivered the lecture "Architecture and Fairy Tales" at Tulane University in 1975. When Moore lectured he referred to a wide array of buildings, all over the world, some famous, many not so famous, in order to focus particular insights. Many of his references were to vernacular buildings (some are not likely to exist any longer), which carry strong parallels to folk tales in that their lessons and traditions are carried down from generation to generation; as Italo Calvino wrote in his introduction to Italian Folktales, *"Taken all together, [tales] offer, in their oft-repeated and constantly varying examinations of human vicissitudes, a general explanation of life preserved in the slow ripening of rustic consciences." Travel, of course, was the source of all of these references and discoveries—not to mention abundant slides—and "Impressions of Japan" displays just how much Moore would see (and remember) when he went on trips.*

The close study of typologies and the variety of things that can extend from this base, and the poetic abstraction of those types (which Moore describes as a game of "chicken"), is described in his review of Vincent Scully's The Shingle Style Today. *H. H. Richardson and Sir John Soane were two particularly absorptive, "vulnerable" architects, and this set concludes with reviews of books about their works and lives.*

Architecture and Fairy Tales

This talk is based first on a series of recollections of the feeling I used to get from John Lawrence, who for years in his very gentle way made me feel that it was right and necessary to think the thoughts and design the buildings that seemed to me to make sense—even when they seemed eccentric or altogether irrelevant, not what people were doing. It's based too on something Lou Kahn said when he gave the first John Lawrence Memorial Lecture here three years ago, and it is based most recently on six weeks in Rome—which is almost half enough time to make it seem possible to restore magic to its rightful place near the heart of our world. It was about that—the magic—that Lou Kahn spoke here at Tulane three years ago. I quote him: "It's the

Previously unpublished; delivered as the John William Lawrence Memorial Lecture, Tulane University, 1975.

fairy tale," he said, "that is so important. I know if I were to think of changing my profession at this moment I would think of one thing—that I would love to write the new fairy tales." Of course he did, in his buildings, make magic and write architectural fairy tales at a time when the world most desperately needed them. And I hope you won't think it is too presumptuous or too academic if I try tonight to describe what I take to be the realm of the architectural fairy tale, or, at the very least, to establish that there is such a realm. It is the realm, I think, of immeasurable dimension—of insides bigger than the outsides—of edges near the center, of places where the familiar rules are for a time suspended. A characteristic of great fairy stories is that the quite carefully established dimensions of everyday reality magically open up, like the back of the wardrobe in which the children hide in C. S. Lewis's Narnia chronicles or like Alice's famous looking glass. Both open up in an everyday way to a surprising new world of incalculable dimension. Perhaps closer to our everyday experiences (since few of us have wardrobes like that) are the magically dimensionless breezes which come sometimes into our familiar world from a mysterious place which may be far away or may be very near. Such breezes suggest the presence nearby of infinity, and I think it is that nearbyness of the magical, of the infinite from where the breezes blow and onto which the openings open, that we care about. It is the infinite toward which the water flows, the time in which time has been curiously transmuted. Tonight I will use slides because I don't know how else to do this, but the slides are only visual and there are no breezes blowing from them. If while the slides are showing you think about breezes, that will bring you closer to the spirit of what I will try to describe.

My real concern, though I will talk about real fairy tales a little bit of course, is with the composing of architectural fairy tales—the kind that Lou Kahn was talking about. I would like to consider how to make the tales that matter without changing profession.

I am not—let me quickly say—trying for a general Procrustean-bed-like theory of architecture which would subject all buildings to a Fairy Tale Test, but I do think that the almost complete absence of that mysterious or other immeasurable dimension in twentieth-century architecture, which has thrown that important part of our lives into the really quite limited realm of Walt Disney, makes ours a drearier world. Very probably it would be just as bad to have an architectural literature that was all fairy tales as it is to have one that hasn't any fairy tales at all. But we don't need to make that choice, I think. The words are difficult and dangerous to use—semiologists have been pocking the ground around us with pitfalls—but let me try to make some distinctions:

The architectural fairy tale, I think, is not fantasy in the sense in which that word is generally used, when it figures in situations in which the architecture of reason is pitted against the architecture of unreason—the rational against the irrational. I wouldn't like to categorize them in that way, since I can't imagine how anybody could design a building irrationally—it takes some kind of reason to make any decision at all—and I don't think that the people who claim some kind of late Teutonic logic behind their work have been doing work more reasonable than the rest of us. There is, however, the realm of fantasy in which some have worked, or at least sketched. I don't think that is the realm of the fairy tale, either, since fantasy seems to be something which starts and stays separate from the possible, from our real lives. The fairy tale doesn't. It partakes of myth, surely, but myth again is a bad word: it is usually used in titles like "Exploding the Myth of Soviet Supremacy" as something that you are meant to do away with, if at all possible. What fairy tales do, and why they are especially interesting to me and to many people who make architecture, is to start from the familiar—from the familiar wardrobe whose back opens up to let you into a land from which you can just about always return in time for tea. Whatever span of fairy-tale time has elapsed in the meanwhile, there is a beginning and end in the familiar and even in the cozy.

I am not trying to enlist everybody whose work I mean to describe in the camp of the fairy tale makers, although I am mostly going to be showing things that I believe partake of what I regard as the positive qualities of fairy tale. I don't know whether Mr. Jefferson would have been pleased to be a fairy tale teller with his architecture or not. But I start with him because the little house he brought his bride to through the famous snowstorm at the beginning of his inhabitation of Monticello is really the essence of house. The little familiar cottage became like the wardrobe, the kernel and the beginning for the grand extrapolations that marked the buildings and rebuildings of decades later, that became for Thomas Jefferson a lifelong passion.

And all the time (not just once upon a time), people built castles like those two Portuguese ones which really do look like good solid castles capable of providing a base to dump boiling oil and expel dragons and do all the things that should be done from castles. Those castles are a part of a story that also includes cottages. In the story you have to go from a humble cottage to the castle. Then after you have been in the castle perhaps for decades you get to go late in the afternoon back to the humble cottage.

I have no limiting definition of the realm of the architectural fairy tale. What I have done instead, because such things must come in sevens, is to select three *wonders,* three *yearnings,* and a *surprise* as realms wherein the architectural fairy tale can fit. The three wonders have titles: they are called "Introductions," "Obeisances," and "Suspensions." Before I introduce the "Introductions" I think it is worth considering the manipulations of all of these—not so much in our standard architectural terms of composition or putting things together to look at from some external point of view, but rather as choreography, as arranging (in this case) the familiar and the unfamiliar in ways that make sense of both without losing the wonder of surprise and delight. I have been working in Rome on what I call the "Doctrine of Immaculate Collision," which I can't yet make work. The idea is that two things—these familiar and unfamiliar items that are waiting to be choreographed—can collide—smash into each other—and that what remains is the shape of a wonderful new architecture. The immaculateness comes in that the pieces that have collided or have been overlaid or jammed together aren't destroyed by this act, as railroad cars are when they engage in the same action. Both remain whole—but the collision forms new shapes full of surprises and powerful things occurring. So in this choreography of the familiar and unfamiliar an important act is the introduction of a set of pieces like the castles and cottages I have described.

I think it is extraordinary in a time as complex as ours that almost all of architecture the world over is based still on columns and on walls. I used to regard that as an interesting but probably irrelevant historical note, but more and more I have come to believe that there is in this powerful ancient pair of forms still the stuff that magic is to be made of; the carefully proportioned and related and considered columns of a Greek temple have provided ever since they were developed the pieces from which architecture is made. Thomas Jefferson's University of Virginia is a campus made with columns big and small, pitted against one another and choreographed to move in stately ways up and down the Lawn. Together with walls, either powerful enough to keep things out as at Carcassonne or just suggested as in a graveyard in the California mother lode, the columns constitute just about the whole architectural world (figs. 69, 70).

69
Carcassonne, France

70
Mother lode
graveyard, California

With just those pieces made by columns and walls we can introduce choreography of the familiar and unfamiliar. One such piece is the porch like the porch on a fire station in Auburn, California, which perhaps has gotten out of hand and has become more important than the building behind it (fig. 71). But it still serves as a powerful introduction, so that if there is magic in that garage (which I doubt), it has at least been properly introduced.

71
Auburn, California,
fire station

The wonders that lie behind the doors of San Zeno in Verona, more likely to be magical, are introduced too by a set of pieces really quite standard for that part of the world: a porch of columns on lions' backs with a little roof over, to make what Aldo Van Eyck would call the in-between realm to prepare you for the excitement of two really mysterious and wonderful doors, then for the church itself (fig. 72).

72
S. Zeno, Verona

There are doors as introduction, too: these are in Korea, the one quite properly in a wall, the other made movable so that if the Chinese come you have the chance to cart the entrance south (fig. 73). I am delighted that the owners of that door should have shown a proper appreciation of magic to know that the door, the portal that invites one into and introduces one to their realm, is indeed so important that it could be carried away when it is time to flee (fig. 74).

73
Korean gate

74
Korean portable gate

There are enclosures of various other sorts as well. A wall at Katsura Villa separates a portion of the outdoors on this side of the opening from the portion on the other side, while it makes of going from one space to the other an intensification of excitement and mystery and magic. The great shrine of Ise in Japan has as its most prominent feature a wall which affords only glimpses of a very remote building nearby. Mysterious temples to which access is forbidden to most people lie just the other side of the protecting wall.

Enclosures can be just suggested, as at the Wies church where paired columns and some plaster hoopla over them make an inner shell which creates a second layer of enclosure more special than ever, an inner inner space (fig. 75). In Sir John Soane's house in London a thick wall with mirrored reveals makes transition from outside to in much more important and gives further enclosure and importance to the inside.

75
Pilgrimage church, Wies, near Steingaden, Dominikus Zimmermann

In the first of my dirty tricks I juxtapose myself and Bramante. However, the same kind of encapsulation of enclosure to create a special introduction to a place is going on in his Tempietto in San Pietro in Montorio as in a recent house of mine in Florida, where a little gazebo is fit, in order to keep out of the winter winds off the Gulf, inside a jungle-filled courtyard. In each instance the temple/gazebo peg is shaped differently from the hole it is in, so that the tensions between the item encapsulated and the capsule intensify the sense of enclosure (fig. 76).

76
Rudolph House,
Charles W. Moore
Associates

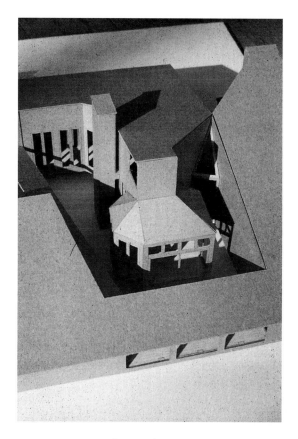

In Bramante's case there was an original intent to surround the Tempietto with a bagel-shaped courtyard in which it would fit without tension. Luckily, for what I take to be the magic, that was never built.

The second of my wonders is "Suspensions," of various things: of gravity, of time, or of the rules. Suspensions too often get passed off as mannerisms or mannerism, as some sort of freaky inversion in the mind of the architect who is simply trying to show his smartaleck contempt for the system. I think that showing off isn't at all the main point in developing suspensions, but rather the achievement of a heightened awareness on the part of the onlooker or the participant, when he sees, for instance, that the Queen of Heaven and her attendants are shooting right up through the ceiling on the altar at Rohr, in Germany. Even if you sit or stand there in person and look and wonder, they hang invisibly; though they don't ever actually make it through the roof, they very clearly could if they meant to (fig.

77). Suspensions of time happen in curious ways and places. In Middleton Place near Charleston, a great deal of effort was expended to establish symmetrical land forms with a pair of butterfly lakes which required an enormous amount of earthmoving by hand and basket in the swampy South Carolina lowlands. But then on top of that quite rigid geometry there grows a jungle of green things with, in the right season, the incredible and very temporary blooming of the azaleas, for a splendid but fleeting occurrence on a strong and permanent base in rather the same spirit that causes flowers to be put for the day on the altars of Indian temples that have been there for millennia.

77
Priory Church,
Rohr, Germany

There are other Suspensions in time that seem to me to have some magic in them; one is the Corn Palace in Mitchell, South Dakota, which is, unaccountably, made of ears of corn. These get old as ears of corn will, and the building is reconstituted in some slightly different way with new ears (fig. 78). Another instance is a pair of churches near Beaufort, South Carolina, which have many contradictions built in. The congregation presumably already had the right-hand one and then built the left one and then, seeing they had both, they kept them. The new one is smaller but more solid so each one has its own virtues, which I suppose are seen as creating a kind of desirable tension between old and new (fig. 79).

78
Corn Palace,
Mitchell, South
Dakota

The same kind of thing happens at the Ise shrine in Japan—except that there obtains there a more regularized way of copying and of timing the construction of a new temple, with the demolishing of the old one in 20-year cycles (fig. 80).

There are, too, Suspensions of the rules: Jefferson again at the University of Virginia brings you through a low porch, covered, in order to get you inside by way of a higher porch, really not covered, which inverts your expectations, twists your mind, and makes a kind of magic at pavilion IX.

At Versailles a look down the long allee toward the canal causes you to suppose because of the architectural frame of urns and regularly spaced trees that you are looking at a flat parterre and that the canal is therefore tipping

79
Beaufort churches

80
Ise shrine

up; until you think about it for a while and realize that even at Versailles the water doesn't tip that easily. An so you are caught in a wondrous paradox in which you have to decide for yourself what's going on, and so get involved.

My third wonder I shall call "Obeisances." One of the things that people do in fairy tales is go off and pay their respects to somebody, as witness, for instance, the crowd which sings "We're off to see the Wizard" in the *Wizard of Oz.* It's an elitist scene, I guess, going to see the Wizard that way, or the King, or the princess or whomever, but it always seems to work out well; the Wizard or the king or princess or whomever never seems at all ashamed of receiving the troop of small children, who are typically the ones making the obeisances, into the royal midst and generally letting them take over the kingdom or whatever seem suitable; so that a kind of democracy ensues, however hierarchic the beginnings.

There are architectural places too, of course, that are based on obeisance: an altar like the Bavarian one shown here or a temple with a place to get near it to make the obeisances as at Ise (fig. 81). I think there is a great wonder in pavilions too—I have been noticing in Rome that there is on the skyline another part of the city above the part that's packed with people and rooms; the skyline is sprouting with little pavilions like this one above the Forum of Trajan (fig. 82). Inside John Soane's house in London a saucer dome with light coming in around the edges in the breakfast room is employed to make a special place, an aedicula, a gazebo, a place that you know is more important and good, more magical than anywhere else around.

And over time that sense of specialness stays with a great many aediculas. The one illustration is at the tomb of Akbar in India, which is composed of lots and lots of four-pillared aediculas each with a little dome over (fig. 83). The other is a former shower of my own in which I sought to enshrine myself while I was getting wet (fig. 84).

Little gazebos used as garden houses maintain an air of importance, as in the Farnese Garden on top of the Palatine in Rome, or in this solid pavilion in a fountain at the Villa d'Este at Tivoli, which you can't even get into, but the sense of its specialness, its capacity to have the world pivot on it, is undiminished (figs. 85, 86).

Edges too are places of obeisance, of the presentation of oneself to what lies beyond. This is an edge of a park in Rome and the edge of a garden with a pool in a house that I have lately designed in California (figs. 87, 88). The latter garden has a framing wall which reaches across a corner of

81
Bavarian altar

82
Above the Forum
of Trajan, Rome

83
Tomb of Akbar, Sikandra, India

84
Moore House, Orinda,
shower, Charles W. Moore

85
Farnese Garden,
Rome

86
Villa d'Este, Tivoli

87
Roman park

88
Burns House,
Moore Ruble Yudell

the pool so that a special sense of separateness is maintained from the not really wonderful views that lie beyond. The wall becomes an edge behind which your privacy is quite carefully maintained. Another edge is the bank of the Tiber in Rome. Again a special Roman pavilion rides high above the palazzo that lies under it (fig. 89).

89
Lungotevere, Rome

Windows we usually consider as something we might look in at, so they function as the eyes of a building to give expression to it, but the act of looking out a window is another part of its function. Kresge College at the University of California at Santa Cruz appears in one picture and the Nathaniel Russell House in Charleston, South Carolina, in the other (figs. 90, 91). Those places are lining themselves up, getting organized, to face the outside which lies just beyond, in another kind of obeisance. Even as buildings of all sorts and degrees of fanciness on many continents pull themselves together, get themselves organized to face the world that lies in front of them, so that however poor and shriveled are their miserable selves—as in these shanties in Utah—they put on a face, cover as much facade as possible to help make a street, a place outside them where the public action can take place (fig. 92). A much grander example from Mantua quite straightforwardly does the same thing. It pulls itself up almost as if it were on parade (fig. 93).

Then a fountain, the Acqua Paola in Rome, does the same thing with even more mystery and wonder; as you look through the facade, you can see that is what it is—a facade where there's open space out behind that lefthand window. So its air of presentation of obeisance to the space in front is undiminished by any enclosed space that is being sheltered (fig. 94).

The Santa Barbara County Courthouse attends to, even insists on its own facade similarly by carving into it, by making a curious three-dimensional big-arched little doorway. Our own monumental Laundromat at Kresge College, like the Santa Barbara arrangement, slips around behind a facade that's standing at attention. These two examples both are thought of not as three-dimensional buildings but as two-dimensional faces paying homage to what lies in front of them (fig. 95).

In addition to my three wonders, I have assembled what I am choosing to call Three Yearnings. The notion of yearning, of quest is central to fairy tales. The main thing people do in fairy tales is go look for something or somebody that has been lost, in order to restore it or them to its proper place. It seems to me that three particularly powerful yearnings are yearnings for the depths of the sea, yearnings for the vast distances of time, and yearnings upward, toward the infinite. We have been told earlier in this century that we don't care about those things which are not rational or sensible. As the century wears on I believe that it becomes more and more apparent that at least some of the time, and for whatever reasons, we do indeed care about

90
Kresge College, Santa
Cruz, MLTW/Moore-
Turnbull

91
Nathaniel Russell House,
Charleston

92
Utah shanties

93
Mantua

94
Acqua Paola, Rome

95
Kresge College, Santa
Cruz, MLTW/Moore-
Turnbull

those yearnings which take us out of the claustrophobic confines of whatever boxes we have built for ourselves. It's the nature of water, I am told—and it seems to have been agreed upon for the past millennia—that any little piece of water in the world is related, in the minds of mankind, to all the water everywhere else in the world, so that if we can get connected with it in our minds, then it is an inevitable and even as easy trip to make the imaginary journey down to the bottom of the sea where mermaids are and Endymion went. In order for that to work, a number of things have to manifest themselves clearly: the sources of water are important, and the way it falls and runs, the edges of the body of water you connect with it, and the way it disappears. Then the islands in it and the engulfments of them, their disappearing into the mysteries of the deep, are all essential to give that sense of mental leaning out over, of connection, that the mystery works for us.

The flowing of water from a source takes the mind's eye with it, as in this village in the Cotswolds (fig. 96), in ways that an asphalt road would hardly ever do, while the actual motion of the water in a rill at the Villa Lante carries the eye and the mind along as well.

96
Lower Slaughter,
Cotswolds, England

97
Lovejoy Fountain,
Portland, Lawrence
Halprin with Charles
Moore

At the Villa d'Este, the water slides and splashes. Similarly, at our Lovejoy Fountain in Portland the water makes its own complex shape as it goes over simple 6-inch concrete steps, or as the water flowing is countered by water squirting back up or bouncing (fig. 97). The edge, and one's own capacity to make connection with that edge, becomes very important in Portofino and many another town along the Italian coast, where the town's central piazza actually slides down under the surface of the water while around the little bay one can stand right at and lean out over the navigable and (until recently) clean waters of the Mediterranean.

Islands standing in the midst of the isolation of the water and therefore very special places have occupied the minds of humankind for a long, long time and form the basis of many intricacies. They focus Japanese art and thought, as in this garden in Tokyo, and they stay in the mind even as they allow defense, as at the island of Mont-Saint-Michel off the coast of France. At Mont-Saint-Michel an engulfment even more dramatic than the ocean's itself is achieved with quicksand (figs. 98, 99).

In Lisbon at the edge of the river are steps descending into it, then at Queluz near Lisbon is a curious boat that seems to be about to sink into a very murky pond. Both draw our imaginations into the mysterious deeps (fig. 100).

98
Koraku-en, Tokyo

99
Mont-Saint-Michel

100
Queluz fountain

Parallel to this yearning for the depths of the sea there is, at least in many people, a yearning for the depths of time, with a chance of finding things lost in time. A fairy tale goes back through time in some way that changes the standard rules of chronology. A city like Rome, too, is full of buildings that are busy changing the standard rules of chronology, that, as here in Trajan's Forum, heap medieval forms on top of ancient forms with modern forms on top, within, next to, around, on, so that a palimpsest, a collage of all these things is in front of your very eyes, all of it laden, to my mind, with magic (fig. 101).

Here's a kind of peekaboo in a building near the Tiber that seems to have some ancient and some medieval pieces put together for heaven knows what purpose (fig. 102). The mystery of each piece, however, deepens the mystery of the whole. In a town in the Apennines a building seems to have a wall which is marching to the rhythms of one drummer and a roof which is marching to the rhythms of another (fig. 103). I take it as a good example of my "Doctrine of Immaculate Collision"—there the pieces are collided and just an attempt to trace the wonder of it all is enough to give one a sizable journey in time, space, and magic.

101
Forum of Trajan,
Rome

102
Building near Tiber

103
L'Aquila, Italy

A pair of places that suspend the rules of time give us a chance to move freely in it. Over the hill at Sven Markelius's Crematorium outside of Stockholm is something else. A grove of trees suggests that the center of everything is just out of sight. It fills us with wonder (fig. 104). In this window arrangement in Bologna one quite urgent set of convictions about the making of form that was based on the arch has been tossed aside by somebody who wanted the window somewhere else, leaving not exactly magic in this case, but some very strange tensions between what is and what might be (fig. 105). What happens when the arch decides that it has been wronged?

Recollections I find of very special interest these days, since for decades we have been told that it is wrong to suggest in the things we do some preexisting things we like since that isn't modern. That has left the whole realm of making some connection with the past (as I was noting before) to the Walt Disneys of this world, who make some very interesting

104
Crematorium,
Stockholm,
Sven Markelius

105
Bologna

things but who rob us of a freer and more real chance to make those connections ourselves.

I don't know where Jefferson got his notion for his Pavilion IX at the University of Virginia. Perhaps he wouldn't have admitted any connection with Sir John Soane—certainly Ledoux interested him, but in his manipulation of the Pavilion's half-dome entry he was clearly recollecting a set of forms that led back toward Rome. In Rome, somebody, I suppose in the 1920s, made this—to me—wonderful facade that is based on some Renaissance recollections very much transformed (fig. 106). It starts up as paired columns which perhaps too soon are capped off in little temples; then the paired columns start up again way behind and come sweeping back out as if they had forgotten they had to hold up the facade higher up; then they go through quite a few subtle changes until they emerge triumphant in an arcade with a cornice through which they go on their way up to being tinier

106
Rome

temples which are probably chimneys as well. I think it contains just about everything that any of us ever tried for with columns (as well as quite a few things that none of us ever tried for).

These are designs containing some things that my office has been trying for. They are for middle-income housing in the outskirts of Williamsburg, Virginia. Some dwellings are combined into six-packs (named in honor of Anheuser-Busch, the clients). Some are based on the Charleston single house, with its end to the street and a garden beside in which a car can be parked, which represents a proven, successful way of coping with a pedestrian neighborhood fairly dense with parking without undue expense (fig. 107). There is another notion here recollective of Charleston too, in which the houses face the street with gardens behind part of them. The cars vanish through an arch in the building wall to be parked in a lot in the center of the block out of sight for the people who are walking or riding up and down the streets. I am pleased to think that the pieces of these houses are modern—if modern means that you can't afford to have anybody shape them, so that corner pilasters are made of plywood, etc. But I flatter myself that the shadows are Federal. (It hasn't been established yet whether they are, because we haven't managed to get this housing built.)

But all this is part of an increasingly overt and for my part necessary attempt to make a connection backward in time with the forms that are es-

107
Kingsmill,
Williamsburg

tablished as especially characteristic of a place—in this case Williamsburg. Their existence, I believe, is an important part of the reason why the people who are meant to buy theses houses have come there in the first place. The importance of this local idiom therefore justifies, it seems to me, a more overt recollection than might be appropriate somewhere else.

Another yearning is a more formal one—let's call it deformation— that honors form by messing with it, that celebrates the half-dome by squashing it, as in one Roman example, or as in another Roman example honors a nonexistent pediment by carrying corners up into a dormer window on each side, and inserting some very strange little pieces of railing that almost recollect a whole shape that might have been there once, but wasn't.

Deformations of other sorts show up in this building in Guimarães, in the north or Portugal, where a set of separate houses are made into one by one great flight of steps up to some entrances conjoined (fig. 108), or in the fenestration of the jail in the Santa Barbara County Courthouse, where a kind of syncopated carrying on is, I think, legitimately recollective of the simplicity of the forms that were there before the windows started dancing around on it.

My third yearning is for upward and the infinite. Those two are in some ways connected, as in a temple complex like that at Monte Albán above Oaxaca, on top of a mountain in the first place, then full of great

108
Guimarães, Portugal

109
Monte Albán, Mexico

flights of stairs up farther (fig. 109). Sometimes you have to go down again in order to have the chance to climb yet again so that you always have the sense of moving upward, in this already enormously high place, as a part of your use of the place—of your connection with it. Moving upward in a baroque staircase is rather like the same experience, although the decor is a little bit different.

In some other European examples, you move up the stairway of the Doge's Palace in Venice past a set of humanoids who welcome you onward, or perhaps threaten you a little bit from the top of the stairway (fig. 110). The stairs themselves make an important part of the choreography, as they do in the Wells Cathedral chapter house (fig. 111).

That thrust upward is expressed in another way in towers; that must be one of the main reason for having towers. There is surely no need to get to the top either of the one on Michelangelo's Campidoglio or of a church spire in South Dakota (fig. 112). They are there mostly to point up to the sky and make some reminders about our hopes for connections in that direction.

110
Doge's Palace, Venice

111
Wells Cathedral

We wanted a tower at our Sea Ranch Condominium, but felt obliged to look for further justification (fig. 113). We filled it, therefore, with bedrooms so that we could afford the space; but what we really wanted was a tower, partly as a pin to stick the building into a slope so that it didn't seem to be sliding into the sea, partly to suggest upwardness. The remarkable building illustrated next—which I will try to further the reputation of—was built in Rome in 1926 (fig. 114). It has a tower and some towering chimneys and quite a few other things as well, including recollections of more places than I ever heard of. It's part of two or three blocks full of buildings that look like that, and are in the aggregate almost more wonderful than you can bear.

113
Sea Ranch
Condominium,
MLTW

114
Rome

Which brings us to my seventh category—that of Surprise. I think that the most efficient and most powerful tool that architects have to create surprise is the manipulation of scale, to allow inside to be bigger than the outside, to command your attention. Surprises of scale can make things seem much bigger or much littler than they are—or let them seem to be bigger in spirit or smaller in size or vice versa. A windowless building in the street in Guanajuato, for instance, painted that way looks as if some Martian giant child had dropped it there (fig. 115). It becomes in that way a magic interloper, maybe from outer space.

This tombstone in a cemetery near Cuernavaca, energized by its bright painting, becomes at once a toy and a really powerful and moving object with considerably more monumentality than most great monuments I have ever seen (fig. 116). Again, I insert an item of our own—a wading pool at the Faculty Club at the University of California at Santa Barbara where littleness is sought after, and a kind of intimacy which makes it important whether that bird that is hopping around in the gutter is fitting or not, or whether a ten-month-old child (which is about the biggest child that will fit in that gutter) is being accommodated, and how deep the water is as it splashes from the child over to the gutter, so your attention is pulled down to a fine scale.

115
Guanajuato,
Mexico

116
Cuernavaca, Mexico

Your attention is drawn to a miniature in something like the same way in this cabinet at Biltmore House in Asheville, North Carolina, which is full of mirrors in very special places, so that we do not know how extensive that little miniature landscape is (fig. 117). It seems enormous as it pulls your mind and your wonder into its interstices.

The things I have been showing have, I hope, a common participation in some kind of fairy tale, so they share mystery and magic. They partake of other things too, of course, and I want to say again that I am not trying to preach an architectural revolution that would require all of us to produce unending architectural fairy tales, but I do think that it is time to reject the restrictions that have made us ashamed to do things with an element of mystery, so that we can explore this realm, which is, I believe, an important part of our own minds and of the world around us.

117
Biltmore cabinet

Japan has a very special quality; more, I think, than any place else in the world. Its surface is a mirror or, perhaps better, the dark waters in which Narcissus saw himself. When he looks at Japan, each Western visitor sees something of himself, or rather himself as he would like to be. It is hopeless, I am afraid, to suppose that a Western visitor's observations reveal any new truths about Japan. Ralph Adams Cram's enthusiastic *Impressions of Japanese Architecture,* based on a trip in 1896 (he came to design a parliament building in Tokyo), told me a lot about Ralph Adams Cram but not much about my Japan. He wanted evidence of the uplifting qualities of the feudal system, and he got it, with a bonus of Buddhist architectural splendors. He liked traditional farmhouses but found Ise barbarous, though it is not clear whether he ever saw it. But it is captious for me to complain about that, since I never made it to *his* favorite, the Hoo-doo of the Byodo-in which reflected everything he wanted to see. What *I* saw in Japan (in the month of October 1977) were 1) the most voracious (and to me, most splendid) eclectic urges on this planet, 2) the capacity, not yet just a memory, to live close together in cities with a close connection to a garden and the earth and sky for everyone, 3) structures of great elegance derived from and not inimical to the commonplace, 4) other structures, almost as elegant, of the most uncommon and unbridled voluptuousness, and 5) magic gardens of purest peace. I did not feel any desire to emblazon on my mind forever the endless degrading urban sprawl; the bad air; the shapeless, scattered mass that disconnects the suburbs from the land, engulfs the real places, and dims the hopes for continuing occupancy of the planet. I can see all that at home, where I am in a slightly better position to combat it (at least I can help vote the rascals in power out, sometimes).

The Japan I visited comprised Tokyo (including a swimming pool with waves, at Summerland as well as Korakuen and Rikugien), Nikko, Takayama, Ise, Miyajima, Kurashiki, Okayama, Kyoto (for the Katsura and Shugaku-in palaces, the Kiyomizu-dera, the Nijo Castle, Daitoku-ji, Tenryu-ji, Ryonan-ji, Saiho-ji, and so on), and bits of Nara, Osaka, Kobe, Naoshima, Takamatsu, Kochi, Kompira, and villages on the way to Fukui and the Sea of Japan. I had seen some of these places before, long ago, and a few more recently. This time I was fully and blindingly transported (an emo-

Originally published in *Japan Architect* (1978).

tion previously limited, for me, to the Athenian Acropolis, Chartres, the Alhambra, Batalha, the Villa Giulia in Rome, John Soane's house in London, and the University of Virginia) by the Saiho-ji and the Yoshijima house in Takayama.

There are other places, too, that I shall always remember: the Katsura palace, of course, and the Daitoku-ji (where it all came together for me twenty-three years ago in a garden I could not find this time—but there were others), the Shugakuin palace, the Yoshimura house near Osaka, Isamu Noguchi's house, and Mr. Yamamoto's museum in Takamatsu, Kochi Castle. (Wow! Now *that* is a castle! I get very excited with small stone castles, like Kochi or the one in Guimarães where Portugal began or the one the Villehardouins raised in Cyprus. I grow testy with big, fussy castles, like Windsor or Cardiff, or prissy perfect ones, like Himeji.) I was excited again by Ise and by stroll gardens in Tokyo, especially Korakuen (which none of my Japanese friends would recommend, probably, because a brand-new building is casting an embarrassment of bright yellow reflection over it). Then there are ancient buildings in the mountains near Fukuji; a tiny, narrow, new row house by Tadao Ando in Osaka; a gymnasium by Kazuhiro Ishii in Naoshima; the climb to Kompira; and the Itsukushima (which should probably be on my four-star all-time list); and some *ryokan* (inns)—Essaen in Miyajimaguchi and Hiragiya in Kyoto. There is no better way, I think, to experience great architecture than to wake up in it. My real tour of the architectural wonders of the world would feature naps in each wonder, a way, however marginal, to surrender to the great place and make it your own.

What I *did* in Japan was to ride on many trains (all of them on time—this is as dazzling to an American as elevators are to the residents of New Guinea); see these buildings; spend pleasant times with American and Japanese people; eat a stupefying amount of endlessly wonderful food; stay in delicately detailed rooms with tatami floors; and bathe in great, wonderful vats of hot water (missing only the soft towels which are an essential part of the Westerner's sybaritic syndrome).

But what I *saw,* as every other foreigner sees, was what I was looking for in the reflective depths of a murky extension of ourselves. I am interested in being candid and even joyous about human eclectic urges.

Item one: Therefore I am very excited by this country, outstanding in the world for bringing the mouth to the food, where it can have it all, instead of, as in the West, bringing the food, in carefully censored sequence, to the mouth. In English, for instance, if one uses a French word, like *hors d'oeuvres,* it is in embarrassed italics. In the midwestern United States, the use of such a term vacillates between the pompous and the furtive. The French do not go even that far: they translate everything into something that sounds French (however preposterously, like *le weekend* and *le camping*). In Japan, three of the four concurrent alphabets are used for foreign words, or words of foreign origin anyway; and a cheerful simultaneity (almost all shopping bags are in English, God knows why) of all of them is everywhere evident. Neon and tatami can coexist, to the destruction of neither. This, damn it, is the conceptual triumph that may save the world, if there's any air left in it to breathe.

Item two: Though everybody knows about the Japanese genius for making a garden in a space three feet (or one meter or two *shaku*) wide, one forgets. The possibility of helping to save the world by putting our roots into one tiny piece of it becomes, for an American, exhilarating. One sees it every day, in Japan, at the entrance to a bar, or in a house, or in the noodle shop at lunch. To cite examples is superfluous, except for maybe the Daitoku-ji, which must be the richest and most exciting assemblage of tiny and medium-sized gardens in the world.

Item three: The way a merchant's house (maybe because it was bound by the sumptuary laws of the Tokugawa shogunate, maybe just because truth will find a way) starts from the ordinary and brings it to the sublime in a kind of Olympian version of cooking scrambled eggs: they lie there all gooey and inert and hopeless until their magic metamorphosis into fluff, if you are lucky. The difference is that the merchant's house starts with the spatial glories of a high, beam-crossed smoky space, breathtaking in itself, against which (or on which, or with which) comes the intimate elegance of tatami-floored private rooms. At the Yoshijima house in Takayama the tatami rooms have the further excitement of a gradual progression to an upper level. Those rooms, by themselves, are worth a trip halfway around the world.

Item four: The voluptuous. Two decades ago, when I was in Japan young and purposeful, I would not go to naughty Nikko. This time I wallowed in it. Maybe it is the trees that save it. Like the buildings, they grow lush and complex without seeming at all absurd. I do not share Ralph Adams Cram's worry about whether the shrines are architecture or just decoration. Are the trees structure or just branches and leaves? And who cares? Somebody obviously did care about the building: therefore, I can too. It is not the manner of caring that puts me off; it is the absence of care (as in the endless outskirts of Nagoya, or anyplace else) that freezes me—and, I think, everyone else too—out.

Then, beyond all else, come the magic places, not all that numerous on our planet, where we look into the dark reflecting surface and see (I have to suppose) more than ourselves and are in the presence of something way beyond all that. God lives. At the Saiho-ji.

Scully's Revenge

Review of *The Shingle Style Today, or The Historian's Revenge,* by Vincent Scully

Everything Vincent Scully writes delights some people and infuriates others. *The Shingle Style Today* will be no exception, except perhaps that some Scully fans will have their enthusiasm diminished by the rather special limits of the subject. I for one am delighted with it (not, as some naysayers will instantly presume, just because I am mentioned). For decades, almost uniquely, Vincent Scully has been making the history of contemporary architecture interesting. This book furthers that grand tradition. Rather than a book, really, with all the angst and spread that implies, this is a published lecture. A lecture, by its nature, does not cover the whole world; it is just a single facet, ingeniously polished, and not the whole damn Kohinoor.

The facet is the set of visual images that architects bring to their work, when that set includes American Shingle Style houses of the late nineteenth century. (The medium of description is pictures, and their comparison, along with some beautiful Scully prose describing how the place feels and seems. My favorite sentence says: "Inside, as we have seen, the variety was like that of a nineteenth-century landscape painting, where grades of light—partly in full flood, partly shielded by porches; sometimes golden, sometimes thunderous—defined flickering interior landscapes at various levels, broader and more extensive through wide doors and echoing porches." That's more wonderful than any of the houses, even mine.)

The inspiration for this book is a book about poets called *The Anxiety of Influence* by Harold Bloom of the Yale faculty. Bloom develops a theory of poetry around the observed tendency of the strong young poet to go after the work of his most admired predecessor, then at the very last minute, in a thrilling adult version of chicken, to swerve, so that if he is successful, the mark seems to have moved and the young poet to have hit it, leaving his predecessor peripheral to the new center, in a kind of poetic left field. Scully applies a parallel pattern to a group of architects in their 30s and 40s, most of us connected with Louis Kahn, or Yale, or both (though a few of us insist on the importance of Princeton in all this), who have acknowledged influence from the Shingle Style (which is of course another Galatea to Scully's

Originally published in *Progressive Architecture* 56, no. 4 (April 1975), pp. 112, 114.

Pygmalion; I'll leave it to Peter Eisenman to cast it in terms of Dr. Vince Frankenstein and his architectural monsters—I feel no bolt in my throat).

The problem, of course, is that architects are, as Scully suggests in his foreword, receiving influences not only from admired predecessors, but also from clients, colleagues, and the bank. I wince at invoking another Yalie, but there is the great Cole Porter line. When he was asked what inspired his latest musical he replied, "A phone call from the producer." The trouble is that people who try to make a full statistical analysis of the sources of inspiration often make it seem all very dreary. Scully may be wrong about sources of inspiration. I don't think he is. I acknowledge that his story is incomplete (one facet on the giant gem), but I certainly found it interesting.

There is somewhere along here, too, a milestone that shouldn't go unnoticed. For an incredibly long time it was regarded as damaging, or at least tasteless, for architects to acknowledge influence closer than Cro-Magnon Man. Then when a few went public with their admissions, there was some suspicion of a sinister attempt to mislead. Now (and it must make a historian feel really good) influence, like sex, can be openly discussed. It didn't even need a Supreme Court decision, but I count on it doing wonders to open the minds of young architects. Vincent Scully, having been instrumental in setting up the milestone, signs the book (I think) by showing up behind us about three-quarters of the way through with a story about Frank Lloyd Wright: "'Son', Wright once said to me in response to a perhaps rather naïve question of mine about Bruce Price, 'Architecture began when I began building those houses out there on the Prairie.' Authentic old American tall talk and corn. How we miss it." Thank God, Vince, we're not missing it yet.

Review of *Selected Drawings: H. H. Richardson and His Office*, by James F. O'Gorman

This altogether fascinating catalog by James F. O'Gorman of selected drawings from the Henry Hobson Richardson exhibition is as revealing a document about the modern practice of architecture as I have ever seen. It commands one's attention, to begin with, because some of the drawings are so simply, hauntingly beautiful (1b of Trinity Church for example, or 19b and 19i of the Marshall Field Wholesale Store, even hard-line drawings like 8b of the Hay house) and it rivets one's attention for its continuing revelation of the power of economy.

Economy of effort is not a quality I had ever thought to associate with such an apparent biterminal candle-burner as H. H. Richardson. Mrs. Van Rensselaer's biography concentrates on his expansive charm; Professor Hitchcock's concentrates on establishing him as a "modern" architect, which seems to me a dubious proposition to begin with, and especially worrisome when so many of the tenets of "modern" architecture are fading, and Richardson's reputation remains secure. But this catalog makes a vivid case for the efficacy of concentrating and conserving one's professional energies, so as to create (in this instance, anyway) a powerful architecture in direct response to the limits on that energy.

It is astonishing to realize that all that profoundly important work came out of just eight years in the Brookline atelier, with Richardson frequently ill and, apparently, aware of how short a time remained to him. The parallel is striking with Michelangelo, for instance, who reached the acme of his architectural career when he was seventy-one, so could have similarly divined that time was short. Both men made powerful simple drawings and lavished their attention on the building itself with an altogether different budgeting of energy from, say, Paul Rudolph, endowed with extraordinary stamina, an early start, and the expectation of a long career, who can afford to lavish his attention on dazzlingly complex drawings. I kept hearing, as I read O'Gorman's pages, the voice of Jean Labatut teaching at Princeton, continually urging "za maximum effect wiz ze minimum of means," and I wonder if that problem—of parlaying a limited amount of energy into a large and influential oeuvre—isn't really the central problem of the professional practitioner.

Originally published in *Journal of the Society of Architectural Historians* 34, no. 4 (December 1975), pp. 323–324.

The catalog sets out quoting Sir John Summerson's persuasion that "an architectural historian should, from time to time, look over the shoulders and under the feet of the conventionally accepted heroes and try to see what went on around them and on what they stood." This text, aided by those wonderful drawings, does that, illuminated by the surprisingly rare perception that "no building above the level of a hut was the product of one man, alone and unaided. The architect cannot function in isolation. He works at the center of a host of interrelated personalities." The conservation of energy, however, which this book (it seems to me) is about has to start from a person, and the wonder is how a set of tiny Richardson sketches (tiny? Richardson?), often done in a sickbed, had the power to summon from his associates contract drawings which produced, with Richardson's "constant criticism" and "final oversight" (Van Rensselaer's phrases), the "massive and simple" buildings that have provided the image for a whole age. The medium itself provides a clue: the drawings were developed in pencil, the firm (for the moment) decisions overlaid in a decisive thick pen line. The very technique banished the likelihood that the finicky crocketed silhouettes of some of Mr. Richardson's older contemporaries would appear; it also militated against the possibility that the sharp-edged lithic curves which give so much power to the work of Frank Furness would be a part of the Richardson idiom.

But I confess I still don't see how he did it, even though the drawings show such a careful conservation of the designer's energy, and such clear concentration on the massive and simple. The number of buildings, from Boston to Chicago and beyond, that had to be traveled to (by train) and fought over and charmed into being (even though his charm was the wonder of his contemporaries) by one sick man during those eight remarkable Brookline years is truly staggering, even given the extraordinarily highly controlled discipline of this design process, and the generous grandeur of the impression he gave. Hitchcock, looking forty years ago at why Richardson's presence was so commanding—and so enduring—called him modern. It seems to me more helpful, forty years later, to think of him rather as the quintessential full-time architectural *professional,* the undisputed leader of a complicated team that accomplishes things (the building of buildings of lasting power) with a beautiful economy of effort and a knowledge of how to be effective, driven by ambition, to be sure, but led on by a vision of how things have to be.

Review of *John Soane, the Making of an Architect,* by Pierre de la Ruffinière du Prey

The architect in all of history that I (and I think quite a few others, these days) feel the closest affinity to, and the most excitement about, is Sir John Soane. Soane lived his long life in London and bequeathed to England in the year of his death (which was the year of Victoria's accession to the throne) his house, which was his museum. The Soane Museum, at 13 Lincoln's Inn Fields, is, as they say, a magpie's nest, laden with the detritus of a messed-up life, an incredibly fruitful and fascinating career, and one of the most driven and unstoppable collector's instincts of all time.

Soane came from what is for us a particularly fascinating time, at the turn of the nineteenth century, when the Western world, at the height of the industrial revolution, was turning at once forward and back; artists and architects were (very sensibly, it now seems) turning directly to the classical past for inspiration, for sources to be transformed, not just reused, to meet the challenges of a world in the throes of change. Soane's younger contemporary Karl Friedrich Schinkel was doing it in Berlin, with staggering energy and skill and verve. And his older contemporary in America, Thomas Jefferson, was advocating the architecture of the Greek and Roman republics as the only model suitable for the experiment in political democracy for which he was also the chief architect.

And here we are, in the midst of another dizzying advance, our powers vastly extended in an electronic revolution, trying to place ourselves. We are, to boot, the immediate inheritors of the modern movement in architecture, which seems to have thrown the historical baby out with the admittedly murky bathwater. So it is no wonder that the generations of Schinkel, Soane, and Jefferson make fascinating models for us: They latched onto the past to get their bearings in the present, and the courage to plunge into the quickly changing future; and they seem, whatever their other problems, to have found a dazzling amount of joy in it.

Especially Soane. His works are eccentric, odd, crazy—though right on target, and often beautiful and moving. He wreaks transformation on classical themes that nobody else has gotten away with before or since. But it is very hard to find out much about him. Dorothy Stroud's picture book

Originally published in *House and Garden* 155, no. 3 (March 1983), pp. 38, 40.

John Soane is straightforward, extensive, and almost impossible to find. There is a catalog from the Soane Museum, much more readily available. And there is an evocative piece about the Soane Museum in Robert Harbison's *Eccentric Spaces* (New York: Knopf, 1977). But Sir John Summerson, who is the curator of the Soane Museum and maybe the most lucid, interesting, and influential writer about architecture in our time, has never turned his attention directly toward Soane. The announcement, then, of a new book, *John Soane, the Making of an Architect,* was for many of us a major event. Written by Pierre de la Ruffinière du Prey, who got his Ph.D. at Princeton, it promised sound scholarship and, of course, a fascinating subject. It has both of those, maddeningly mismatched, as though the definitive biography of Groucho Marx had been written by St. Ignatius Loyola. The wondrous thing, I believe, about John Soane's work (much of which has been destroyed, so the printed page has become the important testimony) is its *wit,* its astringent (but never abrasive), lunatic, inventive, surprising, amazing delight in summoning up in hard, clear lines a misty and romantic past. It's real Zen-archer stuff, where a deft incision into a smooth plaster surface seems to reveal a whole rich world beyond. Or it's a fairy tale, aided with mirrors (nobody else has ever used mirrors with such skill) that open up dazzling but altogether implausible dimensions, through the looking glass or out the back of the wardrobe.

M. de la Ruffinière du Prey, on the other hand, is a scholar, painstaking, thorough, indefatigable. I would trust him just about always to be correct, and always to be precise about it. And his method, his device for being original is indeed ingenious and admirable: He came upon Soane's notebooks, ledgers really, hopelessly uninteresting for most of us, full of small bills paid to bricklayers, and similar heady stuff, and he reconstructed from them and from other more inaccessible sources that must have required prodigies of detectival scholarship a detailed account of Soane's career up to 1785, when he hired his first employee, thereby becoming "established" and swimming out of the focus of this book.

I was grateful, as I read the book, that M. de la Ruffinière du Prey had gone to all that hard work, and had discovered so much. But I was increasingly offended at what came at length to seem a prissily judgmental point of view, snobbish about Soane's lower-middle-class origins, downright nasty about his techniques for getting work, haughtily disapproving of "the specter of copied drawings." Our author seems caught in the grip of the twentieth-century fetish demanding endless originality; and devoid of the understanding that architects copy, and copy carefully for a long time, before they are ready to transform their models into marginally original worlds; Soane's subsequent originality would seem to justify a lot of copying. The author sports an unseemly phobia about guides and models and influences; even the guidebooks used by Soane and his confreres on the Grand Tour in Italy are seen as instruments of the devil. "Snide," I have written in the margin on page 171; "nasty," I have written often. "It is easy," it says on page 318, "to judge Soane harshly." Apparently. But at the expense of missing the point. On the penultimate page of the text, finally, the author writes: "In the final analysis, Soane's early career discloses the basic 'modernity of the 18th century'." Hooray. But wait: it goes on: "His career touches upon the foundation of our architectural profession with its uniform qualifications and standardized fees." No, no, no, M. de la Ruffinière du Prey, that's not the point.

But buy it; it is a book with exciting pictures and miracles of scholarship. And it's beautiful. Remember that before you fling it at the wall.

"Creating of Place" leads this next set of pieces Moore wrote while leading a post-professional graduate program at the University of Texas at Austin, where he founded Moore/Andersson Architects with Arthur Andersson. Two pieces also deal with Moore's own work to create places: the Hood Museum of Art at Dartmouth College (with Centerbrook) and the Piazza d'Italia in New Orleans (with Urban Innovations Group). Soon after it was built, the Piazza d'Italia became an icon of the postmodernist debate, which Moore addresses in a small piece for Don Canty. These are followed by two interviews, with Drexel Turner and Leon Luxemburg, respectively, in which Moore discusses sources and influences. Finally, "The Qualities of Quality" was presented at a University of Texas conference "Ah Mediterranean! Twentieth Century Classicism in America." Moore introduced the conference with:

> *Legitimate questions about classical architecture include: "is it good?" and "is it real?" Goodness is sometimes ascribed to structural clarity. Early in this century, classical architecture scored high on structure: the very bulge of the Doric column was seen as the almost perfect echo of the human musculature that responds to uprightness and support. After midcentury, though, the models changed and classical architecture was thought to be structurally less direct than simpler stuff, though I, for one, was never quite clear exactly why Mies's habit of gluing H-sections of metal onto facades in order to replicate the pieces found in the concrete behind was especially straightforward.*
>
> *Anyway, fashions in criticism change, too, and in the past decades structural clarity has taken a back seat to linguistic clarity. Again, the classical language scores high, for some, as the most highly developed, best articulated set of architectural systems that there is—familiar enough to be widely accessible. For others, though, the remoteness of the classical sources ("not of our own time") and their suitability to the likes of Solon and Cicero render the idiom suspect and irrelevant, and certainly not real.*
>
> *We find solace, as we seek to sort this all out, in "integrity," though that is an uncomfortable judgmental word with precisely puritanical overtones, or, better, in Marin Filler's "decorum," with its intentions of doing the right thing gracefully. So far, the only sure bets are the plants of the garden, which can confirm linguistic redress—full of memories and associations, even classical ones—with realness (how could a living thing not be real?). Now, if we could only get our architecture to do that.*

This article started as a discourse about our times and their relation to Le Corbusier, and ended as a discourse about our times, with Le Corbusier making occasional appearances as prophet and scapegoat. It is a measure, certainly, of his greatness that even in this unsympathetic bit part he functions so importantly. We start not with him but with ourselves, and we can start by looking for a framework (not the only available framework, not the inner truth that shows everything else to be false)—specifically a framework for looking at what the problems are, what has been done and what might be done in ways that dislodge some of our standard assumptions and leave us freer to try to figure out what to do with the environment that we have taken on the responsibility for doing something about. In order to try to throw out our standard notions about shape and the making of it and about space and its importance, I have employed the perhaps vaguer notion of *place,* the ordering of the whole environment that members of a civilization stand in the middle of, the making of sense, the projection of the image of the civilization onto the environment. This projection can be manipulated by the architect in ways spatial and formal, but it has as its purpose not simply the making of shapes or of spaces but the making of a sensible image of a culture, to give people a sense of where they are in it and to make the framework for whatever happens in the civilization.

To place ourselves in Corbusier's time we can note his Swiss dormitory of some thirty years ago, showing that it seemed important then to explore an interest in the orderly and expressive shape of things. Here, the building relates to itself, to its immediate landscape, to the sky and trees and the ground and the park and the orderliness of its structure in ways that had seemed very important in the years after 1922 when Corbu made his first manifestoes. The building is related in ways which seem a little tarnished, now that almost every city across the United States is half torn down in mid-apocalypse, awaiting urban renewal in the image of Le Corbusier's 1922 vision of skyscrapers in a park, but with the skyscrapers dinkier than in his vision because there's not really enough density in a mid-American city to support the big skyscrapers. And the park in his vision is now replaced by automobiles because there are a lot more of those now than there were in

Previously unpublished; written 1984.

118
Spanish Town,
Jamaica

1922. So the pamphleteer's diagram is turned into a real estate developer's
dream of divide and prosper.

We stand two generations later. We have watched Corbu's glorious vision of a city, of skyscrapers in a park, turn into the mediocrity of much urban renewal. We have watched Frank Lloyd Wright's vision of a noncity, of
a Broadacre City of a decade later, turn into the nightmare of uncontrolled
suburban development. Each of these flourishes quite without the meaning
with which Wright and Corbu had invested their dreams, but carries forward in time the same system or nonsystem. Before any of them or any of
us, there was a much more durable demonstration of a hierarchy of importances; it shows up, for instance, in Spanish Town, Jamaica, which was the
British capital of that island—not, one gathers, the seat of a really admirable
civilization by our own standards, but nonetheless a clear demonstration of
a hierarchy of importances in simple buildings that come to a clear
culmination.

The houses of the wealthy, aligned on the gridiron plan, make no assertions except clear, simple, formal, Georgian assertions, and the climactic
ones (fig. 118). In the midst of this simple system, at the heart of it, comes
a square park, in the middle of four buildings whose similarities are by no
means formal but which with more whimsey than strain manage to indicate in
the same formal terms as the houses around the corner that this is the center of
the scene, the top of the hierarchy, that each of these is not just a building in

itself, unrelated, as Corbu's Swiss dormitory was unrelated to the university city or to Paris, but related to the whole cultural environment, the place.

Across from a building with two kinds of porches is a building very different, but asserting itself in the same way. The Governor's Palace (only its facade is left) was the most palatial building in the Indies, it was said; on the third side, a little bit later, a building of more local importance, a courthouse, was built with a small brick pavilion squashed into a long simple facade (figs. 119, 120). Along the fourth side of the square, it was considerably

119
Spanish Town,
Jamaica

120
Spanish Town,
Jamaica

more gala. A hero of a battle against the eternal Spaniards, divested of his Admiral's clothes to don a marble toga, is memorialized in a pavilion flanked by some useful office blocks with a park behind a hemicycle.

These four government structures are important not as four separate buildings isolatable from one another, but as part of a hierarchy of events based on the central square, which by now has some high palm trees growing up in it. They are nice, careful, Georgian buildings, but in addition to that, they combine (without ever having had to worry about combining) into a clear center for this town, dependent not on enormous density of population or activity, but just on people's understanding of what this place was in relation to the whole Jamaican subcivilization.

The same understanding did not illuminate the twentieth-century planners of Philadelphia when they, having interested themselves in buildings which predated 1830, found these buildings enmeshed in the fabric of the city, a much more complicated fabric than the one in Spanish Town. It seemed to them that these were separate objects like Corbu's Swiss dormitory and that they had to tear down all the Victorian buildings around so that the little red buildings that were once discovered down alleys could be seen from afar and separately, like giant ashtrays, whose only proper neighbors are much more giant twentieth-century glass ashtrays. The absence of any sense of a hierarchical system (I've been calling it sense of place) which in some way relates things that have been to things that are going to be is more than evident here.

There exist some old-fashioned but still perfectly useful devices for manipulating a sense of place. First comes the provision of boundary, distinguishing *inside* from *outside,* from the Chinese Wall to much gentler things. A fountain in Coimbra, in the north of Portugal, shows the distinguishing of an inside from an outside in subtle but powerful ways, including stairs down into a sunken walkway which leads between pools of water to stairs back up into a raised island where a fountain plays. That island is already remote from everything including a street immediately adjacent, but from it the opportunity exists to go across bridges one further remove to tiny chapels. Here the breaking away of inside from outside without actually going indoors until the chapel is reached is accomplished with great subtlety and skill. Place is manipulable as well around axial or spinal organizers that relate a group of structures either because they are in a straight line, like the buildings on an axis in Peking, or because they are on an identifiable spine, related to one another as at the Villa d'Este.

This country is similarly full of axes: even two-lane highways and certainly the enormous freeways which have superseded them serve more clearly than most buildings to structure the landscape.

The manipulation of the vertical direction can increase the sense of place in the same way that the boundaries and the axis do. At Monte Albán, thousands of feet above the valley of Oaxaca, the horizontal plane serves as the basis for manipulation through the priestly act of ascending the stairs onto a platform from which one goes down again to an intermediate place from which the ascension begins to a more important place. This set of movements is evident everywhere, from the seats on the ballcourt to the forecourts of the set of now vanished temple pavilions.

We seek with all these devices to make places. I take it that one of the things about a place is that it is distinguishable from other places because of the specific circumstances that created it, so that when you are somewhere you are not somewhere else, and so that the particular characteristics of a spot on the earth's surface are in some way understood and responded to in making a place, which in its ordering of the environment is a function of the civilization which created it.

In the late twentieth century we get into all kinds of problems because the people who once made one place different from another place, who were citizens of cities they would have died for, these citizens who once were special, city by city, now are interchangeable. Each of us moves on an average once every five years to somewhere else we're expected to be citizens of as interestedly and effectively as we were in the previous location. In this movement of people, just about the only thing that remains specific to places on the face of the earth is the land: the structures of the land and its particular characteristics. Barns, better than most other American building types, seem to respond to this structure of the land; they are a size that is commensurate with the size of the hills and trees around and they often rise above the land because of the functional requirements of the barn in ways that keep clear the form of the land, while the structure responding to its own specific requirements responds as well to the terrain that it sits upon, and takes its place with other simple buildings in relation to fields, forests, and the shape of the land. The excitement of the industrial forms of the landscape, like the clarity of the natural forms, has become as important to our vision of what shape to make things as the architectural forms of a previous generation. The excitement of the things that are doing what they are made to do, however complicated that gets to be, the exciting changes between big and small, the changes in scale that make some specific human-sized things happen against a great industrial requirement, can pull us up short as we relate ourselves to them. The pleasantly mechanistic clarity of the workings of a set of related forms like this is probably well out of date; architects perhaps are doomed to be out of date in a world where the really forward-looking achievements are not available to the eye but are rather subatomic or superterrestrial. Nonetheless, within the simple limits of delivering hot air to rooms or electricity to plugs, the same excitement attached to the industrial forms attaches to our own architectural efforts.

Bernard Maybeck picked up the industrial materials newly available to him, skylights and corrugated siding, to make in the High Sierra (which accounts for the rocks) a set of camp buildings (fig. 121). The simplicity of doing something in the way it is easily done manifests itself too in Guanajuato in the middle of Mexico, where automobile traffic is restricted naturally to the bottom of the town's valley where cars can maneuver, though they maneuver at the scale of little plazas and very narrow streets, not at the scale of superhighways. Up the steep slopes where the cars cannot go, another system takes over of pedestrian streets and stairs. The citizens of

121
Maybeck camp
buildings

Guanajuato, faced with automobile traffic past the capacity of their single
street, with the expenditure of considerable money and considerable attention to their town have lowered the river that forms the town's valley and put
running cars where the river once ran, under eighteenth-century vaults. The
system doesn't solve a New York-scale problem of parking and handling of
the automobile, but with the very carefully understood limits of a small and
tight-packed eighteenth-century town, it maintains at once the excitement
of travel of the twentieth century and the fabric, the density and structure
of this pedestrian-scaled town.

The concerns that animated the citizens of Guanajuato I don't think
have so clearly moved the more numerous citizens of Pittsburgh, Pennsylvania, on one of the great American sites where two rivers come together
under enormous hills which allow a prospect of the whole (fig. 122). The
downtown of Pittsburgh is as imageable as San Francisco or Quebec. It is a
place where the water and the hills provide the open space, and the chance
to pack in between really tightly functioning and excitingly dramatic urban
scenes is a splendid one. What happened, of course, in the lee of Corbu's
manifestoes of 1922 was that the planners supposed that what they needed
for the city was a park, and what they needed to have under the freeways was
a monument to the past which turned out to be Fort Pitt, so the excitement
of the place where the land meets the water is out beyond the limits of hu-

122
Pittsburgh

man exploration, and the chances to make clear the fabric of the city and the nature of this place are missed.

Only rarely in our society does a single building function beyond its own outlines to make some sense of the larger environment, to create a place. Two that do sweep the rest of the environment into their framework are Corbu's Carpenter Center and the Santa Barbara County Courthouse in California. The Santa Barbara County Courthouse serves not as a tight-closed neo-Spanish fortress but as a forecourt for the great mountains behind and for the whole Hollywood-based notion of sunny southern California's Spanish past. It was built in 1929 and I think it owes more to the jazz rhythms of Chicago of that year than to anything historically Spanish. The syncopated holes in the wall are extraordinary. Fragments and almost surreal pieces of half-imagined other civilizations emerge one by one so as to make the building as a total object almost vanish, though the relationships are still strong enough to allow great jumps of scale, from big arcades to little windows and tiny details, endlessly to stimulate reactions. But then, under the great tower that centralizes the whole, it develops that the main entrance goes not into the building but through it, to the mountains. Immediately beyond the entrance, a sunken set of grass panels sweeps the foreground out of the way so that the great hillside with a mission on it is what is there instead of a building. The building manages to reach out and physically to join, as well as to organize, that whole landscape, while from the other side it serves also as a backdrop for whatever mythical early California activities are organized in front of its white walls. (Since California doesn't really have a history, a highly colorful one has been invented for it.) The pictures convey some of the sense of poking holes into the space and the leaping over space, the inclusion of great gulps of space in this not-all-that-solid but still enormous structure.

In the realm of buildings which organize what is around them, the only proper companion to the Santa Barbara County Courthouse is, I think, Corbu's Carpenter Center for the Visual Arts at Harvard. Here on a street between fake Georgian buildings, the Fogg and the Faculty Club, it starts out seeming to agree with them about what a building ought to do in the street, then twists itself so that it sets new sets of things happening and in the process teases, disembodies, pokes fun at, and cheers up these old things on the sides which were pretty dull and stuffy before their new neighbor came along to render them surreal.

If the Santa Barbara Courthouse is a commentary on an invented history of Santa Barbara, this is a commentary on Corbu's invented vision of America (fig. 123). Naturally it includes a freeway, a bit small for cars but great for motorcycles (though driving through is against the rules). From the ramp as it sweeps around and up, the reflections of all the buildings around begin to show in the glass, so that Corbu, who knew that glass is not transparent but reflective, was able to set up a way to reflect all the buildings around when the glass is in the light; when the glass gets back into the dark, they vanish. The glass surface of the building itself now, because it is all at an angle, starts reflecting disassociated fragments of the buildings around; from inside, one looks at pieces of those other buildings only, at single windows or hunks of pediment always at an angle.

123
Carpenter Center for
the Visual Arts,
Harvard University,
Le Corbusier

As in Santa Barbara, the great entrance goes up toward the building only in order to squirt out through the other side, so that one moves through the building, and then the building itself chews out into space while with all the devices of the freeway it becomes a part of the great space that it hangs out over and chews into. Thus it becomes a part of the whole environment, not just an object sitting by itself.

Here with the kind of industrial devices which we glanced at earlier is a building not designed for much programmatic activity, but capable of handling it. Pitting its own devices as in its egg crates of concrete against

Georgian devices of the Fogg and creating at this point a repetitive architectural background for the entrance of the great ramp which slides down and lands by the Fogg, it deals with it and the Faculty Club as it deals with the space around in ways which make space and idea and the shape of the civilization into a part of the same hierarchy of importance. It is an importance that transcends that of Snow White and the Seven Dwarfs, and yet I put Snow White's Disneyland castle behind it, or better Disneyland's Matterhorn on a Swiss cable car, and you can see the bobsleds inside the mountain running downhill in a space like something out of a Piranesi prison drawing, in ways more action-packed than on the real Matterhorn which only has a surface on the outside so that inside there's nothing doing.

This represents only a tiny fragment of what we think of when we think of our civilization, but what I think is curious and important is that this opportunity for people riding through space and walking around to relate to other people in a social context is so seriously necessary that people will spend a great deal of money for it because it is missing otherwise. The kind of hierarchy to which one can be sensible (which we started out by examining in Spanish Town, Jamaica) is pretty clearly not to be found in Los Angeles except within the fake but important confines of a place like Disneyland where the Matterhorn is.

All this has been to say not that the idea of place is one that need supersede any other we've ever had but that to look at what objects in the environment do as places and not what shape they are as objects may be a help in making not only better buildings but a more useful environment on which the buildings find their place, so that they matter again. (It will turn out that Corbu prophesied this, too.)

The crucial issues involved in planning the Hood Museum of Art surfaced before we became its architects. Even in early 1981, when several firms were being considered for the commission, there was great uncertainty about the site of the building. The Hood was meant to be next to the Hopkins Center, working in close connection with it, but no site seemed ideal. In fact, I had been introduced to the problem of siting the Hood the year before. James Stirling, the eminent British architect who was teaching at Yale, had assigned the problem of the Hood to his students. I sat on the jury. It struck me that although many sites were available, there seemed to be no correlation between the site chosen and the excellence of the buildings produced in the student problem. Buildings that were placed on what seemed an eminently logical and correct site often lacked qualities manifest in buildings on less obvious sites.

When Dartmouth selected our firm to design the Hood Museum, my experience as a juror had already persuaded me that there was some virtue in not making a highly organized decision about which site to select. It seemed best to hold a kind of architectural beauty contest, in which we took advantage of our capacity to produce schemes quickly. We decided to design a building for each of the available sites and then discover which found the most favor. The task of selection was vested in a committee of about thirty people, representing many of the groups who were interested in the building. It was guided (with amazing skill and subtlety, I thought) by Leonard Rieser, who was then Provost, and Peter Smith, Director of the Hopkins Center at that time. We set up shop in a room adjacent to the snack bar in the Hopkins Center, at the heart of comings and goings on campus. Our goal was to be, as much as we could, the opposite of mysterious: we wanted to be continuously available. We did this for weeks at a time, working on alternative schemes and welcoming the visits and intervention of anyone who was interested. We established ourselves as willing to talk. This receptivity is at the heart of our beliefs as architects, and it is one of our strengths. We are interested in listening, and in responding to people's images and ideas about the buildings they are to occupy. By now we have become fairly adept at picking up and making use of the things people tell us.

Previously unpublished; written September 1985.

Our procedure began with devising schemes for six sites, which were then considered by the committee of thirty. (They came to be known as the "Gang of Thirty.") We were asked to forget a couple of the sites and to make an alternative to another of them, leaving us with five sites for the next round. We projected buildings for each, describing them with plans and models. People from our office were turning out models at high speed. These were all looked at, reconsidered, rejected or accepted, until finally we were down to three schemes on three different sites.

The proceedings then began to resemble what I imagine a Republican convention might have been like in the 1880s. The museum's face onto the Green had always been an issue of great importance in discussions of the site. We had one site to the right of the theater entrance of Hopkins Center, as you look at it from the Green, and one to the left, between Hopkins and Wilson Hall. The committee had also retained a third possible site, a dark horse indeed, which was down the walk toward the courtyard between Hopkins Center and Brewster Hall, a dormitory to the south. At the time it seemed most likely that the party favoring the building to the right of the Hop (thereafter known as "Tweedle Dum") would find common cause with the party favoring the building to the left (thereafter known as "Tweedle Dee"). Thus a compromise between the best of each might have occurred. No such luck. Again, it was like a political convention: the people in favor of one site could not see any virtue in the other, and vice versa. When the smoke cleared, the site tucked back in the center of the block had surfaced as the only one that made sense. The building was brought up to the Green by a connecting link between Wilson and the Hop, with an entrance and a sign and nestled among all the pieces of a very complicated block (fig. 124). I find it a fascinating choice and am delighted with it. Everyone on the committee seemed to be delighted when we arrived at it. Yet it is a choice that I am sure no one would have thought to leap straight to at the beginning of the design process.

Then we came to the issues of image and style. Now that we had a site, what might this building look like! At Dartmouth, of course, there are a number of historically important styles of building. Perhaps the one that is most powerful in people's minds is the big white "clapboard" colonial, with gable roof, small windows, and green shutters. Several important Dartmouth buildings are in this style. Then there are the buildings of the later nineteenth century—the chapel, for example. At Dartmouth these tend to

be quirky and very special—not pretentious and not staid, but wonderful, almost goofy little buildings that I am particularly fond of. Wilson Hall, which was built in 1885 as the library and president's office, is a particularly delightful example. Dartmouth also has a number of neo-Georgian buildings from the early twentieth century. These are at once traditional and calm, and in some cases (like Baker Library) extremely handsome, grand, and at times even bombastic in their quiet New England reticence. Twenty years ago, the Hopkins Center appeared in this setting. This important American building, one of the two or three masterworks of the architect Wallace K. Harrison, may have been the model for Harrison's Metropolitan Opera House in New York's Lincoln Center.

The Hood Museum, then, was to go between Hopkins Center and Wilson Hall. Now, the Hop is of an age that makes it extremely difficult for the architect. The building is full of heartfelt principles of planning, design, and style of exactly one generation before. It is easy for me to love Wilson. It is just far enough in the past to have romance and wonder, and I find it a charming building. But the Hop has a kind of assertiveness about it, an insistence—with its barrel vaults and modern shapes—that we are now in the midst of reacting against. Even so, it is a building of great conviction and power. To be churlish about its stylistic concerns would certainly be unbecoming. Here is a building not to copy, any more than we would want to copy Wilson, but to try to be a good neighbor to. Indeed, one of the tasks of the Hood is to be a good neighbor—to Hopkins Center, to Wilson, to the other buildings around, to the Green, and to the entire campus. Our task was to mediate between these very different architectural persuasions.

The best solution in this effort of mediating, it seemed to us, was a building that did not have one big overpowering image, but rather a number of images (perhaps smaller in scale, but not necessarily) that one would come upon in the course of wandering toward and through it. The first of these is the gate facing the Green. Next, we were interested in having a big room, something that you could remember when you went back to New York and thought about your visit to the Hood. In that room, we felt there should be some natural light from the top (not falling directly on the paintings, of course), and there should be a way to reach and adjust the lights up high, to make it easy to work with the place. We decided on a skylight with a catwalk running beneath. We also had occasion for flights of stairs to become important things to look at and to remember. In the choice of the site, we acquired a connection with the Hopkins Center snack bar at a part of the campus that we were able to enlarge and reshape, making it one of the festive gateways to the Hood.

Within the museum, we were excited by the prospect of organizing some of the small rooms into an equivalent of the long gallery in stately British homes of the sixteenth and seventeenth centuries. This series of smaller rooms—for works from the permanent collection or for temporary shows—provided a vista down the length of the gallery. Thus the whole would be considerably more than the sum of its parts, but the parts would also be special. Among my favorite museums are the little ones with lots of special places—like the Phillips in Washington. I wanted this museum to be a series of rooms of very different proportions, grandeurs, and characters, where the art would not just appear in some anonymous matrix but have the opportunity to enjoy its own environment.

As for the fabric of the building itself, we were extremely anxious to make it solid, and we chose brick. We would have loved it if some of the building could have been granite, expressive of our location in New Hampshire, but that was unaffordable this late in the twentieth century. We settled for bush-hammered concrete—not quite as everlasting but very close.

For the main section of the building, we liked the idea of a big vertical piece, like a New Hampshire industrial building, given a certain layer of civilization by the copper roof. We were also concerned to introduce some distinguishing feature that would not break up the solidity of that vertical mass surrounded by the less vertical masses. We settled on a cornice band—in gray brick, as it turned out, with a green-painted wooden cornice above. It looks so simple and inevitable, but of all the details on the building, it was the one that received the most attention, concern, and even, at times, the most worry. We needed a material that would be distinctive without being showy. It also had to have permanence, unlike the glazed brick we once thought of using, which in some terrible cases was spalling and destroying itself in climates like that of Hanover. But the expressive possibilities of ornamental brick intrigued us. It is obviously not what you find on every post office building, nor, for that matter, on every academic building. We welcomed the chance to vary its dimensions, to make suggestions about what lies within—suggestions that were not meant to be too specific or to occasion too much wondering. Another fascinating task, also extremely difficult, was coordinating the green of the wooden cornice with the color of the copper roof as it now is and as it will become in time.

The style of the Hood Museum was not intended to be an assertion of a new idiom, as complete and on its own as the Hopkins Center had been in its day, and I would have been very upset if it had tried to be. I would have been equally upset if the new building had tried to ape any of the other persuasions that surround it. By the device of making a few things particularly ours—the cornice and the cupola, for instance—and by the interesting shapes and spaces that are, I hope, attractive to move through and into, we allowed the building to develop its own special character. We were seeking something that supports and mediates between the fascinating buildings that lie around it. With any luck, the Hood will enhance all those other buildings and will make them even more fascinating.

I have some friends in New York who have a name for this kind of style—or nonstyle. They call it "free style," which is an interesting way of considering it. But it also misses, because it suggests that you can just do anything that comes into your head. We like to think that making something that enhances everything around it is not that easy. Maybe it has to do with animating the familiar, with bringing to life a set of things that strike chords of familiarity in us. This may call for shapes that are not exactly like what we are used to, but are close enough to it that we, the inhabitants, can feel as though the building is ours.

We had a party—a little festival—on August 18, 1983, in the Piazza d'Italia
to celebrate issuing a poster for the 1984 World's Fair. It was very hot and
threatened to rain, most of the neon was broken, and most of the jets did
not work, and the mayor did not show up, but there were tables set up with
linen and luminaria and a 400-pound cake, and it seemed a fine party. These
days the Piazza is in a fully Latin state of disrepair, apparently ignored by the
city's maintenance people, but recently I received a heartening report from
a friend who was walking there at 7 A.M. It seems that the benches, as usual
at that hour, were covered with the sleeping figures of the vagrants who constitute the place's only regular inhabitants. Then one of the sleepers awoke
and rang a little bell. Everyone got up, picked up all the trash, and went back
to hanging around.

This is, I choose to think, welcome confirmation that this public space
is not just flexible but special, and able (I think) to support the particular
needs of groups with very different needs. In addition, it is built around a
fountain. Surely, making a fountain is one of the most exciting chances to
make a place. A fountain makes a place by manipulating the most richly
evocative of all locations, where a source of water has the uncanny capacity
to suggest all the water in the world. Fountains, being made of water, have
the capacity (and have had since the beginning of civilization) to suggest life,
and death, and the creators of life and death (fig. 125); but they do not serve
so well as satire or nursery rhymes do to develop political themes, or to reinforce insights into the stock market or the vicissitudes of, say, the Shah of
Iran.

I was surprised, therefore, when an article about the Piazza d'Italia,
published in *Progressive Architecture* with a very supportive critique by Martin Filler, brought an avalanche of mail (architects' avalanches of mail are
of a size that would depress a rock star), much of it criticizing the Piazza
d'Italia for failing to produce adequate political insights. A couple of the cor-
respondents, indeed, blamed us, or me, for the excesses of the Shah of Iran,
on the one hand, and his upcoming demise, on the other. There was, I was
told, more mail about the Piazza d'Italia than about any other project report
published by *Progressive Architecture* during that decade. I was pleased, of
course, and my pride in the project was amplified by the vigor of the re-

Originally published in *Places* 1, no. 2 (Winter 1984), pp. 28–30.

125
Piazza d'Italia, New
Orleans, Urban
Innovations Group

sponses. I had noticed long before that what I regarded as the best works I
was involved in had drawn the heaviest fire; that makes the Piazza our best
effort to date, with the Sea Ranch condominium a close second.

What is for me a much more interesting phenomenon is a shift (which
involves more than just us, and is neither good nor bad) from a high degree
of abstraction in, let us say, Lovejoy Fountain in Portland (1964), to more
literal references at the Piazza, to some veils of abstraction again in the Wonder Wall for the 1984 New Orleans World's Fair. When Lawrence Halprin,
William Turnbull, and I were working on the Lovejoy Plaza, though we all
had images of waterfalls in the high Sierra, we had no doubt that a built object would abstract those images: therefore, a set of 5½-inch steps, readily

formed of concrete behind 2-inch by 6-inch board edges, became our format, with the water itself splashing over the steps providing the family of fluid forms we thought a fountain needed. Ten years later it seemed appropriate, bolder, and stronger for Allen Eskew, Malcolm Heard, Ron Filson, and me to be more straightforward and less abstract at the Piazza: What could be a more Italian shape than Italy? And what more direct, and therefore effective, cultural reference in a piazza dedicated to the Italian community could there be than the architectural orders—Tuscan, Doric, Ionic, Corinthian, and Composite—which the Italian civilization had developed after heavy initial assistance from the Greeks? Making the orders out of water seemed an adequate abstraction to keep us out of the lifeless blind alley of "correct" copying. Now almost ten years later, most of us, plus Bill Turnbull, Leonard Salvato, and Arthur Andersson, are working on the Wonder Wall for the 1984 New Orleans fair, which is only a few blocks from the Piazza, but is, I think, far bolder still, and has far more unbridled architectural fantasies.

In boldness there is almost bound to be a modicum of naughtiness, and I will not deny that I felt a tinge of excitement at having my Vignola out on my desk (the book open to Doric) at U. I. G., the practice arm of the UCLA architecture school, where the work was being done when the school's accreditation team came by. (I had been educated at the right moment to regard the written-down orders as wicked sorts of bootlegged notes standing directly in the path of originality and innovation.) So maybe it *was* naughty (I am sure I hoped so) in 1976 to have those classical orders. I would not have liked, then or now, to have been pretentious or condescending with them: I was relieved a few years ago when a friend reported that he had seen a man with two small children at the Piazza pointing at the fountain carefully explaining the differences between the Tuscan, Doric, Ionic, and other orders. Surely the orders give pleasure to more than just architects, even as someone who is not a musician might enjoy noting the difference between a sonata and a tone poem.

Perhaps it is in the same spirit that I am enjoying the shift (I will not call it progression nor retrogression) from our attitudes toward the givens (nature, the past) in work on the Lovejoy in 1964, to the Piazza after 1974, to the work on the New Orleans fair of 1984. One of my favorite pieces of the 1984 world's fair is a set of seven Centennial Pavilions, gazebos of varying sizes apparently randomly disposed in and around a lagoon—that, from just one spot, snap into place to resemble (with considerable abstraction) the great main pavilion of the 1884 world's fair in New Orleans. It seems an appropriate comment on history to say that you have to choose your point of view very carefully to make any sense of the past.

Our three projects seem to demonstrate an increasing easiness and more casual familiarity in dealing with what is, in fact, in our minds (nature, the past, fantasy), and an increasing freedom from a reliance on abstractions to distance ourselves from a messy reality. How much abstraction is needed? How much is enough? How much is too much? I do not know. Is a lack of abstraction an automatic ethnic slur? I really doubt it.

For Don Canty

The decade 1978–1987, according to the crustier old-line critics of architecture, was the decade that saw postmodernism elbow its way onto the urban scene and promptly die there, leaving a residue of cleaned-up classical reminiscences high atop new buildings otherwise indistinguishable from their modern predecessors. The little cries of triumph from these same critics made it evident that they believed that the postmodern fiasco had brought a new lease on life to their own otherwise moribund modern constituency.

If, however, the central architectural question of our times is whether the Princes of Corporate Power should have Greek temples or more abstracted shapes on top of their ziggurats, then it is perhaps appropriate to characterize the ten years just past as the Decade of Critical Lobotomy. If the statistics don't mislead us, it seems that in 1970 one half of all American families could afford a freestanding family house—the house of the American dream. By now, it is said, the number is under 12 percent and the majority of us are not part of a nuclear family anyhow. So most of us are not going to have the house of our dreams, the government has no housing policy to help, the codes become increasingly restrictive, even substitute dreams are in short supply. Might architecture schools inaugurate programs for critic/poets or critic/dreamers?

The one really heartening architectural arena was also born of despair: for several decades, preservationists had been noticing that when old buildings they were fond of were torn down, they were generally replaced with something they were much less fond of—crassly scaled, drearily undetailed—but, beset by timidity, they often seemed to panic when they had a real chance to save something. Then it all changed and the mild-mannered preservationist stepped out of the telephone booth as Super Saver. Even architects caught on, and now most of us seem comfortable saving old buildings, building around them. We honor them by being congenial with them. But there is little agreement about when congenial ends and domination begins. Our future critic will doubtless remember Gwathmey Siegel at the Guggenheim, Michael Graves at the Whitney, and I. M. Pei at the Louvre, with the brouhaha they set off.

Previously unpublished; written 1987.

Or it may be that our critic, like many already, will breathlessly be asking, "What's new?" and what was new during those years 1978–1987. Well, it seemed new anyway that a few architects were getting rock-star exposure in the magazines. Michael Graves and then Frank Gehry took the honors there, and their influence was enormous. Graves's shapes and colors were everywhere; Gehry's high-energy casualness has been electrifying, though at the hands of some of his California followers it has been reduced to a post-modern minimalism which bears a remote resemblance to the kind of fifties retrofit that seems to be the season's determinant idiom in other parts of the country.

So there's a mixed bag for the critic, who won't be interested in all of it (or perhaps in any of it). It describes architecture for a wealthy country that can't accommodate the dreams of its people, produced by talented designers who are lionized for all the wrong reasons, getting better (and more sophisticated) in its connections with the past as the clients realize that what is put up new is too often inferior to what is taken down. So the critic's view is bleak. Fortunately, though, quite a few of the buildings have been really nifty.

Reflections of a Less Critical Regionalism and Other Burdensome Matters

Interview with Drexel Turner

DREXEL TURNER: Let's begin with the importance, real or imagined, of being regional. You have lived and practiced for extended periods in the Bay Area, Connecticut, Los Angeles, and now Texas. How has this affected your work, or has it?

CHARLES MOORE: I think locale does matter. One of the ways of looking at architecture is to say that there are two kinds of architects. Some are cosmic, like Aldo Rossi, and interested in general ideas, as free from specifics as they can be. Then there are others who are interested in particulars, in the sense of place and places. I've come down very much in favor of the latter. I don't have any particular desire to be cosmic, and I do like very much the notion of making something that fits into the site and with specific people and circumstances. So I'm very proud when somebody says that they can't see any thread of consistency in my work, that it's all special to the place and the arrangement that it's in. And I'm a little embarrassed when people say, "Oh yes, no matter what you do in all those places, it's all the same stuff." I hope that isn't so. It seems to me that obviously it's the same stuff in the sense that I did it and that I now have a set of preferences and prejudices and attitudes. But I like to hope that what I run up against and what I listen to each time is more important to me than the baggage carried from somewhere else.

To follow this point a little farther, I think I learned something from the example of my great-grandfather, who was a farm boy in Michigan. He was self-taught, and yet he kept his farm records in Latin and his personal diaries in Greek until the 1830s. He introduced coeducation at the University of Michigan, the first state university to have it. He introduced the resolution in Latin and since it was in Latin, they thought it must be right. Obviously he wasn't standard, but I think he was an interesting phenomenon, somebody who was of the soil and operating in that part of the world, but who also felt some connection to the classical world and a lot of things that lay way beyond his own experience in space and time. I like to think that that kind of thing is still possible, and I am my great-grandfather's great-

Originally published in *Cite,* Spring 1987, pp. 12, 13, 16.

grandson; that it's still possible to have some hook on literature and history and other things and still be operating in a particular place in the way of that place.

DT: But isn't it more difficult to deal with a place in very particular terms today when so much, perhaps all, of the country seems to be becoming so much alike? Is it possible, without nostalgia, to render such distinctions credibly?

CM: It's probably not possible to do without nostalgia. The thing to do is to get rid of the notion that nostalgia is in some way unworthy of us. It seems to me that if you take some high-minded pleasure in nostalgia and see it as something altogether worthy of building on, then the problem improves some. It isn't necessarily solved, but the prospects are improved. Yet it's true that there is more and more sameness. Like the Howard Johnson song: "Someone you know wherever you go." The world is Howard Johnsoning at a breakneck pace, and our only solution is to die before it gets much worse, or to try to counter it as a romantic with a great deal of nostalgia.

I thought when I came here to Texas that one of my reasons for coming was that Texas is a lot like California was twenty years ago. I think it's less so now, but Texas reminded me of that California I remembered from my childhood and which I inhabited from time to time during my adult life, which started out to be a place where anything goes. . . . That old Noel Coward thing I quoted over and over again in my LA book about a place where what's phony seems real and what's real seems phony. That back-and-forth between fantasy and the real I liked very much, and my sense is that in the last twenty years in California things have become increasingly and overpoweringly and suddenly earnest and bureaucratized and tangled up in themselves, desperate to maintain their qualities. And so the California of my joyous remembrances is not very much like the LA of today, which has got more suicidal regulations than any governmental entity that I know of. And it seemed to me three of four years ago when I was pondering a move to Texas, that Texas still had (and to some extent still has) a looser, more laissez-faire, less tangling sense of itself, and the Texas of 1984 was in that sense more Californian than the California of 1984. So I didn't see myself as giving up something to pick something else.

DT: Lionel Trilling once observed that a twentieth-century public is "likely to be unschooled in the comic tradition and unaware of the comic seriousness," and "our suspicion of gaiety in art perhaps signifies an inadequate seriousness in ourselves." This was written in a piece called "E. M. Forster and the Liberal Imagination," where Trilling noted that Forster "is sometimes irritating in his refusal to be great . . . [that is] . . . greatness with a certain sternness and a touch of the imperial and imperious." He goes on to specify "serious whim" as one of Forster's virtues, as well as "the very relaxation of his style, its colloquial unpretentiousness" and a "worldliness without the sentimentality of cynicism and without the sentimentality of rationalism." Doesn't that describe your work as well?

CM: I like to think that's so. There is a distinction that can be made between low camp, which is just horsing around, and high camp, which requires a certain command of the situation. Mozart, who had his stuff very well under control, would fashion a sonata as an act of play, no matter how dire his circumstances were. Beethoven was a very skilled, non-high-camp person who was struggling through his material as a matter of personality, and he made great stuff too. But I like Mozart better. I find that most people I admire have their act sufficiently together to enjoy it, and the people who feel that suffering and gloom are essential to genuine OK-ness are, by and large, less impressive to me.

DT: This general penchant for seriousness and the suspicion of gaiety seems to surface as well in David Littlejohn's book about you. If you read between the lines, he seems to approve of Sea Ranch and its near relations with an enthusiasm that doesn't extend, in all cases, to the later work, which seems to make him uncomfortable at times. But it is just this later work which strikes others as most challenging and rewarding. How do you account for this?

CM: I think that at Sea Ranch and a few other little houses from the same time we found ourselves particularly interested in the land and local buildings. The idea was about fitting the buildings to the land and being sensitive to the land. What came later didn't represent for me a step backward from the gestures of Sea Ranch but rather trying something new.

Marty Filler wrote a not very positive piece in *Artforum* several years ago where he announced that I had had it. Yet again. His point was that I was always talking about freedom of speech in buildings, about the need for buildings to speak in many voices, presumably the voices put there by their designers. He said I was saying things that were chatty, and were not to the mark or important enough. I found that odd, not because I deny it, but because it appears to me that would be a reasonable expectation from a desire to test the freedom of speech of buildings. One would say things that were of very different sorts and some of them would be considerably less monumental, ringing through the halls of history, than others. I've taken it as a part of my mission, I guess, to deal with things which were not central to the culture. I've known of architects who felt that every building, everything they did, had to be dead on to the main, throbbing pulse of the civilization, which seems to me gives us a national architectural heritage of branch savings and loans as a building type that is determined to be serious beyond its capacity. I don't want to do branch savings and loans. So it seems to be quite proper, as far as my own agenda goes, to do things that seem appropriate to the circumstances attending them. I don't have a very extensive system for getting jobs, so I take the jobs that come to me and some of them have called not for pearls that will ring down through the ages but for making something that was pleasant in the circumstances. Every building does not have to be wildly important.

DT: The tunnel vision of critics is something that Trilling remarks as well when discussing Forster as a critic. Although he finds critics in general concerned, as never before, with the need "to make distinctions and erect barriers, to separate thing from thing and to make salvation depend on the right choice," he finds Forster, as a critic, to be accepting in an almost mystical, non-Western way, and admonishes him for "excessive relaxation." Yet what he goes on to describe seems to suggest the considerable merit of such a course, whether pursued by a critic or artist.

CM: I guess it's a matter of what one wants. I've been in a discussion with Charles Jencks about why Michael Graves is the only important postmodern architect, in which he points out that Michael Graves is the only one who hasn't relaxed some, who made up this thing he was going to do, and the style he was going to work in, and works in it. He has excited people by the things he has done in that very special manner and has gotten more and more, and bigger and bigger work so is succeeding at being what he set out to be, which is the inventor of a style really. It hasn't seemed to me that that was what I particularly wanted to do, I suppose partly because the notion of being on the edge of all that ambition makes me tired to think about and also because one of the things I've wanted to do, and have done with some frequency, is to design buildings with people who are going to *use* them instead of separate from the people who are going to use them. The ways are varied and some work for some groups and not for others.

I had a long talk with the rector of St. Matthew's Church that we designed (or they designed) in LA, and we seemed to notice that in some professions—clergy and architects for two—some things you do are in the nature of working yourself out of a job. Clergy don't save people's souls; they help people to save their own souls. And architects don't move in to inhabit people's buildings; they try to help the inhabitants to inhabit their buildings. But these require a certain self-effacing set of activities. My claim is that they require far bigger egos than the obvious ego trips, and it's also clear that you belong to a different kind of profession that gets itself more and more into the center of things, instead of less and less, like doctors or lawyers; those people get paid increasing amounts of money while the clerics and architects seem to get paid increasingly tinier sums of money. But no matter, it still is more interesting to me to try to get closer to the basic truth of dwelling and inhabitation so as to make that act more and more available to people, rather than inventing and purveying a special, personal view like Frank Lloyd Wright did.

DT: So that architecture might become a cottage industry, more or less?

CM: Yes, I think that's a noble desire to inherit, to become more and more the property of the people who mean to dwell in the buildings. And so from that point of view I've gone in the direction I've meant to. Not by any carefully planned set of moves but by being pushed around where I was pushed. But anyway, that kind of desire to vanish is I think easily hookable to the kind of relaxation that Trilling fusses about in Forster or Marty Filler fussed about in me.

DT: How does that idea apply to the design of public, civic places? Is it more relaxed or less so?

CM: The way I see it is that buildings are solid objects that have to perform a number of quite specific functions efficiently and have to be maintained and have to do all the things that we know buildings do. Public spaces, on the other hand, are something like gardens. They are fantasies. They don't in many cases perform a specific function like most rooms and most buildings, but are meant to be nice places for relaxing and enjoyment. I think it's right to say that public spaces, like gardens, could and should be lighthearted, sybaritic, and, I guess more than I had realized, ephemeral. Certainly they are more difficult to maintain and there is less pressure to maintain them.

We had a visiting Chinese student who was asking me why our Piazza d'Italia in New Orleans was so unloved and uncared for. I was trying to think of the reasons why, and I found myself giving a long speech on how the great value of gardens as a civilized building form is that it doesn't work just to build them. You've got to keep on loving them and taking care of them or they very quickly go to pieces. And we had loved our piazza, but I guess hadn't known how to ensure that there would be continuing love for it. It's our fault that we didn't perceive past what we were enjoying doing ourselves—not *really* our fault, but we can't expect others to pick up on the attention we were giving it at one point. I suppose that's the way it is with all these spaces in Texas that we snarl about. They're gardens and maybe somebody loved them once, but we've left them alone for a long time and some lovers will have to get found if any one of them, from Republic Square to Hermann Park, is going to get turned into anything that people can actually enjoy.

DT: It has been reported that one of your fantasies is to do a tempietto atop a turtle, a sort of Celliniesque maneuver. Is that so?

CM: I do like the notion. There was an ad some time ago in which Noel Coward stood on rocks at the edge of the ocean with the surf rolling around, his tuxedo trousers rolled up a little bit, barefoot, casually clutching a glass of Smirnoff vodka on-the-rocks. The pun was silly but the whole business of extremely cultivated architectural arrangements or lifestyles happening on the edge of chaos and disaster has always appealed to me. Which is why the tempietto on the back of the turtle appeals to me or why I, at one stage, invented a whole set of aerial turtles borne aloft on balloons carrying whole tropical islands and made a thing of flying turtles bringing palm trees to Catalina Island.

DT: In a less threatening way, fantasy seems to be marketable in Texas, from the crescent in Dallas by Philip Johnson to any number of amusement parks. Have you visited any of them here?

CM: I find the Crescent astonishing. I was there once to have breakfast with Robert A. M. Stern. I just can't get over how big it is and I can't figure out whether it was done out of conviction that this was the way to do it or simply out of a desire to get the job done. Maybe somebody was mean to Philip Johnson in Dallas once. The business of putting a piece of Paris, I guess it's Paris, probably at 2.7 times normal scale, is staggering. Strangely enough, I haven't visited any amusement parks in Houston or Dallas. I've been to a whole slew in Los Angeles and have very careful gourmet reports of the differences between Knott's Berry Farm and Magic Mountain and Lion Country Safari (now closed) and all the others. I started my book about LA with a mention of a young fellow who was clerking in his father's curio store in Kashmir and as he took my address in LA his eyes brightened up and he said, "Oh! I spent my honeymoon in Los Angeles, California, and we went to Lion Country Safari."

DT: Bringing it all back home.

CM: Bringing it all back home. And was delighted with that. So I think the worries that architectural critics seem to forever have about places like Lion Country Safari or Six Flags Over Texas are all very interesting. I find the critics dead wrong. I'm especially fascinated by this business that many architectural critics (they mostly seem to be British) have developed; a passionate fear of kitsch, as though if one were guilty of liking or causing any to be built, or having any, or inhabiting any, that somehow one is rendered unclean. That it's kind of like getting herpes, and you want to hold yourself clean.

DT: Recognizing that one culture's kitsch may be another's art?

CM: Well, I don't see how they can tell. It seems to me that the things that I'm interested in—ways of getting at peoples' desires to dwell in places, and, therefore, their connections with them—are going to land me sometimes in kitsch. It is the twentieth century after all; they are not hearty peasants, running around close to the ground, that we're trying to make houses or buildings for. They're sophisticated people in a complicated environment where kitsch is everywhere. I don't see any point in wasting my energy trying to steer clear of it.

DT: Fear of kitsch at the expense of memory and delight. Just as Robert Stern has been raked over the coals for lingering in places like San Simeon, or going there at all.

CM: It would all be so much better if everyone would relax a little. We don't even have to learn to love kitschy things; we just have to get over the stark and debilitating fear of being tainted by the ordinary.

DT: The design of public spaces today seems beset by an evasion of what Forster posed in *Howard's Way* as the need to connect, whatever the risk. The Piazza d'Italia makes such a connection and so does Western Plaza in Washington, D.C., although neither has been well repaid for its effort. So, too, might the premise of a truncated freeway interchange downsized for Pershing Square—a sort of belated Fine Arts Square trope as skateboard heaven—or your colossal steers for Sesquicentennial Park in Houston. Perhaps if we considered monuments initially to be somewhat disposable commodities available for later stabilization where warranted, like Maybeck's Palace of Fine Arts, the results might be more worth keeping?

CM: Exactly. Or at least the process of designing them wouldn't be so painful. I got a particular thrill out of designing the Wonderwall at the 1984 New Orleans fair, built for six months. When people asked, "But will it last?" I was able to say, "No." Temporariness removes a heavy burden.

Interview with Leon Luxemburg

LEO LUXEMBURG: Could you give us some background about how you became interested in architecture?

CHARLES MOORE: I think I was always interested. I had a grandfather whom I adored who was a newspaper publisher, so I thought I wanted to be a newspaper publisher. Later, I realized that I really wanted to become an architect. Not long ago I found a notebook full of designs that I had done when I was, I think, thirteen. So I went to Michigan as an architecture undergraduate when I was sixteen and I kept on being interested. Most of the teaching that I have done has been in schools like Yale and UCLA where students come after they already have a bachelor's degree and subsequently decide they want to be architects. That is the route I have observed, and most of the architects I know came late to it, but I didn't. I think the turning point for me was when I was thirteen and my family built a room onto the old house for me. I don't think the young man who came to plan it was an architect, I think he was a building designer, but the whole presence of blueprints and renderings for my room was, I thought, the most exciting thing I had ever seen. I guess that is when I got hooked.

LL: You designed a great many houses throughout your career. Is there any reason for that?

CM: I suppose the real reason is that those are the jobs that came, architecture being an art of the possible. I went to San Francisco when I first got out of school to work for architects who did houses. After that, I was teaching and working at the same time, and the jobs that came were almost all houses until some years ago when bigger projects started coming, and then the houses vanished for a while. Nobody wanted houses, and I missed them. Lately, I seem to be back doing a number of houses, some of them very expensive and some them still cheap. Of course, I don't make any money doing them, but I still like doing them partly because they happen while I still remember what it is all about. The bigger buildings take at least a decade, sometimes two, to happen in many cases. The houses are going up in six or eight months, and in another year they are finished. Houses too have more immediate involvement. I have found that buildings I feel the closest to are

Previously unpublished; interview conducted 1991.

ones where I have really been in on the whole thing. Those are usually houses or small buildings, and I have found myself less intimately involved with projects where other people make decisions that I might not even have found out about. It is egocentricity, but that sort of thing bugs me.

LL: What was your first project of which you were really proud?

CM: I think probably the first things I was really proud of were some little houses in San Francisco, shops, and a cabin in Palo Colorado Canyon, and a cabin in Boulder Creek near Santa Cruz. They were all tiny houses with the most expensive costing $12,000 and the cheapest coming in at $7,000. They finally represented something that was my own and wasn't a direct derivative from somebody or something else. Not that they are original. They are full of things I already had seen, but I felt in some control of the material and geometry as I had not felt before. That was when I was thirty-six, I guess. Before that I had done many things I was excited about, but they were still student work.

LL: Could you tell us what you think about the idea of surprise in architecture?

CM: I think it certainly is important. I am fond of saying that architecture ought to be looked at as choreography of the familiar and the surprising. As I get older I pay more attention to the familiar, which I think is a natural result of growing older. It is like cooking: if it is totally unfamiliar, people won't be able to relate to it and probably won't like it; if it is altogether familiar, you hardly notice it because it is dreary. So what you need is some combination of the familiar and the surprising. With the surprise to make you aware of what is already there. If the surprise is just shot or worn out it doesn't do much. If the surprise is what gets you involved, piques your interest to be excited about the familiar, then that idea becomes a very important piece of work.

LL: How do you feel about the controversy concerning your work in the Piazza d'Italia in New Orleans?

CM: I guess I like it when something that I think is a particularly good work draws angry letters to the magazines and stirs violent controversy. The Sea Ranch Condominiums, when we did them over twenty-five years ago, promoted violent letters from people who would drive along the road and see them, and then stop to write saying how awful they were, and how insulting to their intelligence. I figured it must be pretty good if I upset them that much. When the Piazza d'Italia came along and we got really noisy letters saying how awful it was, I figured that must be pretty good too. So I think the way to deal with controversy is to be glad that we have gotten some people to the point where they are screaming.

LL: Your architecture seems to display a fun image through forms and coloration and material use. Is this style a reflection of you or a philosophy of your architecture today?

CM: I don't think I know the answer. Architecture would have to be either profitable or enjoyable to have anybody do it. Since I have not been able to figure out how to make it profitable, I am happy to settle for having it enjoyable. I don't understand why some architects seem to think it is sinful to enjoy the work, and that it has to be in some way self-inflicted punishment. I used to have students at Yale quit and go to Harvard because it was too pleasurable, and they wanted to suffer some. At Harvard they were good at whipping them. I just don't get it. I think architecture ought to be a pleasure for the people who do it and the people who inhabit it. That to me is a very good reason for doing it. I guess that makes it a theoretical stance, but I don't think it just comes from me trying to show off my own personality, because I don't have one. I don't think I could bear to do things that were not a pleasure just for the sake of having them be disciplined.

LL: Do you feel this is why your work has gained so much attention?

CM: I think so, because in the last several decades it has changed greatly. For several decades it was presumed that architecture was fairly dreary, and I never could see the point of that. Of course it made people angry, controversial is the word, about things that were not conventional. I figured out that if most architects had their way the whole world would look like a series of branch savings and loans, and I would hate to see the quintessence of importance used for dreariness.

LL: What are your feelings on public education on architecture in the United States today?

CM: Do you mean of people who are going to be architects or of the public in general?

LL: The public in general.

CM: Well, there isn't much and it's pretty sparse. One of the great advantages of most modern architecture, which everybody seems to find uninspiring, is that the weekly news magazines like *Time* and *Newsweek* run buildings in color, so buildings are in a sense news, which they hadn't been for years and years. For most of this end of the twentieth century, buildings have just not been interesting enough to cause people to think of them as new, or to cause the public to want to find out about them. So I think that we should be making the buildings more interesting in the first place and involving the public in the design. One of the unfortunate things through history, but which only shows up as a real problem in our own time, is that architecture is seen as some mysterious thing that architects do. Doctors have gotten away from that, but lawyers are making their field so arcane and impenetrable that we just give up on being involved in it at all. Especially in the case of doctors, it is when one's own life is at stake that there is lots of interest. Architecture has seemed to most people, for most of our time, to be something other people do for God knows what reason.

LL: How do you think you can improve this?

CM: I think one thing that will make architecture more interesting is to be more open and work with people, and have them involved in the design of buildings. There is a real job to do making magazine and TV series and textbooks for the schools that will make architecture an interesting thing for people. Maybe it is because there have been so few people interested in teaching it to the public. There seems to be a general lack of confidence; for instance some teachers are at home with works of art, paintings and sculptures, but architecture is beyond them. So, anyway, I think we need to do things. This includes most of you; architects getting out into the world and volunteering some teaching to elementary schools and high schools.

LL: That's very interesting, but do you think that the direction that influential architects are leading the public is appropriate?

CM: No, I think there is altogether too much concern with the latest in constructivism, which I can't figure out the usefulness of, and I'm sure that the public in general must be severely brainwashed and can't figure out the usefulness of it either. The very real social purposes of architecture have been potentially shortchanged by the famous architects and by the architectural crafts, so that you would think there was no purpose to architecture except making a set of powerful shapes that command attention and reach the magazines. I don't know if it's time for a general uprising, whether we should burn down the magazines or whether some other solution is at hand, but I do notice in schools in general a real absence of the proper social concerns of the architect, the desire to make places for people to live which they can inhabit. Instead there are excessive concerns about what's the latest formal rage.

LL: Are there some special guidelines on the method of teaching design problems?

CM: One of the things that I've been particularly interested in as a teacher has been in giving students, especially beginning students, a courage of their own convictions. It seems to me that too much of architecture education, less now than formerly but too much, has been involved in watching the students and making them ashamed of the things they've come to enjoy and feel part of during their first two decades, wiping the slate clean and replacing it with a set of enthusiasms forced on them. I think what people come with in architecture is something of their own that they are familiar with. Their own enthusiasm is a very good place to start in architectural education, which should build on those things that students are confident in and feel comfortable about. Then we can take it into levels of sophistication way beyond where the students start. I think we don't give enough credence to what people already know in life.

LL: You spoke earlier about the involvement of the public in your design or the design process and I'm presently working on my thesis on town planning and working with the community. Could you give me some idea of what some of the do's and don'ts are in that process?

CM: I think the chief do is to listen. I just came back from a week of working with a group designing the addition to a museum on the Penn State campus, and we had a very good week with them. Everybody seems to be pleased with it and we think we can afford it. What they seemed very positive about was that they had been listened to; nobody had said anything that we didn't note and try to do something about, and this was with a group of maybe fifteen people who were part of the museum, and the campus, and art history, and the architect's office. I felt bad that they seemed to regard it as so rare that anybody was actually listening to them, and they had some really good ideas. I would say the big don't is don't get defensive. When we were working on the St. Matthew's Episcopal Church with the whole parish, some woman—frightful woman—was screaming at me that Jesus was going to get me because the ceilings were too high and Jesus, as it turned out, was extremely interested in energy conservation. She also announced that the organ was going to suffer greatly because it has to be warmed up. I smiled. I'm sure she knew Jesus better than I did, but I was rescued by the organ committee who said, on the contrary, the organ has to be as cool as possible and the high ceilings were essential, of course they were, for the acoustics of the organ too. So I was out of it, I was saved, and afterwards the rector, who had been a little dubious about the whole process when we started but was beginning to think it was worthwhile, said the thing that had saved me and saved all my partners and all of us who were working on it was that we never got defensive. I didn't get defensive because my metabolism just doesn't work that way at all. I don't get angry—until later. I think once you start defending and shouting at the attackers in a real job you are sunk, because it's you and them . . . you versus them. You're not going to have anything that people feel good about, that they could inhabit, until they buy into it, till they see that it is theirs too, which they won't if you pull the Howard Roark number. I'm delighted when people are presenting a scheme that I have worked on with them and say, "Mr. Moore was hired to work with us and he did, but this was our scheme." I couldn't be more pleased, because if it's their scheme they will work for it and raise money for it and see that it gets built, but if it's my scheme, well, they just won't. So I think you should take whatever steps to insure that it is a shared scheme, which I realize is harder with a thesis than with a building that people are about to build. But to whatever extent you can simulate it, this is worth doing to make it genuinely a work *with* the clients, the users. I guess it's understood, but a lot of people don't believe that you really can't go in with your own scheme that you are waiting to put over on the people and have it come out as theirs. You have to go into it with a genuinely open mind and have what shape it takes come out of what they say and do, and certainly from your own abilities and energies too, but not so that you go in with your mind made up, because you will kill it.

LL: You come from the Midwest and we were speaking about the decline of the midwestern town. I wonder if you could elaborate on this?

CM: I feel rather urgently about it. A few weeks ago I was in South Bend for a lecture and my hosts drove me up to my hometown, Benton Harbor, which is only thirty-five miles. We lived in my grandfather's house and I hadn't been back in almost forty years. It was a shocker because Benton Harbor, I guess, is worse than almost anywhere. I don't know how many people there are but it used to have almost 15,000. Now I understand their total budget for the city last year was $125,000, and I guess they didn't need it anymore because everything has been torn down. Both grandfathers' houses were still there, although one of them was abandoned and one was falling apart. The downtown, which was a pleasant little midwestern downtown, is almost entirely wiped out. I'd say that three-quarters of the buildings are leveled, not even parking lots because there is no reason to park. I didn't see a single business open, except one laundry, in the whole downtown that used to have everything. I don't know whether I should call it a crisis, but the devastation of towns, and the country really (you especially notice it in the Midwest), is a major loss for us and wipes out memories and connections of where we come from; and that cannot help but be disastrous. We all know the reasons: we make more money than we did forty years ago, shopping malls have moved the scene of activity from the towns to suburban locations where they are making profits for some developers, but the new locations are simply not as public as downtowns were, not as interesting, and have no connection with our past or with any kind of continuous activity that lets us have a sense of where we are and who we are, and how we might connect with someplace. It is also the case that we all move so much that hardly anybody in any town at any point seems to come from there, or has been there for very long. Certainly I am an example of someone who has been on the move all of my life, but it's a major shocker and I'm trying to figure out how to deal with it. The longing is there on the people's part for a village with some intimate situation that the people can all feel a part of, which they can't do with your typical shopping mall because it doesn't include anything but shopping. I think we are going to have to come to some structure for our cities that we can feel connected with and a part of. The way we are doing it now is disastrous. That's not an answer, that's a long wail about the problem.

LL: What do you think are the elements that make a place special?

CM: The elements that make the place special probably have to do with the buildings themselves. I will come back to that in a minute. They also have to do with the society that goes on in a place and with the fit of the physical structure to the kinds of activities that people do there. Those things are in the realms of expertise of political scientists, and economists, and sociologists, and many others. As far as the physical part goes I don't think there is any clear answer, but there certainly seem to be some spatial dimensions to the problem. There have to be spaces that are at once intimate and grand, able to make people feel comfortable and sheltered, to hold enough people to do things together, to extend the imagination, and to invite the human bodies to move in them and to experience them. I keep thinking that this is a more or less definable, very critical question, and it is an extremely useful task, maybe one of the most important ones there is, to figure out what are the spatial dimensions of making places. I have done some seminars to try to arrive at that. So far, I have not had any precise or successful outcomes. Reading the literature is discouraging because most of the books that talk about space, from Bruno Zevi to Giedion, refer to space, time, and architecture, but don't really tell you in terms that are useful to the architect. It is a very important field of attention that ought to get some directed energy from people like you and me.

LL: A few years ago you designed a house for a blind gentleman and his grandmother, and I would like to know what issues you were forced to deal with that you had never dealt with before because of the special circumstances, and also how you applied what you learned to other projects.

CM: One of the most specific requirements was to figure out some way of communicating concerns of plan and space to the client. Fortunately he had been sighted until a few years before we met him and was an extraordinarily intelligent and active person. I think one of the reasons he hired us was that one of the partners in the firm had been working in the basement during his vacation and had built a vacuum-forming machine, so we were able to vacuum-form the plans. It worked extremely well and the guy could read them. It was all linear work, the Gutenberg Bible, rather than all simultaneous like the twentieth century, and he would go through and wonder about some place: "Now if I were walking here where could I go? How would I know which way to go to the next place where I could get my bearings?" It involved sound. He told us the places where he felt comfortable, which included his sister-in-law's living room which was in a house with stone walls, and the University Club in New York. We took note of the quality of sound in these places and tried to reproduce them. One of the reasons he hadn't hired his brother, who is a famous architect, is that his brother wanted to make a modern house with open space and the sound of that just drove him crazy. He had an office that was altogether modern, and he had pretty colors and a pillar in the middle of the space which he kept banging into with his forehead. He didn't want that kind of amorphous space. He wanted concrete spaces that he could hear the sounds in and feel comfortable. I think for me what is quite fascinating, what was lastingly important, was the need to listen to see what he was really driving at, which was more urgent than programmatic requirements usually seem to be because we can usually empathize with them. It is a little bit like zoos, which used to be a popular program for school problems: if you do it wrong the animals die. People are normally very adaptable, and if you make idiot mistakes they will get through it somehow, but if you put kangaroos in a place and don't set it up right, they die. People with a specific handicap like a blind man are somewhere in between. They have to adapt, but you just can't make it work unless it is set up so that they can function without great disruption. Until the move, he was on top of what everything was supposed to be, but during the period of moving nothing was where it was supposed to be, and he got really angry because he would fall over boxes, and things were totally out of control. He didn't like being out of control, as most of us don't.

LL: I am from Berlin. I read an interview with you in a book where you stressed that you liked tight schedules and low budgets because they force you to improvise. Could you tell us about the Tegel Port project in Berlin?

CM: Let's see, as for the cost on Tegel, it's social housing, subsidized housing for people who can't afford expensive housing. It wasn't as tight as subsidized housing budgets in the United States are because in Berlin there is a considerable subsidy by the West German government to induce people to live there in circumstances that had some restrictions. As I understand it, a young man who went there during whatever period was relieved of his responsibility to do military service, and various activities like that encouraged people to be there. For the developer, this project was a greater opportunity than it would be elsewhere. We were able to get far more dimension into the facades of the project then we otherwise could have because the developer was part of a precast concrete company in West Germany and therefore was able to realize the thoughts for the building. There were pretty tight limits on that. We have been criticized for accepting the West German government's very tight standards. They aren't very much different from the ones the US used to have when they built housing, but they are more specific. They are very tight, and we all accepted that, and did not try to toss it over because we didn't have the time, or the money, or the power to do that usefully, so we did the housing accordingly. There were lots of restrictions on making the housing, and we were very proud soon after it was open because there was a very long waiting list. A friend of mine heard a woman walking around there who said that this thing was being built for rich people, but when she was told that it was subsidized housing her first statement was "where do I sign up?" So we were proud that subsidized housing was mistaken for rich people's housing, and that is how I think it should be, and the way it has never been in the United States.

LL: What is your idea of the civilized man, and how is this view expressed as ritual in our culture?

CM: This will take a week or two. I am tempted to look up the definition of civilized man, with the various definitions of gentleman as someone who never knowingly does hurt to anyone. As far as how that is expressed in a complicated eclectic culture, the role of ritual is to define a place for people which they can tell apart from other places, and so make the place their own. That is a really important part of what to do and what architecture is important for. I think probably the most important aspect is being aware that ritual does form an important part of people's lives in a society that is sophisticated and scornful of most people's rituals. I realize all peoples have rituals, and have to have them. Architecture has to support them. It is critical. In December I went to a groundbreaking for a housing project in Japan and they had built an extremely expensive and fancy tent, and had gravel on the floor and a Shinto priest. We all took part in an elaborate ritual of handing around branches and simulating cutting grass, and making mountains of sand, and bowing at a Shinto altar, clapping our hands and doing the traditional Japanese forms of sanctifying this place that was having its ground broken. I, being somebody not of that culture, was like a participant in a play, struck by how affecting it was, how much more important it made the enormous amount of time we had spent working on it to that point. The ritual was a powerful addition to the process of making a place.

The Qualities of Quality

There is a tendency to equate any subject at hand with what is good. I have been, for instance, to a number of conferences on vernacular architecture in which anything good managed to be swept into the vernacular category and things that were not so well regarded failed to be vernacular. And so with classicism. It might be salutary, therefore, to look at the question of quality, of what is good, and see if we can relate that to qualities that have to do with classicism. We might admire work of high quality, putting aside for the moment high-mindedness—low-minded high quality seems to me a nice Mozartian possibility—and recognize a scale that goes from what is incompetent, not admired by anybody; past competent, which is okay; to good, which is competent plus; to great, a work of genius, something that thrills us, that does not happen very often.

There are other scales that are also interesting, but not related to that scale from incompetence to greatness; these other scales measure quality by measuring qualities. We have discussed *passion,* which is human energy focused on something that could even be classical architecture. We have examined *invention,* which seems both bad and good. Mies van der Rohe said, "discovery, *not* invention," and we all remembered. Invention as we know it is an invitation to excess and general badness, in addition to being a good thing, something interesting enough to help keep the passion going. There is another question of quality; I will call it *appropriation,* which measures the distance from the model in the original—classical building or whatever. Then there is, after appropriation, the question of *appropriateness,* the decorum that this magazine has enjoyed discussing.

The question of authenticity is a much more difficult one to argue, as for instance in the very different positions held about the Getty Museum in Los Angeles, which claims to be an exact reproduction of some buildings buried in Herculaneum that nobody has ever dug up. This seems to be a problem only for some of us. Then, presumably, a quality that must figure in our apprehending buildings is not only the passion of the designer but the enthusiasms of the viewer, the juror. And it is through the jurors' enthusiasms, the viewers' enthusiasms, the experiencers' enthusiasms that buildings and landscapes are seen and judged.

Originally published in *Center* (University of Texas Center for American Architecture) 2 (1986), pp. 121–126.

I submit for discussion an almost finished project of our own—an Extension Center for the University of California at Irvine. I include it here not only because I am especially fond of it, but also because it is a fairly literal copy of three little chapels on the Celian Hill in Rome, designed in 1607 by Flaminio Ponzio. Two chapels stand in an overgrown garden beside the steps to San Gregorio Magno. I was smitten with them when I first saw them some years ago. I do not know why exactly they appeal to me so much. Maybe it is their false-frontedness, 1607 or not—quite a lot like false-fronted buildings in western towns that I admire. I like too that they are jostling each other for position (like my colleagues) and I thought that it would be nice to do something about them. I had designed a couple of houses for myself (never built) that were based on them. So when clients came from the University of California at Irvine saying they wanted a building with a number of classrooms and offices that would face the public, I thought this might be the chance for my multi-faced building. Here, a few years later, those three chapels reappear. I wrote a description for their opening noting that the image of little baroque false fronts only goes for the building; the image for the landscape full of pepper tress comes from the Tyrone Power movie, *The Mask of Zorro,* that described a southern California pepper-treed, dusty, and romantic. It is not acceptable now to do a university campus in dust—too fragile—so what we had to do was a masonry replication of dust, which is more permanent so it may stay looking like dust longer (fig. 126).

Here are views of the three facades jostling each other. Behind the representational rooms up front, a long spacious wing with places to work hooks itself around a courtyard where a dry riverbed has been reconstituted of rocks from the nearby mountains. The wing is meant as a pleasant place to work and has not at all the same functions as the exhibition function of the Roman facades.

It seems to me (of course) that the fact that our building started life as a copy does not rob it of passion, or of legitimacy, or of authenticity. Our building has a new life for new people in a new place for a new function. It is a safe bet that a few, if any, of the inhabitants have ever seen Ponzio's chapels on the Celian Hill, so the new buildings will have to stir up their own connections with the inhabitants' memories. I was delighted to be told (without asking) that, at least for some, they do.

126
University of
California, Irvine,
Urban Innovations
Group

There *are* questions of legitimacy. I submit the Parthenon. One is in Athens in Greece, and one is in Nashville in Tennessee. The builders of the Nashville temple went to some pains to make theirs look just like the Athenian one. It does not look like it to me. It interests me to wonder what is wrong with this copy. I naturally think that my copy is fine, but the Nashville Parthenon has me worried, maybe because its very literalness makes impossible the modicum of invention that is necessary to engage the passions of the designer. So it never comes alive.

There is certainly no problem of inventiveness, of passion, of excitement at seeing it that goes with the classical shapes of Bernard Maybeck's Palace of Fine Arts at the 1915 San Francisco fair. Nor, in a very different spirit, is there any lack of authenticity in the architecture of Thomas Jefferson—the model keeps recurring during any discussion of classical architecture in America. Here, a Roman republican past is passionately referred to as part of Jefferson's powerful intention—with its architecture—to make his new little republic a great one. He did it the best way he knew: by following available models of previous greatness. He thought the Greek and Roman republics were the very best bet, perhaps the only suitable one. It might be useful, as we consider quality and the areas of agreement about what constitutes it, to regard the design jury, a ceremony in which four or five worthy senior professionals gather to look at the designs or the built works of their colleagues. The thing that strikes me about those juries—and I have been on a great many—is that most of the decision-making about what is adequate and what is not is very easy, and people of many different viewpoints seem to be able to agree. They look at the patterns in the plans, or in the elevations, or in photographs of the building, seeking some kind of integration of the parts with the larger patterns of the building, some knowing capacity to handle the multiple functions of a building within the structural and formal patterns that have been selected and developed, as well as within the cultural patterns. And they look too for suitable associations (a passionate replica of Buchenwald would probably not stir up very much support) neatly integrated into the whole.

The jurors also consider the quality of the communication, written and graphic. Detailed niceties of structure and shape and the *construction* would be noticed and quite quickly agreed upon. Failure to measure up in these realms would eliminate, by general agreement, perhaps 80 percent of the entrants. Then the jury, addressing the surviving 20 percent, perhaps talks about inspiration, invention that must appear effortless or unstrained. Positive functional invention to cope with the situation at hand is required to get into this surviving 20 percent. An appeal to the senses—all of them, as we return, these days, to our senses—is more and more seen as a good thing and agreed upon. And in general when classical (or any historical) models are used, transformations rather than embalmings of the distant past are favored.

But then the disagreements begin to balloon, especially if the jury has been selected to represent various points of view. There is disagreement about which models are appropriate, disagreement about how far the building has come from the model—with some people wanting it to come not very far, others wanting it to come a long way—and disagreement about the doctrines, formal and social, that guided the scheme. I find it interesting that the greatest area of disagreement seems to be about the basic principles, the beliefs that people start with. There is a good deal of agreement about skills of surface manipulation and integration of patterns, and hopeless disagreement about the basics. But quality—the subject of this disquisition—is built on competence, given energy by passion and invention, held together by a sense of appropriateness, of decorum. It seems that we are building with some skill and sophistication upon a foundation—an area of social and formal agreement—which shifts as the very sands. We doubtless should heed those structural consultants who argue that sand, properly dealt with, is about as good a foundation material as there is.

"Spain is no less eccentric than England," Octavio Paz wrote, "but its eccentricity is of a different kind. The eccentricity of the English is insular and is characterized by isolation: an eccentricity that excludes. Hispanic eccentricity is peninsular, consisting of the coexistence of different civilizations and different pasts: an eccentricity that includes." These next pieces examine the spread of Hispanic influence in the Americas; the Anglo-Saxon and French influences behind the work of three of Moore's favorite architects, Sir John Soane, Karl Friedrich Schinkel, and Thomas Jefferson; as well as the work of Mexican architect Ricardo Legorreta.

Hispanic Lecture

The Iberian peninsula, though it gets very hot in the summer, is by no means tropical, and only a corner of its south can claim even a semitropical climate. But Spanish conquests in the New World were mostly in the tropics, and Hispanic architecture came into the United States from the tropical south, so the southern tier of the United States has an architectural heritage doubly romantic, with a Hispanic predisposition for massive unadorned walls ornamented only at key points but then with unbridled enthusiasm, that brio combined with a tropical proclivity for shadows and the spatial complexity that produces them, and breezes and the openness that allows them.

Not only does all this look great in the sunshine, but when a century comes along in which it is declared, for a while, that ornamentation must change, or that ornament is indeed crime, it becomes possible to renounce the ornament, as the California architect Irving Gill did, without doing much violence to the architecture. This paper means to survey the Hispanic roots in Spain and Mexico of some structures built in the eighteenth and early nineteenth centuries in California, Arizona, New Mexico, Texas, and Florida, then to see the effect of these buildings (and their predecessors) on skilled eclectic architects early in the twentieth century, and to note the changes that made modern architecture come of them, then finally to note recent shifts in attitude that are producing contemporary buildings that more directly acknowledge their Hispanic roots. Then we might enjoy for a moment the tropical breezes that seem still to blow around them.

Previously unpublished; lecture delivered at Columbia University, 1987.

The Spanish California settlement was most memorably an ecclesiastical one, under the charismatic leadership of Padre Junípero Serra, then of his successor Padre Lasuen. These priests founded a string of twenty-one missions, from San Diego in the south to Sonoma, two days' walk beyond San Francisco, in the north. The missions were about a day's walk apart, along a trail called the Camino Real. They are full of romance today, but they represented bondage and early death for the Indians who were confined in them and set to hard labor. The California Indians were, by North American standards, especially numerous. They had lived in houses of brush, sufficiently temporary to remain fairly hygienic, and were not able to survive in the Spaniards' heavy and permanent adobes, which were cold and damp, unsanitary places ideally suited to the propagation of the white man's diseases. The substantial Indian population of California was all but wiped out by concentration in these labor camps, and the governor of California wrote back to Spain that Padre Serra showed a perhaps kinky enthusiasm for the whipping of the new Christians.

But the missions, fallen into ruin and now mostly in part restored, are handsome buildings that fit superbly in a compelling landscape, and for the past hundred years there has grown a literary tradition which has bathed their adobe walls in the glow of romance. The main source of the story may disappoint the modern reader: Helen Hunt Jackson's *Ramona* was a popular novel about a hundred years ago, when Yankees were discovering southern California. It tells the story of a beautiful young woman raised on an idyllic southern California rancho. She has been adopted into a kindly and generous family of rich Hispanic hacendados, but after she very unsuitably falls in love with an incredibly noble Indian we discover that she too is half Indian as well as half Scottish. She of course has to bear the brunt of injustice: her baby dies, her Indian dies, and in the end, saddened but strong, she marries her Hispanic foster brother (who is noble too) and goes off to Mexico City to live out her days.

Ramona and many successor stories set the romance of California in the American mind, so that the string of missions, by the early twentieth century, became a series of collectibles, suitable, once the automobile had been developed, for being visited separately or in series.

I've chosen three of the twenty-one missions to include here: one is the Mission Santa Barbara, the tenth and the last to be founded by Junípero Serra, and some say the Queen of the Missions (fig. 127). For notice here is

127
Mission Santa Barbara

the temple front, very simple, in this very distant land, with domed towers
and a freestanding wall, a sort of *espadaña,* above the center of the facade. It
seems here to have no discernible architectural function, but I note it because it has a surprising staying power in the states we are examining. Is it
the precursor to the western American false front?

The second mission I'd like to look at is San Antonio de Padua, in a
handsome valley about two-thirds of the way from Los Angeles to San Francisco (fig. 128). Here the main excitement on the facade is the *espadaña* at
the entrance to the church, separate from the simple bulk of the nave behind, holding its own with the long arcade which continues the facade to the
left. In former days, another arcade extended the facade almost as far to the
right, so this signboard and entrance marker has here a major role to play.

The third California mission, San Carlos Borromeo del Rio Carmelo,
is also called the Queen of the Missions (fig. 129). Here on the facade the
major pleasure is a Mozarabic window, the more powerful for being seriously out of kilter. Does this have something to do with Junípero Serra dy-

128
San Antonio de
Padua

129
San Carlos Borromeo
del Rio Carmelo

ing here? Surely the masons could have been whipped into shape. Or is it an expectable quirk of the vernacular, like the *espadañas* themselves?

Arizona received just three missions during the same time, Tumacocori, Tubac, and San Xavier del Bac. It is the latter that has commanded the attention of northern visitors since they started to come: elegantly proportioned, towered with simple but elegant shadow lines of detail that come from a system of channels meant to lead water from the occasional hard desert rain harmlessly down the soft walls (fig. 130).

130
San Xavier del Bac

Just below the border, in the Mexican state of Sonora, are many more missions of early foundation, smaller, simpler, and full of unexpected strengths (fig. 131). Three of my favorites lie just southwest of the border town of Nogales, little adobe buildings whose fronts are distinguished by the application of bright white plaster so that what are otherwise almost unadorned blocks become strongly frontal. Even more astonishing is the church on the plaza at Bacadehuachi, farther south in Sonora almost on the Chihuahua border and still almost inaccessible by vehicle (fig. 132). Its plan of pierced concentric chambers has cousins in Bavaria and Brazil, as if a south German priest, come to this distant land, had memories of home which had gotten somewhat rattled when the Yaqui arrows whizzed by. The facade, especially, of walls staggered inward toward the center, begs comparison.

If it requires, as I suspect, a memorable literary image to set a way of building, a style, in the minds of people after the buildings have been made, an image such as *Ramona* came to provide in the late nineteenth century and after in southern California, then certainly the Hispanic heritage is weak in Arizona. Indian motifs and tales of lost gold mines operate instead. But a little farther east, in New Mexico, in the valley of the Rio Grande, wondrous tales and images have enriched the centuries.

131
Sonora church

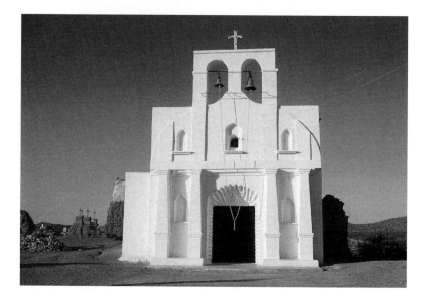

132
Bacadehuachi

Spanish settlement of the upper Rio Grande valley started as early as the sixteenth century: Coronado and his men were drawn on by tales of the Seven Cities of Cibola, whose golden towers were described at least partly, we suppose, to urge the Spaniards on out of the place where they were asking their questions. They found, of course, only the adobe pueblos of the Zuñi, whose walls do glint golden in the setting sun, but the golden image didn't go away. A combination was made of Indian pueblo shapes and the techniques of the Spaniards that is still used, four hundred years later. The native method of making walls of ramped earth was replaced by the Spanish technique of fashioning walls of sun-dried adobe blocks, reinforced with straw, which gleams (in the right light) almost like gold. And the shapes of the church, say, at Acoma, Latin cross in plan, with a towered west wall and a cloister beside, all made out of thick adobe walls, are simultaneously in the tradition of old Spain and of New Mexico (fig. 133).

The Governor's Palace in Santa Fe dates to the end of the seventeenth century, when Santa Fe was being resettled after an Indian revolt had driven the Spaniards for a while out of the upriver country (fig. 134). After 1690 the Europeans came back to stay, and their descendants still prefer to be called Spanish Americans, to indicate their distance from the activities surrounding independence in Mexico in the early nineteenth century. But the one-story Governor's Palace itself, of adobe with round logs for columns and

133
Acoma

134
Palace of the
Governors,
Sante Fe

a modest but continuous arcade along one whole side of the Santa Fe Plaza, owes at least as much to local building forms as to images of old Spain.

There are three churches of at least partial Spanish descent that are especially sought out by visitors to upriver New Mexico: the Santuario at Chimayo, the church at Las Trampas, and the church at Ranchos de Taos (figs. 135, 136). Ranchos is probably the most famous; it is a very few miles from Taos, where many painters work, and its voluptuously buttressed apse has surely been painted by all of them. Its towered entrance face is simple and beautiful, all of adobe with wooden doors, and its interior very simple, and handsome, too. Chimayo and Trampas are both tiny, adobe in their lower reaches and wood above; Chimayo has a wood screen and tower above the entrance, and painted wood panels inside; Trampas is mostly adobe on the outside, with little trellised tops on the towers which speak more of Anglo origin. On both the little churches, the mix of sensuously molded walls of adobe and delicately trellised upper pieces is wonderfully engineered, and of that place, and speaks at once of a Spain a long, long way away and of a strong local tradition.

135
Chimayo

136
Las Trampas

The Spaniards came early to Texas, as well, but some of the Indians, it is said, were cannibals, and not nearly so much fun to talk to as the New Mexicans who were describing the Seven Cities of Cibola.

The building fabrics, however, around San Antonio, to which the padres repaired after their first settlements turned out to have been too optimistically spread apart, were more elaborate than in California or New Mexico. San José y San Miguel de Aguaya, completed in 1768, has the most elaborate—and most beautiful—facade of the missions built in San Antonio, and recalls more clearly than any other early Hispanic building in what is now the United States the Iberian practice of dramatically concentrating lively ornament at key places or otherwise plain walls (fig. 137). The Governor's Palace of 1749 is far simpler. Its garden endows it with the same dreamy charm that clings to Ramona's early California, but of course in Texas the salient legend is of blood and death at the Alamo, where a small group of Anglo settlers demonstrated great personal courage though a weak grasp of tactics when a superior Mexican force wiped them out. The Alamo

137
San José y San
Miguel de Aguaya,
San Antonio

itself, the mission of San Antonio de Valero, receives far more public attention (in ads and collages) than art historical acclaim, and indeed it turns out that the top of its *espadaña,* which provides its memorable Hispanic silhouette, was completed by the U.S. Army after Texas had become a United State in 1845.

To the east of the four states that border on Mexico lies Louisiana, which was also Spanish for a while, from 1763, when France ceded the whole vast Louisiana Territory to Spain, until 1803, when Napoleon took it back for France in time to sell it to the United States. Except for some wall tiles with Spanish street names in the Vieux Carré (not Cuadro Viejo) in New Orleans, there is little architectural evidence that bears the mark of Spain.

The eastern end of the US Sun Belt, Florida, received Spanish attention early, when Ponce de León went there in 1513 to look for the Fountain of Youth, a suitably lyric enterprise to merit our attention, though neither he nor those who came after produced much memorable architecture to link their fringes of the New Spain to the Old. There is a fort, Fort Marion, at St. Augustine, made interestingly enough of blocks of coquina, a tiny shell packed solid, but it isn't a patch on the archbishop of Seville's castle at Coca, near Segovia, finished by 1500 (fig. 138). There is a house in St. Augustine, too, which is the oldest in the US, unless one in Santa Fe, New Mexico, also said to be the oldest in the US, is instead. Neither speaks very forcefully of its origins.

Together these simple though sometimes poignant buildings constitute the Hispanic heritage in the southern tier of United States: there are missions the length of California built of simple stuff by friars far from home, in a beautiful place, bathed by now in the golden light of legend; there are a few more missions in the Arizona desert, then around Santa Fe in New Mexico a whole world like no other, where Hispanic and Pueblo visions combined (and combine still) into an architecture unique to that place. In San Antonio, there was the most sophisticated of the Spanish northern outposts, and in Florida, some more legend.

Just about all this was in place (except the legends) by the early years of the nineteenth century. Later in that century came the years of Yankee influx, of bringing Monterey and Santa Barbara and Tucson and Santa Fe and San Antonio and St. Augustine up to date with buildings that looked as much as possible like the ones back in Kansas City and Chicago and Buffalo

138
Coca, near Segovia,
Spain

and Springfield. Then, not long before the turn of the twentieth century, the breeze shifted—and it was as evanescent as the shifting of a breeze: the perfume of orange blossoms and pepper trees and visions of shaded arcades and the splash of fountains perhaps relaxed the Yankee drive. Or maybe the industry of the missions had made their scented languor acceptable within the puritan ethic. Anyhow, a way of building developed before the end of the century called the Mission Style, which allowed for everything from simply crafted wood furniture to at least two dazzling hostelries, the Mission Inn in Riverside, California, and the Ponce de Leon Hotel in St. Augustine, Florida (figs. 139, 140). We'll look at the hotels as well as a third, more modest, the Alvarado in Albuquerque.

The Ponce de Leon in St. Augustine may in fact be a touch too sumptuous to qualify as Mission Revival, which is meant to have some edge of spartan simplicity down under the romance. It was finished in 1888 by the young New York office of Carrere and Hastings and is the most romantic

thing they ever did, probably because the young Bernard Maybeck was doing it the way he felt it.

The Mission Inn in Riverside at least started off Mission when one
Frank Miller inherited the property in 1880; but he kept building from
1902 until he died in 1935, so there are parts that are Spanish (all twenty-
one missions are said to be represented here) and even Italian and Japanese.
Myron Hunt and Elmer Gray, among the most celebrated of the architects
who worked here, did most of the Spanish parts; but perhaps the most special quality of the Mission Inn (in addition to the astonishing profusion of
architectural shapes and ideas) is the Mission Style juxtaposition of sever-

140
Ponce de Leon
Hotel, St.
Augustine

ity—here represented by unfinished board-formed concrete—and romantic ironwork and other detail that owes much to its California precedents.

The Mission Inn is presently being restored and refurbished; the Alvarado Hotel in Albuquerque, from very early in the twentieth century,
however, has been demolished. It was a much simpler building than either
the Mission Inn or the Ponce de Leon, mostly just two stories high, symmetrical about a centerpiece that very closely resembled a mission facade.
Flanking wings sported *espadañas* almost as large as one in the center, while
a continuous arcade around the building made a shady porch. The Alvarado, an almost perfect example of a Mission Style building, was one of a

famous series of hostelries that Fred Harvey provided along the route of the Santa Fe Railroad on its way to Los Angeles. (In subsequent decades they would serve motorists along Route 66.)

One other building particularly merits our attention as we review the not-quite-Hispanic impulses that followed on the Yankee building booms of the nineteenth century. In the mangrove swamps of south Florida, just below the village of Miami, a Chicago industrialist, James Deering, and his agent, Paul Chalfant, undertook with their architect, F. Burrall Hoffman, Jr., the construction of what turned into a palace. South Florida had never received the imprint of any architectural persuasion, which left the trio in a quandary about what this palatial intervention should look like. It would be much too sophisticated for Mission, with no hint of the spartan. Finally, Venetian was settled on, a kind of country Venetian (as if there had been anything quite like that) where late medieval flourishes animate windows and arcades and fireplaces and chimneys with a gusto very like the Hispanic. The garden, too, with a stone boat in the bay was a wonder. Vizcaya was completed after many delays in 1917, just in time for the world to change away from it: World War I, a federal income tax and changing social attitudes and the failing health of its owner, all made this vast estate a white elephant almost from the moment it was opened, and it stands at the end, rather than at the beginning, of a chapter in the Sun Belt's architecture (fig. 141).

In California, meanwhile, something new (or really two new attitudes diametrically opposed) was happening. Irving Gill had come to San Diego about the turn of the century and was developing a way of building, beginning with the simple walls and arcades of early California and the missions, then refining the idiom to a condition of clarity and austerity parallel with the contemporary work of Mackintosh or Loos. Meanwhile, Bertram Grosvenor Goodhue, a successful New York architect who spent time in Santa Barbara during the winter, had interested himself in Spanish architecture and had collaborated on a book on *Spanish Colonial Architecture in Mexico*. By about 1910 citizens in San Diego, an extraordinarily ambitious city of 35,000, had decided to have a fair, the Panama-California Exposition, in 1915 to celebrate the opening of the Panama Canal. Irving Gill, at the height of his popularity, seemed the natural choice to design the fair, in his elegant brand of Mission-turned-modern forms. But Goodhue, who was friendly with the Olmsteds, who were the landscape architects for the park, and with some prominent San Diegans, was interviewed and captivated the

141
Vizcaya, near Miami,
F. Burrall Hoffman

committee. As Richard Oliver wrote: "The choice of Goodhue was fortu-
itous for the city. As Kevin Star observed in *America and the California
Dream,* 'Goodhue was just at that stage where he could remarkably fulfill
San Diego's needs: poised between past and present, glimpsing the modern
but filled with nostalgia for an imagined past.' By recalling a romantic Hispanic tradition, Goodhue created a new architecture intended to symbolize

the city's future." The fair's architecture, Churrigueresque ornament running polite riot on simple planar bases, introduced the Spanish Colonial Revival to the United States (fig. 142). No longer bound by the simplicities of the Mission Style, the shapes (at least in Goodhue's hands) are genuine—only the historical provenance is made up.

The planning, too, of the Panama-California Exposition is noteworthy for its Hispanic or at least Mediterranean overtones. As Richard Oliver mentions, Alfred Morton Githens found "no French influence" in Goodhue's "idealized Latin city." He compared Goodhue's scheme with the experience of progression through sun, shade, and space in Rome, where "out of the shadows of narrow streets and alleys between huge palaces, one emerges on the Piazza Colonna, di Spagna, or Barberini; a vivid contrast is felt, the shadow intensifies the sunlight, and the sunlight the shadow."

Gill's popularity, and the popularity of his classically simple and unadorned work, suffered from the great popular success of the fair and the Spanish Colonial Revival architecture that followed, but he worked for another 20 years, refining and clarifying his ideas. My example from his later years is the Christian Science Church in Coronado, of 1929 (fig. 143), a particularly moving little work, one very short step removed from the "modern" that was beginning to be enthusiastically received, especially from two architects come to Los Angeles from Vienna, Rudolph Schindler and Richard Neutra.

In Santa Barbara, the Spanish Colonial Revival furnished the image and then the structure of the town. It seems to have begun, at first, with Goodhue and George Washington Smith, who built in 1916 the Heberton house in Montecito. A blank wall faces the street, with a place to pull up an automobile, and some spiky desert plants—the front yard—and no windows except a balconied French door over the entrance. Beside the house and behind it are gardens to which the house opens wide. Nearby is the Smith house of 1920. (Both houses served as the architect's own.) It faces a paved entrance court, with narrow veranda on the upper floor.

There were a number of houses of Spanish Colonial Revival persuasion by 1925, when a block of commercial buildings called El Paseo was built downtown among some early nineteenth-century adobes by a young Scottish architect named James Osborn Craig. El Paseo, especially its "Street in Spain," is so compelling that when a devastating earthquake struck in 1925, there was a concerted effort to rebuild the city Spanish. A perfumed past was concocted (*pace* Ramona) and white walls shadowed by big leaves

142
Panama-California Exposition,
San Diego, Bertram Grosvenor
Goodhue

143
Christian Science church,
Coronado, Irving Gill

and arcades were brightened by bougainvillea and hibiscus. A drafting service was set up to provide free design assistance to the merchants on State Street who wanted to rebuild, so long as they would do it in Spanish Colonial Revival. Soon a giant movie house was deftly scaled to fit with its smaller neighbors, with dramatic overtones straight from Coca castle. The skilled jumping of scale is, in fact, a special attribute of the Spanish Colonial Revival: George Washington Smith's Lobero Theater, for instance, sports a giant molding along its base.

(It is interesting to note that what seems like a California phenomenon was happening, at almost the same time, in Spain itself: the Catalan resort community of S'Agaró, on the Mediterranean coast north of Barcelona, is astonishingly similar to Santa Barbara of the period.)

The great monument of Santa Barbara's reconstruction, and indeed of the whole Spanish Colonial Revival, is the Santa Barbara County Courthouse, started after the earthquake in 1926 and finished in 1929. The architect was William Mooser of San Francisco, whose other work bears little resemblance to this masterpiece. Some say that Mooser's son was the designer, others that a member of the client group in Santa Barbara had enormous influence. In any case, the building is a dazzling agglomeration of pieces, huge and middle-sized and tiny, of every conceivable shape as long as it is sort of Spanish. There are some breathtaking spaces, especially at the two main stairs, one of them climbing at once indoors and out. The locations of the openings combine to surprise, even after a hundred viewings, and the surface of paint and tile is gorgeous. The entrance arch serves not just for the building, but as entrance to a forecourt for the whole Santa Ynez mountain range; the vast white walls are splashed with the shadows of palms and broad-leaved plants, and doorways of an almost surreal grandeur are collapsed into the walls. Even a precut ruin of a tower guards one corner, while late medieval turrets loom over other towers. Never before that I know of has a fictional history been so lovingly honored.

In Pasadena and its southern neighbor San Marino, some Spanish Colonial Revival houses of the 1920s still fairly glow with a kind of magical correctness. Two architects of particular note in San Marino were C. W. Smith (of Santa Barbara) and Wallace Neff, The Bourne House of 1927 and the Singer House of 1925, both by Neff, are, as I've written elsewhere, "grand and intimate, chaste and flamboyant, modest and sumptuous," and private while admitting the public gaze.

The Pasadena City Hall, of the same period (1925–1927), is the product of a competition won by Bakewell and Brown, who designed the grand Beaux-Arts City Hall for San Francisco. The Pasadena building is a French Beaux-Arts work too, in its details, but its openness, the fully tropical way that it rises all open air into the sky, connects it, in the public mind, with our Spain of soft and perfumed breezes. So the new buildings to be built in 1988 near this Franco-tropical confection have to be Spanish Colonial Revival, which is doubtless the way things should be.

In these same years, Bertram Grosvenor Goodhue, who had introduced the Spanish Colonial Revival at San Diego, was taking the next step, trimming and straightening and shaving and sculpting his masses in the Los Angeles Public Library, a commission he worked on from 1922 until his death in 1924. It parallels in many ways his competition-winning project for the Nebraska capitol, which has a higher, thinner tower surmounted by a dome where the Los Angeles library is topped by a tiled pyramid. Each, though, has laid aside the curvilinear excitements of only a few years before in favor of simple masonry shafts which crystallize into Lee Lawrie sculpture (fig. 144). The Nebraska capitol was not finished until 1932, and disappointments over it are said to have hastened Goodhue's death, but the dazzling speed at which the Spanish Colonial Revival was changing in its introducer's hands hints at remarkable things that might have been (fig. 145).

As it was, though, southern California with its simple white-walled buildings softened by exuberant ornamentation and semitropical planting was an easy place for architecture of the International Style to come: keep the walls plain, skip the ornamentation, and don't forget the plants, and a bloodless revolution is accomplished. In Arizona after the First World War, the work of Henry C. Trost of Tucson and El Paso is of special interest. Trost's early practice produced houses with the look of Sullivan and Chicago about them, but by the 1920s there were taller buildings, too, in an idiom that has since come to be called "Pueblo Deco" after a little book by the architectural historian Marcus Whiffen. It is, I believe, fascinating to see in Trost's Bassett Tower in El Paso, Texas, of 1930 how close he has come to closing the circle on the archbishop of Seville's splendid theatrical Coca castle of just over 400 years before (fig. 146). My favorite of his works, though, is the Luhrs Tower in Phoenix, Arizona, of 1930, a tiny but astonishingly vertical skyscraper that crystallizes at the top, like Trost's Bassett Tower and rather like Goodhue's Los Angeles Library and Nebraska capitol of the same years.

144
Los Angeles Public Library, Bertram
Grosvenor Goodhue

145
Nebraska State Capitol, Bertram
Grosvenor Goodhue

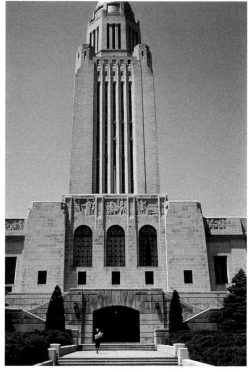

146
Bassett Tower, El
Paso, Henry C. Trost

Goodhue had received a number of western commissions as a result of
the popular success of his 1915 fair in San Diego, and one of them is of special interest to us here, though it involves moving backward a few years, to
1916–1918, through years in which an extraordinary amount of stylistic
change had been going on.

The project was a company town for the Phelps Dodge Corporation
at Tyrone, New Mexico. The excitement for Goodhue was the opportunity
to explore his ideas about urban form, and about buildings in New Mexico.
"The strength of Goodhue's design," Richard Oliver wrote, "was its arrangement into the image of an idealized Mexican town, with all the small scale
urbanity that image evokes." The village was organized around a plaza, with
a church on a nearby hillock. "Around the plaza, the general store and the

bank had ornamental elements in the same Spanish Baroque style used for the San Diego fair, and the administrative building had a heavy cornice and window moldings," but for all the other buildings in the town except the church Goodhue took his cue from the special simple way of building of New Mexico, and from the work of architects like Irving Gill, and designed the rest of the buildings with "not an ounce of ornamentation anywhere, nothing but plaster walls with tile for flat parapeted roofs," relying on the composition of volumes and on soft colors. (Goodhue doesn't mention Spanish precedents, but the early fifteenth-century castle of Olite, for Charles the Noble of Navarre, does come to mind.) Goodhue went to upper New Mexico for Tyrone, to soak up its extraordinary sense of place.

A few years later, in 1920, the young John Gaw Meem, seeking a place to recuperate from tuberculosis, arrived in Santa Fe. Though he had been credit manager of a bank in Brazil, he had an engineering background and was soon immersed in the special architectural concerns of Santa Fe, which had become one of the first American towns to take special interest in its architectural heritage. In 1909 the one-story adobe Palace of the Governors, along one whole side of the Plaza, had become the target of the "progressive" citizens of the town, to whom it symbolized backwardness and poverty and who wanted to demolish it. The mud palace was converted into a historical museum and restored, thanks to a dedicated preservationist group. The same group was instrumental in mounting an impressive exhibit for New Mexico (which had just become a state in 1912) for the 1915 San Diego fair, designed in the Spanish Pueblo tradition. In turn the success of the little exhibit paved the way for a Museum of Fine Arts by the same architects (Rapp and Rapp). The Governor's Palace restoration and the new Fine Arts Museum, then, side by side in the center of Santa Fe, turned the tide in favor of the Spanish Pueblo revival, or "Santa Fe Style."

Into this heady atmosphere of exciting architecture came the young Meem, who guided and developed it and produced an extraordinary variety of works within the idiom (and, for other places, outside it) for thirty-five years, from his first commission in 1924 until he retired from practice (but not from work) in 1959.

The Parish Church of Cristo Rey from the 1930s and the Santo Tomas Church in Abiquiu both show the power of his work at its best, and the Santo Tomas Church even exhibits the *espadaña,* standing free, that is becoming a leitmotiv of this survey (fig. 147). Perhaps his richest stew of

Spanish and Pueblo elements, though, comes in La Fonda Hotel, in Santa Fe, of 1927, where pierced walls and towers and buttresses create an extraordinarily animated large building at the corner of the Santa Fe Plaza, which still manages not to endanger the scale of the one-story Governor's Palace on the opposite side (fig. 148).

In San Antonio, meanwhile, Meem's slightly younger contemporary O'Neil Ford was pursuing a career very similar in some ways (he was rooted

147
Santo Tomas,
Abiquiu, John Gaw
Meem

148
La Fonda Hotel, John
Gaw Meem

in San Antonio, devoted to it, and produced work firmly grounded in the local idiom) but very different in others (his practice was international in scope and he served on national boards and panels; he was even declared, I believe uniquely for an architect, a National Treasure by the National Endowment for the Arts). Another difference is that, surprisingly, no biography or monograph on his work exists. Yet another difference is that from a fairly early point in his career Ford gave extraordinary freedom to the designers in his office. I remember being shown around by him perhaps twenty years ago, when his offices were in a group of one-story houses, one on King William Street, a restored historic district in San Antonio, the others backing up to it from the adjacent street. In every room of each house was an architect, or maybe two, each working, I was told, on his own project, some projects small, some very large. When help was needed to draw a project, it would be sought from people in other rooms. O'Neil Ford would visit these rooms, criticize, urge people on, and go on to the next. I was deeply impressed with the orderly delegation of decisions: many minds contributed to the design, although Ford's personal drive and his love for the flavor of Texas were present in almost everything. But San Antonio is not Santa Fe, and the Spanish heritage, though very much present in Ford's work, is by no means so closely rooted to the place in San Antonio as the Spanish-Pueblo mix is in Santa Fe. Nonetheless, the easy and generous and generally simple row houses with long porches and a few elegant details that were likely to come from Ford's own hands, with craftsmanship by his brother, spoke eloquently of the Spanish connection.

Backward a little in time, and a little to the east, Houston has some very interesting Spanish Colonial Revival buildings. A particularly romantic one, though it has a serious case of what California real estate people call "deferred maintenance," is the Isabella Court apartments, a spatially elaborate and formally amazing concoction for which William D. Bordeaux was architect. Bordeaux had worked in Los Angeles in the heyday of the Spanish Colonial Revival for A. C. Martin, then had moved to Miami, then to Houston, where Isabella Court was built in 1928 and 1929.

Bordeaux's flight from Miami was presumably occasioned by the collapse in 1926 of an extraordinary real estate boom in which the Spanish Colonial Revival had played a central role, though the unquestioned architect-star in the gala performance was the undoubted entrepreneurial and compositional genius Addison Mizner, who owed allegiance to old Spain and Venice too, and in a few years before 1926 achieved a dazzling series of clubs and houses and hotels and even a shopping street for the very rich in Palm Beach. He even developed the industries to make the Hispano-Venetian tiles and furniture and crafted objects for which he had created so avid a demand. The sudden collapse of the boom, three years before Wall Street followed suit, caught Mizner trying to develop a whole new town at Boca Raton, and he paid dearly for his ambitions. But over sixty years later, whole stretches of Palm Beach, especially, owe their unfaded charm to the grandeur of his tropical visions of Venice and of Spain. And the little shopping arcades he made, Via Parigi and Via Mizner, grow more gorgeous with the years (fig. 149).

The years since the Florida boom collapsed, and especially the years since the Second World War, have mostly been unkind to the Sun Belt's double architectural heritage of sunny Spanish walls and tropical shadows. Americans have grown, the statisticians say, more and more mobile, and feel a much reduced sense of wonder upon arriving in Paradise, whether that paradise is Los Angeles or Santa Fe or Palm Beach, so the provision of Spanish Colonial Revival as the architecture of exotic American places has lost most of its point. Also, and even more devastating for architecture, air conditioning by refrigeration has become common everywhere, so that buildings in

149
Via Mizner, Palm
Beach

semitropical places look just as much like tattooed boxes (or refrigerators) as those in the frozen north. And in cities like Los Angeles, where once the building and zoning laws favored (or at least allowed) apartments with the pedestrian intimacy of landscaped courts, later laws have required more and more parking for bigger cars, with less and less room for plants on more and more expensive land. Then too modern architecture, while it held sway, sought generally to approach a universal ideal, so it really wasn't meant to be possible to tell where a building was located from its looks, and internal form-givers—structure, especially, and circulation—were meant to operate, from the inside out, to shape our buildings. Only during the last two decades have the concerns that died with Goodhue and Mizner in the twenties, for architecture that addresses our memories and concerns itself with a specific place, begun again to surface, so that we can look again at the American Sun Belt and see (only occasionally so far) that wonderful combination of plain sunny walls and ornamented chiaroscuro that we think of as Hispanic, with indoor and outdoor woven together in ways we deem tropical. New terms describe the work: radical regionalism, critical regionalism. The backward glance goes all the way to the Spain of Trajan and beyond, and frequently lights on Pliny's villa, or Hadrian's. A house by Andrés Duany and Elizabeth Plater-Zyberk of Miami is an intellectual endeavor that is also dreamily Hispano-tropical, and a house on the shore in Corpus Christi, Texas, by Batey and Mack involves at once a classical and tropical image. Reyna and Caragonne's Guadalupe Center in San Antonio is postmodern with strong Hispanic overtones, directly undertaken here for a cultural center for the Mexican and Chicano community. The plans, again, are a sensitively developed intellectual exercise, but the idiom is strongly recollective of buildings south of the border.

In New Mexico, as might be expected, the strong local idiom provides a real head start for some talented architects. An increasing number of works blending the Hispanic-Pueblo local idiom with a powerful futurism are coming from the architect Antoine Predock.

As a last example, though not a culmination of a powerful heritage, I believe it is interesting, anyway, to look at a hotel in Orange, California, that will never make it to the architecture magazines but has an astonishing amount of innocent vernacular Hispanicism liberally applied (fig. 150). And though this is not the end to which Hispanic architecture in the Sun Belt all boils down, it is reassuring to see that it is accepted by the person in the street, in evidence of which we have the *espadaña* on the Taco Bell (fig. 151).

150
Embassy Suites Hotel, Orange,
California

151
Taco Bell

The chief reason to rummage through the past is to find some friends, people who shared some of our hopes and even some of our limits. For several decades now many architects have looked to the generation that matured in the 1920s—Le Corbusier, Gropius, and others—for models and support. I find it difficult indeed to see how our current concerns coincide very closely with those of half a century ago. Instead I think I spot a close connection with members of the generation that practiced about 1810, including John Soane, Karl Friedrich Schinkel, and Thomas Jefferson. These architects found in the classical past a deep reservoir of shapes and meanings which they made their own, willfully and lovingly misunderstood, transformed to face the extraordinary new challenges of the industrial revolution of the nineteenth century. They made, in the course of coping with these challenges, some buildings to which some of us can feel very close, not only for their low construction budgets but also for the great pressure on them to say something, to speak to a new world anxious for their message.

In the course of looking at them, I hope to allude to the nature of influence: that is, what it is like to borrow and lend. The major source here is a book by Harold Bloom called *The Anxiety of Influence*. His model is an arrangement wherein the young poet (read architect) seizes on the work of an older poet which he extravagantly admires. He heads toward that body of work with his own, and then at the very last second, in a poetic game of chicken, swerves slightly to the side and hits some other target. If he does this just right, he makes the target itself seem to have moved to his point of impact, leaving the older poet with a near miss. If he doesn't do it just right, the target won't budge, and the world will note (if it notes at all), "Oh God, another one." The chance willfully to misunderstand one's predecessors, immediate or distant, is a chance which anybody who is trying to make something (buildings, for instance, which say something) is entitled, indeed obliged, to take. This account of three architects will engage, accordingly, in some willful misunderstanding.

Thomas Jefferson was intent on developing an architecture that would make the rest of the world proud of his undercapitalized new frontier republic. I find it thrilling that he thought architecture might be helpful. Karl Friedrich Schinkel, similarly, was using architecture to make something

Originally published in *An Architectural Life: Memoirs and Memories of Charles W. Moore* (Boston: Little, Brown, 1996); written as a chapter of an unrealized book, "Borrowings and Lending" (with Wayne Attoe).

important, a visible flowering of humanism for a humanist monarch in what might otherwise have been thought of as a muddy garrison town very near Western civilization's Eastern Front. John Soane, meanwhile, from his London base was sympathetically and seriously giggling through those building years, making structures of such deep triviality that they command our thoughtful attention.

I am not the first, certainly, to consider these worthies, and what I see is apt to differ strikingly from what others have discerned. Mies van der Rohe, for instance, when he completed his museum in Berlin, said that he hoped he had done something worthy of the Berlin Schinkel. And I have to suppose, from the evidence of Mies's museum, that he saw a different Schinkel from what I see. But Schinkel remade the face of Berlin and gives us a rich storehouse of works to consider, even after the destruction of the Second World War. Jefferson, who found time during his busy architectural career to be President and Minister and to pursue other interests, also has made some inroads into the minds and hearts of our forebears. John Soane's career was rather more limited, but again has meant different things to succeeding generations.

These three gentlemen, so far as I know, were not close to one another. Jefferson's bias, for reasons known to us, was not pro-British; Schinkel is said to have been a friend of John Nash, whose opinion of Soane's work, I gather, was rather like mine of, say, the current work of Minoru Yamasaki. So the chance of establishing a personal connection among the three is not open to us. What does link them is not just contemporaneity but a shared capacity to elevate the simple, the cheap, even the trivial, to works which speak; to make out of the pressures of the world, of pressed time and restricted budgets and the tumult of social and industrial revolution, a group of buildings with meaning, for them and for us.

Sir John Soane's Debt Redemption Office in London has a complexity of geometries in plan worthy of the Emperor Hadrian or of Louis Kahn. Various geometric room shapes are overlaid and moshed together without losing the clarity of the recognizable parts. It all bears very little resemblance to standard classical planning; but note how effectively the peekaboo qualities characteristic of Soane's work allow the architect, just by opening up a crevice in a very modest surface, to concentrate the inhabitants' attention. He achieves a magnificent effect with a very minimum of means.

This, like most of Soane's work, has vanished. But one wonderful, perhaps the most wonderful, piece of Soane's work is left to us. It is his own house in Lincoln's Inn Fields in London, left by him as a museum for his collections. It is actually the center row house in a group of three which he built. He lived at first in the left-hand one, then moved to the center, which he spread out in back, behind the flanking houses, to give space for the museum, his personal collections of antique trivia. The mind boggles at the cache of disparate objects packed into this tiny bright space, even layered in one rear corner, where overlaid panels flop out to reveal view after view. Next to that is the breakfast room where a handkerchief dome settles down over a space within the tiny space. There are models of buildings and classical pieces of every size, mostly tiny, but hovering around an enormous Egyptian sarcophagus.

A century and a half after its construction, the outside of the house continues the London rhythms of getting sooty and then being cleaned, revealing in the chiaroscuro a series of little classical surprises. One enters first a small vestibule, then an entry hall, which makes use of a big mirror to dissolve the space, to make it altogether impossible to figure out where you are and what's going on, though seconds ago you were on the sidewalk. Beside you (or is it?) is a dining room with red walls and mirrors, the slight curve of arcades, windows somewhere in the background admitting light but indoctrinating it instantly into the rich dark red mysteries of the space, faceted, encrusted with paintings and models and objects congealed but somehow not stilled, caught up in the dance marshaled by light, the changeling.

Just above this dark dream is a pair of drawing rooms all in ivory, where light is admitted to a brighter mystery dance. Here the wonder is geodic. Taut ceiling planes break open to suggest infinite distances in the six inches behind their surface. The light that plays on them has poured through two front walls, and danced and dodged between glass panes in the space between. Little Gothic stalactites hang in the openings pricking the light into frenzy, so it is not Le Corbusier's pure, serious Hellenic light that washes these models of classical buildings (which sit on every surface), but a giggling demon light. It seems to be friendly but it is not domesticated.

Back downstairs, next to the dining room is the breakfast room, whose tiny space, as we've noted already, is greatly compressed from above by a shallow handkerchief dome, itself relieved by a miniature lantern at its center, but seeming to have an altogether disproportionate effect on such space as there is below which shoots up the narrow slots at the edges of the room, into light (fig. 152). All this squirting space is being goaded, as the light was up above in the drawing room by dark stalactites, here by convex mirrors at the pendentives, which give it no peace. And half the spaces are, of course, not spaces at all but only illusions made by mirrors, though some are real, up around the edges, where little extra worlds crowned by skylights are crammed with paintings you can't see until you flatten yourself against a wall. Many other paintings, of Pompeian persuasion, hide themselves in their tininess and make one long to fashion a room like this all out of post-cards, whispering their trivia in unison ("not to the sensual ear, but more en-dear'd, Pipe to the spirit ditties of no tone").

152
Soane breakfast room,
Sir John Soane

In a nearby corner is a room you must now enter with a guide, who will reveal layer after layer of paintings (Hogarths, and Soane's own buildings) by flopping open and then closing a set of big doors on which the paintings are hung. Once all the doors are swung away on one of the sides, you are surprised by a tiny two-story space which opens onto the little courtyard which has given light to the other rooms we've seen, in spite of its being packed with such solidities as a substantial memorial mourning the passing of an ancient dog. Next to all that is the tiny, crammed-full but brilliantly lit urban galleria of a museum, with classical fragments stuffed into every conceivable space and appearing in places you wouldn't have thought of at all.

People dressed for London come as such a surprise on this compression that it is a full astonishment to come upon someone with no clothes on (though he's marble) more than fully lit under the focused skylights of the gallery. The same skylights are pouring energy into the fragments from excavations across the known world, brought out of the underworld and into the light—with a vengeance. The place breathes life into these shapeless classical stones, and Soane's lifelong passion for collecting them and fixing them here, like his passion in his buildings for breathing strange hot new life into cool, cool ancient forms, has made of the classical past a living present.

Meanwhile in a much newer, smaller European capital was unfolding another career which shared with Soane's chiefly its base in the late eighteenth-century Grand Tour of Italy and a continued passion for the forms the young architect has seen there—a passion too strong to admit of rote copying. Karl Friedrich Schinkel came back to Berlin, where the presences of the architect Gilly (for whom he once worked) and a remarkably cultivated royal house were transforming what had been described not long before as a forlorn muddy town full mostly of military barracks into a pleasant capital still, for a European capital, surprisingly middle-class. Pictures of Unter den Linden, Berlin's treed main street in Schinkel's time, astonish us with their bourgeois modesty: the houses along it were only occasionally palaces of nobility. Mostly they were the dwellings of bankers and bakers and clothing merchants, comfortable but not at all grand.

Schinkel's little pavilion at the Charlottenburg castle is altogether chaste and simple and controlled. Inside, it has an exhibition now of some of Schinkel's concerns, especially early industrial ones, like the establishment of a Prussian ironworks. Outside, the classicism of the square structure is established with the most disciplined and delicate illusion. It is hard even to see the thin line which runs along the top of the column capitals and alone marks off the entablature. But that is all it takes to make this box into something far more than a box, a whispered recollection of all kinds of classical riches. The same impulses create the precisely incised porches within the building's cube; reserved for its outside is the altogether modern iron balcony, also lovingly handled, its underside painted blue with stars.

A pair of Schinkel's urban sketches cheerfully mix classical and Gothic elements. They reveal in picturesque hilltop siting city squares with towers and flags, concerns that were soon to be applied to making a special place on the little island in the Spree where the monumental heart of Berlin was developing and was yet to be. The impulses we see here had a classical base but were at heart romantic and theatrical.

Perhaps the most moving passages of Schinkel's romantic imagination start from Tuscan country villas, with spatial warps. My favorite is capped flat on top with an arbor, the spatial splendors achieved entirely by diving down, around a little four-columned temple, the downness reinforced by the presence of Germanic Styx-crossing mechanisms that propel the whole scene to the very edge of the infinite (fig. 153). Consider the problems, which will require magical intervention, of that boat entering the almost-underwater arch which lies just ahead of it.

153
Schinkel's version of a
Tuscan country villa

PERSPECTIVE VOM GARTENHAUSE IN CHARLOTTENHOF BEI POTSDAM, VOM PUNCTE F. IM GRUNDRISSE AUFGENOMMEN.

On another surprising spatial construct, we have a hunting lodge which combines the Gothic possibilities for drafty vertical gloom with a cheery fire, in a classical chimney plunging up through the center of the central space, encrusted with stags' heads.

More domestic, the country house at Tegel for his friend Wilhelm von Humboldt (the brother of Alexander, for whom the current was named) envelops an older, smaller baroque palace, supersedes it without insulting it, and shows a new face to a garden allee worked out by Schinkel, von Humboldt, and their sculptor friend Thorwaldsen; French on one side, English on the other (where there is a hill) with the statuary of a Prussian family graveyard at the end of the allee, it is a piece, in the fading light, of romantic Northern mystical eclecticism without peer.

It does not hurt, on the other hand, to note the points at which our sympathies do not make it back across the years. I submit Schinkel's scheme for shaping up the Athenian Acropolis, whose irregularities our generations have come to extravagantly admire. He lines up the recalcitrant stones like recruits on a Prussian drill field, then domesticates the whole. When he was at home his urban improvements, held in line by small budgets, were more modest and, for us, more congenial. Thus one of the gates for Berlin, the Leipziger Tor, where classical buildings, less charged than the Parthenon, flank an opening in a fence which leads you from one circle into a smaller one, from which streets radiate.

Two alternative (both fortunately discarded) schemes for honoring the Prussian monarch with astonishingly overscaled statues of himself don't transmit a serious message to us either (fig. 154). It is, rather, the smaller pieces, even in the larger work where the architect engages in serious play, skilled and supple, with the size of things, with shaping and—especially—miniaturizing the scale of the pieces, which in their modesty and precision speak to us. The theater in Berlin recalls a little the house, Bocages, in Louisiana (which it antedates) with a double entry of classical piers big and little which engage in lively syncopations. For the designer of Bocages, as well as for Messrs. Schinkel, Soane, and Jefferson, the rediscovery, after the middle of the eighteenth century, of what was left of the real sites of classical antiquity supplied a source more robust and more poignant than anyone had seen since Hadrian.

Another monumental building in Berlin, the Old Museum, develops at its entrance the same sort of vertical surprises that transpired in the shad-

ENTWURF FÜR EIN DENKMAL KÖNIG FRIEDRICH DES GROSSEN.

154
Project for a
monument to
Frederick the
Great, Karl
Friedrich Schinkel

ows under the arbor at Charlottenhof. Here you slip in between the bases of
the Ionic columns and sweep up, in ways which enhance your dignity as a
human inhabitant of the space, expanding your stature and your importance as you enter.

Nearby is the powerful little Neue Wache, purely and simply a monument, full of power. But my favorite is an unexecuted scheme for the same
project, surmounted by mad skeleton signpost-armorials, a proto-Calder
throbbing to the rhythms of very distant Northern drummers. A wall that
I have worked hard on, representing the Doric order in a fountain in the
Piazza d'Italia in New Orleans, slits into almost-armor a pair of stainless-
steel Doric columns in homage to these skeleton warriors of the North.

Thomas Jefferson was born a little sooner, on an even more distant
frontier. His formal education occurred not in Italy but in Williamsburg,
the tiny capital of his province, which he (unlike Rockefellers after him)

thought was architecturally hopeless, composed of wretched misshapen piles of misunderstood English barbarism. It was essential, he believed, while throwing off the political ties with England (to which end he authored an eloquent document in 1776), to loosen as well the cultural ties which had caused his forebears to make these pathetic little buildings. His own models were French and Roman and Palladian. He stood in the street in Paris while the Hôtel de Sâlm was under construction, looking on it, he said, as a lover would his mistress, and then he came back to his beloved hilltop in Virginia to make Monticello, making first a scheme he thought too Italian, not French enough, then tearing that away to make for his home the powerful and personal structure that now graces the nickel. It does not hurt to notice that the scheme for the house of the most populist of our Founding Fathers is an unabashedly elitist one, which puts the proud public rooms and the seat of the master in a highly visible pavilion, fitted with the classical splendors of column, pediment, and dome, astride an almost invisible podium, an H in plan, the vertical bars of which reach daylight in verandas over the edges of the hill. The work of the house takes place in this extensive podium, so that what seems above like a simple, small classical temple is really the tip of an iceberg, except that below, very un-iceberglike, cannily considered and well-running episodes of complex frontier housekeeping were taking place. The tiny house to which the youthful Jefferson brought his bride became, with its later reflection, the visible pavilions at the ends of the podium which very simply state the theme of the house, while the domed and pedimented portico in the center takes on more public tasks, even the development of an architectural idiom suitable for the whole new republic (fig. 155).

Now, when architects are trying to use in our work with pleasure and without guilt the shapes we like and respond to, without engaging in an absurd cult of originality which supposes that we have never seen anything in our lives and have each invented every shape unaided, it is a great comfort to see Thomas Jefferson, too, finding architectural excitement in Paris or Nîmes, and bringing it back across the ocean to his mountaintop in Virginia. Once he got it home, he had no hesitation about mixing the imported forms with the products of his native inventiveness, like the triple-hung window which allows you to slide up the two lower sashes, so you can walk upright from indoors to out. More directly still, a new capitol for Virginia at Richmond, free of the colonial burdens of Williamsburg, is meant to be

155
Monticello, Thomas
Jefferson

as close an approximation as was possible to its model, the Maison Carée at Nîmes.

Most powerful of all, some of us think the most important group of buildings on the continent, was Jefferson's part of the University of Virginia. It was designed, on a hill near Monticello, as an open U, a bay of space that opened to the vastness of the broad mountain valley. The sides of the bay are continuous colonnades, along which are placed ten professors' houses, where classes would meet (fig. 156). At the head of the bay is a central building, with formal antecedents in the Roman Pantheon (a library not a church), set not to dominate the lawn but to center the embrace of the vast valley space beyond. Behind the colonnades and pavilions on both sides are private gardens, enclosed by ingenious walls, one brick thick, serpentine in plan with an additional row of modest habitations beyond.

The wonder of these buildings, it seems to me, is that they are talking, speaking about a great many things. One of the things I imagine they are talking about is a thoughtful coexistence of the populism of the continuing colonnade, behind which students live, and the elitism of the mannered, altogether exemplary ten pavilions which served as homes for professors,

University of Virginia,
Thomas Jefferson

classrooms, and expositions of the glories of the five architectural orders (and then some) to the young persons who were having their minds formed in these precincts. Each pavilion signals a different drama of accommodation between its order and the continuing colonnade. Sometimes the colonnade is interrupted by a big porch, sometimes it glides right on through, sometimes it overtakes the pavilion, and slips right on in front of it. The colonnade steps down, to cope with a falling away of the land, or becomes for awhile a little arcade so that another colonnade the same size but ennobled by its elevation can sit on top.

Along the colonnaded porch are perhaps the most desirable student dormitory rooms on the continent, and at the most elegant of the pavilions, Pavilion IX, is surely one of the magical architectural moments of any time. The apsidal porch, presumably influenced by the contemporary works of Ledoux, contradicts in its height and grandeur the comfortable shelter of the colonnade in front, to set up a complexity of passages from shelter to expansion to front door that achieves clear and powerful monumentality, that tells us what we hoped to hear about the democratic republican new land (fig. 157).

If I were someone else I would have seen other qualities in these three oeuvres. But for now, the simultaneous elitism and populism, the coexistent high art and low, and (especially interesting I think for us) the extreme economy that gave the successful gestures in this work the maximum effect with a very minimum of means, these are some themes about which buildings can talk, and did, when their authors counted on them to help establish a new order in a new century.

157
Pavilion IX,
University of
Virginia, Thomas
Jefferson

Triple Threat Heritage (Inspiration for a New Architecture)

The qualities that Ricardo Legorreta sees in vernacular buildings neatly describe a desirable architecture of the future, a new architecture we might create. Following his twelve points:

Vernacular architecture has direct references to human inhabitation and use.

Surely that would be our first criterion for a new architecture. The urge to inhabit is a basic one, like eating, or sex, or sleeping. Admittedly, you can be deprived of it without dying, which makes it different from food or sleep, but it is nonetheless a universal human need. Inhabiting is a physical act, and a mental and emotional one, too. You have to belong; your body has to fit inside a space that's warmed or cooled, or tight so the rain won't come in; but also you have to feel mentally and emotionally at home there, so that you the individual are at the center of your world. One could certainly make the case that many famous buildings, especially in our own century, don't have any quality of making you feel in repose in the middle of them, don't even have the capacity to let you connect with them, even to the point of finding the front door so you can get in.

Buildings in general are meant to be inhabited, and vernacular ones are typically directly related to their inhabitants. A vernacular building that we respond to tells us what it is. The shapes give clues to what it is used for and what a human being could do with it. Vernacular buildings have to work, or nobody would put up with them. Fancy architecture has some chutzpah of its own that has allowed people to put up with a building even if they're not willing to move into it, yet I know of famous architects who have had the problem that people wouldn't accept what they had built because it didn't feel right to them. Legorreta's buildings feel right.

Vernacular building is logical and at the same time flexible. So it can adapt to changing requirements.

This is really a way of saying that vernacular is not marching to some arcane drummer. That it is adaptable suggests that it is responding to requirements in the first place. Those are humble qualities for a building to have. (It's a luxury of modern architecture to be abstract, to be not logical, to make adaptation difficult or impossible. Vernacular doesn't seem to have or claim

Originally published in Wayne Attoe, ed., *The Architecture of Ricardo Legorreta* (Austin: University of Texas Press, 1990), pp. 163–166.

that luxury.) To be unadaptable to changing requirements is to have a fixed theory that doesn't feel the need to change when anything else changes. A luxury that polemicists allow themselves is to be independent of changing requirements, to be fixed: the luxury of fixity. What vernacular can't do and our new architecture can't do is allow itself that luxury of immobility. It has always to be ready to move, to change, to be different from what it had been before.

Vernacular building is sincere, forgiving, and loving.

This is particularly important and powerful. Vernacular is, of the things we know, among the richest in this quality. Perhaps it is our American anti-monarchist slant that causes us to go, for instance, for songs that say, "Be it ever so humble, there's no place like home"; we do seem to have a distinct bias toward democratic, open, available, comfortable architecture—and vernacular is that.

I value my times with Ricardo Legorreta, especially when he has been showing me and other students pieces of Mexico, the fresh excitement of all the wonderful little things, the way the sun shines on the fruit in the market or glows through a white canvas awning put up over a vendor. All that freshness is what lets him see so clearly into that vernacular that he loves, and that he conveys the love of when he talks of it and when he builds.

It embraces mystery, a quality we are losing in modern life.

Ricardo Legorreta has described his triple threat heritage—the powerful precolonial, the bombastic Hispanic baroque, and a Hispano-Mexican vernacular—which serves as the immediate fount of his dazzlingly complex inspirations. They all pass through Legorreta's work, through a purifying screen of attention and to composition and the learned putting-together of forms in light. Like Le Corbusier's, the search is for simplicity and clarity but with the urgently important latter-day sense of complexity and variety as well, which is not the unsymmetrical in the canon of modern architecture but the circumstantial and offbeat that underlies and brings alive the clear forms. This yields the chaos and related mystery that we need.

Vernacular is based on common sense and not intellectualized.

Most architectural theories that rise from an architect not liking the situation—Adolf Loos saying ornament is crime, for example, or Le Corbusier describing a city of skyscrapers—are flawed; they turn out finally to be wrong. Goldilocks and the Three Bears is a more useful format than the standard pamphleteering one of doctrinaire architecture: Some things are too fat or hot or big, and some things are too much the other way. And some things are just right.

Architectural theories appear always to be wrong: every big enveloping idea has turned out to have some fatal flaw in it. The most famous failure of this century is Le Corbusier's version of *le ciel, l'espace et le jardin*. It was all alright except the green countryside. Nobody knew what to do with it except turn it into parking lots.

Theories are not complex enough but are simple in the wrong way. Christopher Alexander observed, long ago, that the city is not a (mathematical) tree. A simple treelike format is not inclusive enough to allow for the variety and complexity of life in cities. Some architects have believed cities can be drawn on the back of an envelope. The Camino Real in Mexico defies such reduction; it's just too rich.

In a direct as well as a poetic sense, it is functional.

Stravinsky, in *The Poetics of Music*, asserted that the better the artist, the more he limits himself to making his music out of as few pieces as possible, the more he abstracts it. But architecture, being an impure art, does not readily submit to reductions; the architect/artist as minimizer runs the risk of being deceptive and wicked. A psychological study of architects undertaken at Berkeley in the 1950s is said to have included an exercise in which each architect was given a set of colored pieces to arrange in a box. There were two heroes there. The first showed a box in which all but the black and white pieces had been taken out. The other hero then showed his. He had taken out all but the white. So he had clearly won. It's a legitimate artistic victory, and straight out of Stravinsky, but I think that the poetics of an impure art, which architecture is, are the opposite of that. They have to include the richness and clutter of the real world, not just the perfection of the artist's realm.

The vernacular is not related just to poverty and naivete. It is capable of elegance and dignity.

I can't agree with the way Ricardo set this up but do endorse the intention. Poverty and naivete are powerful forces in the world. It's the old story of the

Japanese tea master who takes a very ordinary earthen pot that's rough, the product of poor people, and finds in it qualities of refinement, specialness, and dignity that make it, in Japan, priceless. The very rough utensil used in the ceremony, an exquisite refinement on very ordinary things like drinking tea, preserves carefully the relation between the simple and the poor and the refined. This is something the West doesn't so fully appreciate. In the Japanese imperial gardens like Shugakuin and Katsura, the relationship between the garden and the adjacent rice paddy or watermelon patch is very carefully worked out so that the imperial inhabitant could see ordinary people going about their work and reflect on the virtue of it, and not let his own refinements stray too far from that. The Japanese started from positions farther apart than we in the West are used to and used their artistic efforts to bring poverty and wealth together, as we use ours to push them farther apart. Vernacular architecture in the construct I'm favoring is like the Japanese union of the very poor and rough and the refined. Legorreta achieves this, too.

It is capable, because it is based on experience, of great refinement.

Modern architecture made a mistake in thinking people could identify with altogether unfamiliar sights, sounds, and surfaces, and part of the revival of the classical language recently has centered on the capacity of the classical language, because it's been around so long, to be expressive with nuances of refinement and change. Vernacular, too, though it doesn't have anything like the buildup of symbolic language that classical architecture seems to have, is capable of the subtlety that comes with our experience, and we want our new architecture to have that.

It has an enviable simplicity.

There are kinds and kinds of simplicity, perhaps a bit of a trap for our new architecture. A new simplicity that comes from digesting and then forgetting for a little bit the complexities is worth including in our pantheon. I myself wouldn't mind including the capacity for complexity, which is not that different from the capacity for simplicity and may be easier to cope with. Jean Labatut, my teacher at Princeton, had a four-step rule for making architecture: take in (reach out), digest (absorb), forget, and create. This gives the illusion of simplicity; the stuff of experience is sufficiently ground up inside you so you are not hiccuping back whole pieces, but a reality transformed. Listen to Legorreta talk about designing, about looking and reacting to what is around him, about waiting for all the elements to churn and blend, about the rush of excitement to let something new come out, and you see that he knows about the new, enriched simplicity we need.

It has a capacity for intimacy, hand in hand with elegance.

The Mexican precolonial heritage is not a monolith. There are, on the one hand, the giant pyramids of Teotihuacán, which Legorreta says put him off when he was an architecture student and a young architect. I share his horror at the giant, scaleless, and inhuman monster pieces, although he has managed better than I to get over this horror. And there are, on the other hand, the Zapotec ruins at Monte Albán near Oaxaca (which I have followed him through), admittedly the product of a different pre-Hispanic group, full in its ruins of light, grace, scale, and an intimate connection with a grand landscape, which is a powerful part of his powerful heritage.

Two strongly contrasting examples of the Hispanic colonial heritage are full of the delicate and the brutal, the big and the tiny. Both extremes seem to have their hooks into us. A sixteenth-century monastery like Acolmán or Huejotzingo, built by the conquered Mexican population, has the enormous force of rule and requirement and spirit made not by the conquistadors but by the priests who followed the conquerors. It took a couple of centuries to devolve into the delicacies of a church like San Sebastián y Santa Prisca in Taxco or the ring of churches around Guanajuato—La Cata and La Valenciana among them—where the delicacies are lacy and angelic. Out of the almost beautiful and very powerful and elegant came the delicate and magic/aerial, intimate; it seems to me they are both very much at home in Legorreta's heritage.

There is freedom from rules, which shows up especially in an insouciant use of color, just for fun.

Freedom from rules comes partly from the existence of a set of possibilities for people to express their interests and enthusiasms, which Mexican vernacular is so incredibly rich in. But it's also the case that vernacular, like our proposed new architecture, has a set of automatic rules in it based on enough repetition for us to have figured out which things work and which things don't. That distinguishes both the vernacular and a forthcoming architecture.

Wayne Attoe talks about the formal and informal, the play back and forth between composition strictly ordered and the excitement of circum-

stantial color and shape, light and scale. My own excitement about all this I
cast these days in the terms of an interplay between order and chaos. Our
predecessors in the modern movement were very concerned about order and
tried to expunge chaos from the system. But by the 1950s this effort had
brought about an order whose life was not apparent. I used to quote T. S.
Eliot to the effect that it was the function of the playwright (read architect),
by giving a perception of order *in* reality, to let us develop a sense of the order *of* reality. I keep insisting that Eliot was right and that architects were forgetting about the reality part as they paid attention only to the order.
Legorreta reminds us that the real, the lively, is what the order is about.

Now mathematicians and physicists are making a substantial and illuminating study in favor of chaos, which they show the order of, a nonre-
peating, subtle, fascinating, and mysterious order, like the order of the
waves. Interlocking order and chaos, formal and informal, highly controlled
and spontaneous and accidental, all perhaps invested with a more complex
and great order than a simple order of things, is a part of a vision that Legorreta certainly has which seems to come most clearly out of the vernacular,
which is almost by definition endowed with especially large quantities of
life, not held back or disciplined by an order sufficiently heavy to knock the
life out of it.

It can reflect the country's sense of humor.

The Hispano-Mexican vernacular is of course of every stripe, from the delicate and subdued to the crazily interplanetary-visitor-like—a house apparently hit by a checkerboard, or a broadly and brightly striped shed I once saw
in the middle of a street, a child's toy misplaced by a Jovial visitor. I used to
collect pictures of humor in buildings, and it should be noted that there are
kinds and kinds of humor. Some sophisticated architects indulge in building the one-liner. Architecture is an extremely clumsy vehicle for one-liners
because we have to look at architecture for a long time, and if it depends very
heavily on a joke which you get the first time, or a perception you get all at
once, it's lost some of its punch for subsequent encounters. The good kind,
which happens in Legorreta's Mexican vernacular, is the kind that grows on
you, that gives you pleasure, a change every time you see it, from then on. If
you get it the first time, it probably is too simple.

The Zacatecas cathedral front is an extraordinary piece of work
straight out of the hearts and hands of a large number of people, unlike any-

thing else in the world, full of Mexican Indian spirit and of a pre-Hispanic sense of organization, as full as the various tableaux on a Mayan plinth, or the patterns of Mitla. The Zacatecas front has a life of its own, unreproducible. To use it as a rich vein for mining for our own purposes is difficult because it is so complex. The incredible, unique, cockeyed spirit of it is one of those things that constitutes a heritage and lets us say that Legorreta is taking the spirit, not just the shapes of the heritage, to make his architecture.

Humor and energy have a lot to do with each other. Humor that just comes from solidifying something that is out of whack gives you only a one-liner; humor that comes from energizing something that is out of whack gives you the Zacatecas cathedral front. Such phenomena are generally group manifestations because they take more energy than a single human has. It is a capacity of vernacular architecture (because it is well enough understood) to be dealt with by a group. Zacatecas cathedral has more energy than any single architect could have put into it. One of the key qualities of the new architecture has to be that it picks up the energies of the community, not just the energy of the individual creator. How sad that we cannot see built Legorreta's conception for Jurica, which would have brought together the dreams and craft of so many people to make a community.

So it is that with Ricardo Legorreta we see a series of lessons from the Mexican vernacular which turn out to be the very qualities one would wish to have in an architecture newly made up. The lessons are not for Mexican architecture alone, either. They have applicability everywhere. We see, too, Legorreta's own remarkable efforts to find a way to embody those qualities in an architecture that is not vernacular but is enriched for knowing, understanding, and loving it.

The last piece that Moore wrote was commissioned by Alex Caragonne for The Texas Rangers: Notes from an Architectural Underground.

Foreword to *The Texas Rangers,* by Alexander Caragonne

The events that occurred at the University of Texas over thirty years ago partly were heightened by the magic attached to Austin. After living in Austin for almost ten years myself, I can attest to the enchanting sense of place that makes things that happen here seem especially important.

Austin is situated in what is known as the Texas hill country. It is uniquely forested and hilly terrain that is a pleasantly surprising scene for those who arrive expecting legendary Texan landscapes that usually come to mind with images of the Texas Rangers. What makes the green hills green is the Edwards Aquifer—one of the largest in the world—which lies beneath the region and feeds Barton Springs and Lake Travis along with many other water features, distinguishing the area as one of the few surviving, authentic oases in the world.

This natural oasis, surrounded in all directions by rangeland, serves as a kind of metaphor for the cultural and political life of Austin. The social magic has roots in the late fifties and sixties when Austin became known as a stronghold of liberalism isolated in the center of a state know for its good ol' boy conservatism. Austin has also succeeded in resisting the development that has transformed Houston and Dallas into mega-cities built upon seas of asphalt. To this day, Austin is a small city grown a little too big, but still possessing those appealing qualities of a capital and university town.

The impressive Texas State Capitol, design by Elijah E. Myers in 1882, and Paul Cret's 1935 university tower form the symbolic heart of Austin, though the dome and tower now compete with an assortment of curtain-wall office towers and dormitories. The architecture school is situated in the historic section of Cret's Beaux-Arts campus plan, housed in a trio of buildings—Goldsmith and Sutton halls, also by Cret, as well as an exquisite Cass Gilbert library located on the main mall facing the tower. An endowment made cyclopean by Texas oil revenues, and later the leadership of Hal Box, led to permanently establishing the architecture school in these inspiring facilities, so in contrast to the concrete bunkers that most archi-

Originally published in Alexander Caragonne, *The Texas Rangers: Notes from an Architectural Underground* (Cambridge: MIT Press, 1994), pp. vi–viii.

tecture schools in the country find themselves housed in. It is a genteel and sophisticated arrangement, one that exudes an aura of southern manners and elegance.

The times also had a lot to do with the events at the university described in this book. It was the straight-laced age of Ike, an age of conservative idealism grown out of proud optimism. There seems to have been a timeliness connected to reforming architecture education that seems distant from our somewhat contented era. In hindsight, the time and place both contributed to the making of the Texas Ranger days that now seem to be the stuff of which tales are made.

Much of the Texas Rangers' magic was, of course, due to the presence in Austin of some genuinely extraordinary people. Though I cannot claim to speak for the personal divisions that still today color reactions to the events, this book tells the story of those characters in a sympathetic way, paying attention to the heroes and even the villains.

One of the primary and most urgent things about reading this book is that it contains the finest discussion anywhere of Colin Rowe. His principles, which are difficult at best, come out clear here as we see Rowe's ideas building the Austin curriculum. Rowe's influence in the realm of architecture education is still too frugally acknowledged, despite the fact that his *Collage City* and *Mathematics of the Ideal Villa* are now *de rigueur* reading in most architecture schools. Since most of us could not study directly under Rowe, these testimonies allow us to bear witness to his *ideas in action*. Given Rowe's temperament, an autobiographical work is unlikely, making Caragonne's account even more precious.

I was myself a part of a scene at the University of Utah between 1950 and 1952 that in many ways paralleled the events in Austin, although events in Utah were not cast in the emotional *chiaroscuro* of opposing viewpoints. A former professor and mentor from my undergraduate days at the University of Michigan, Roger Bailey, had started the architecture school at Utah in 1949. The story is that he had gone to Salt Lake City for an architecture conference and was so struck with the place that he called on the president of the university and suggested opening an architecture school. As usual, Bailey's enthusiasm was catching and the president said yes.

Bailey then hired a young Canadian architect named James Acland, whose interests were in teaching design and history, and they immediately set about forming the school. Meanwhile, I was traveling throughout Europe and the Near East looking at and photographing buildings. When I returned to America, I drove to Salt Lake City in my imported Citroën (probably the first one ever to reach Utah) and joined the young faculty. Bailey had hired some local architects as well, including Steve Macdonald, and a year later Gordon Heck arrived from MIT. By the time I arrived, there was a common cause, with the school already going with an impressive energy, and for a wonderful two years we reinvented the curriculum every day.

One memorable design problem involved the urban layout of downtown Salt Lake City. We assumed that we could close off some streets and divide the enormous western-sized blocks into smaller ones more fitting for human-scaled dwellings. What we hadn't anticipated was the Power of the Church. Apparently Brigham Young had laid out those blocks so that a cart and a team of horses would be able to make a U-turn in the street, and the design was therefore partially sacred. Suddenly I was the focus of very loud opposition from the students to any tampering with Brigham Young's legacy, and realized that any design development in Salt Lake City would need to be proposed with far gentler and more sympathetic means.

Too soon, however, it all ended for us, as I was drafted into the Army for service in Korea and the others were called on to other enthusiasms in Canada and the University of Arizona. The excitement had been in thinking about new ways to educate young architects, and developing a program without having to struggle with an established academic order—starting it all from scratch, as it were. For a long time, we all looked back (as Rowe and Hejduk presumably do for Texas) to the days in Utah as a kind of vanished golden age. But our experiences in those halcyon days in Utah were not made bittersweet by the sense of battles and loss, as seems to have been the case in Austin. The story, then, that Caragonne chronicles here is a gripping saga of exciting ideas and youthful energy that were vigorously resisted by stubborn academics. While Rowe and the others may have suffered great frustrations of having dreams stymied by entrenched adversaries, it is important to realize that Rowe and the others went on to other places and, armed with their experiences, changed the face of architecture education.

Page numbers in boldface indicate illustrations.